T0348795

Fostering Open Source Culture

Increase Innovation and Deliver Faster with Open Source

Arun Gupta

Apress®

Fostering Open Source Culture: Increase Innovation and Deliver Faster with Open Source

Arun Gupta
Intel
Santa Clara, CA, USA

ISBN-13 (pbk): 979-8-8688-0976-7
https://doi.org/10.1007/979-8-8688-0977-4

ISBN-13 (electronic): 979-8-8688-0977-4

Managing Director, Apress Media LLC: Welmoed Spahr
Acquisitions Editor: James Robinson-Prior
Development Editor: James Markham
Editorial Project Manager: Gryffin Winkler

Cover designed by eStudioCalamar

Distributed to the book trade worldwide by Springer Science+Business Media New York, 1 New York Plaza, Suite 4600, New York, NY 10004-1562, USA. Phone 1-800-SPRINGER, fax (201) 348-4505, e-mail orders-ny@springer-sbm.com, or visit www.springeronline.com. Apress Media, LLC is a California LLC and the sole member (owner) is Springer Science + Business Media Finance Inc (SSBM Finance Inc). SSBM Finance Inc is a **Delaware** corporation.

For information on translations, please e-mail booktranslations@springernature.com; for reprint, paperback, or audio rights, please e-mail bookpermissions@springernature.com.

Apress titles may be purchased in bulk for academic, corporate, or promotional use. eBook versions and licenses are also available for most titles. For more information, reference our Print and eBook Bulk Sales web page at http://www.apress.com/bulk-sales.

Any source code or other supplementary material referenced by the author in this book is available to readers on GitHub. For more detailed information, please visit https://www.apress.com/gp/services/source-code.

If disposing of this product, please recycle the paper

To all the change agents in enterprises who are tirelessly transforming open source from a possibility into a sustainable reality

Table of Contents

About the Author

Arun Gupta is Vice President and General Manager of Developer Programs at Intel Corporation. He has over two decades of experience building, growing, and fostering large developer communities at companies such as Amazon, Apple, Sun Microsystems, and Intel. He has taken these companies through systemic changes to embrace open source principles, contribute, and collaborate effectively in open source. His leadership has empowered countless developers and organizations to thrive in the open source ecosystem, driving transformative change across the tech industry.

As two-time elected chair of the Cloud Native Computing Foundation (CNCF) Governing Board, Arun works with CNCF leadership and member companies to grow the cloud native ecosystem. He is also the elected Governing Board Chair of the Open Source Security Foundation (OpenSSF) focused on securing the open source software ecosystem. He also participates on the Linux Foundation Governing Board.

Arun has delivered technical talks in 50+ countries, authored multiple books published by O'Reilly and McGraw Hill, and is a Docker Captain, Java Champion, and Java User Group leader. He also leads the TED AI open source hackathon. He is a fitness and kindness enthusiast, practices mindfulness, and is passionate about promoting technology education among children.

About the Technical Reviewers

Hilary Carter is the Senior Vice President of Research at the Linux Foundation. She leads a team dedicated to creating insights into the impact of open source technologies across various sectors, including financial services, healthcare, and energy. Before joining the Linux Foundation, she served as Managing Director at the Blockchain Research Institute, where she led the development and publication of more than 100 research projects. She holds an MSc in Management from the London School of Economics and has a background in financial services, digital media consulting, and content marketing. Hilary is inspired by the opportunities to leverage open source for mass collaboration, sustainable growth, and creating positive global change.

Russ Rutledge is the Senior Director of InnerSource and Collaboration at WellSky, a leading technology company offering a range of software solutions that help organizations across the healthcare continuum. In this role, Russ is leading a transformational change in the company towards broad and pervasive InnerSource as the normal way that work gets done. Russ's drive and passion is to enable all software engineers to achieve incredible technical and business throughput via quality tooling and streamlined work process.

Russ is a founding member of the InnerSource Commons Foundation and currently serves as the foundation executive director. Previously, Russ founded and led the Developer Collaboration effort at Nike. He began his career as an engineer on feature and infrastructure development on the Outlook and OneDrive consumer websites at Microsoft.

Acknowledgments

Writing a book is a profound journey that transforms an initial idea into a published work. It involves navigating the challenges of crafting a narrative that resonates with readers, enduring countless drafts and revisions, and overcoming moments of doubt. It requires a blend of creativity, discipline, and the invaluable support of others. Along this journey, I have been fortunate to be surrounded by individuals whose guidance, encouragement, and expertise have played an essential role in bringing this book to life.

First and foremost, I want to express my deepest gratitude to the 50+ contributors who generously shared their stories and expertise. Your 40+ case studies are the heart of this book, providing invaluable real-world insights into how enterprises worldwide have successfully embraced open source. Your willingness to share your successes, challenges, and lessons learned makes this book a practical guide for others embarking on a similar journey. I recognize the effort required to write these case studies, secure a buy-in from your management, and obtain approval from your communications teams. This is not an easy process and requires an extra level of perseverance. Please know that I deeply appreciate your contributions, and I am committed to returning the favor in any way I can.

I also want to acknowledge those who attempted to get a story approved within their organization but were unable to do so. Your efforts are greatly appreciated, and I recognize the challenges you faced in navigating the approval process. I hope this book inspires you to become change agents within your companies, continuing to advocate for open source culture and contributing to future endeavors. Your dedication to this cause is vital, and I believe your persistence will eventually lead to meaningful change and the opportunity to share your stories in the future.

ACKNOWLEDGMENTS

Several executives from different enterprises have provided insightful quotes that highlight the relevance and impact of open source culture within their organizations. These leaders have shared their perspectives on how fostering an open source culture has driven innovation, collaboration, and business success in their respective companies. Their contributions add valuable context to the book, demonstrating the critical role that open source plays at the executive level in shaping the future of enterprise technology. I am deeply appreciative of their willingness to share their thoughts and experiences, as their voices underscore the importance of embracing open source as a strategic advantage.

A special thank-you goes to the organizations I've had the privilege of working with, where we launched significant open source initiatives. These experiences have been instrumental in shaping my understanding of what it takes to build and sustain an open source culture in large enterprises. I have a deep appreciation for my mentors in these companies as they provided guidance, shared their wisdom, and encouraged me to push the boundaries of what was possible. Their support and insights were invaluable in helping me navigate the complexities of cultural change, and their belief in the power of open source has been a constant source of inspiration throughout my journey.

I'd like to specifically acknowledge Eduardo Pelegri-Llopart, who believed in me during my time at Sun Microsystems and played a crucial role in helping me teach tricks of the trade early in my career. His efforts in driving open source cultural change at Sun were highly influential, shaping my approach to open source and inspiring me to think, "How would EPL handle this?" later in my career. Additionally, he helped me validate and clarify the GlassFish story, which is featured later in the book.

I want to thank the countless developers and open source advocates I've met at various events and meetups over the years. Your passion and dedication to the open source movement have been a constant source of inspiration. The conversations we've had, the ideas we've exchanged, and the challenges we've discussed have all contributed to the content of this book.

I extend my heartfelt thanks to Hilary Carter from the Linux Foundation who meticulously reviewed the entire book and provided invaluable feedback. I am also very grateful to Russell Rutledge from InnerSource Commons Foundation for reviewing the chapter on InnerSource. Their expertise and critical insights have greatly enhanced the quality and accuracy of the content, ensuring that the book meets the highest standards of technical rigor and relevance. Their dedication to reviewing the intricate details and offering constructive suggestions has been crucial in refining the chapters and shaping the final manuscript. I deeply appreciate the time and effort both of you invested in this process, and I am grateful for your contribution to making this book a meaningful and authoritative resource.

The book would not exist without Apress believing in my dream. I'd like to express my deep gratitude to Shobana Srinivasan, Gryffin Winkler, James Markham, and James Robinson-Prior at Apress, and every other person that I did not interact with who helped define this book. From navigating the intricacies of the publishing process to ensuring the final manuscript was polished and ready for readers, your team has been an invaluable partner. I am deeply appreciative of the opportunity to work with such a professional and supportive team, and I am excited to see how this book will reach and inspire its audience thanks to your efforts.

I want to express my deepest gratitude to my family and friends for their unwavering support and understanding throughout this process. After writing six books, I thought I might not write another, but my wife, with her unwavering positivity, kept believing in me and encouraged me to write again. I had countless discussions with my boys on the structure and stories coming into the book.

Last but not least, I want to thank everybody else who contributed to this journey and is not mentioned above.

Preface

Newton's first law of motion says, "An object at rest remains at rest, and an object in motion remains in motion at constant speed and in a straight line unless acted on by an external force." People and organizations tend to remain in their existing state, especially if they have been accustomed to a certain culture or way of doing things for a long time. The deeply ingrained cultural beliefs and behaviors in an enterprise act as a form of cultural inertia because there is fear of the unknown. There is often discomfort associated with change and can create resistance. It is analogous to the objects at rest or in motion described in Newton's first law. In an enterprise, this cultural inertia manifests as a reluctance to deviate from established norms and practices.

Similar to how an external force is necessary to alter the trajectory of an object, cultural change initiatives must address and overcome the resistance rooted in entrenched cultural elements. Leadership plays a crucial role in applying this force by steering the organization toward the desired cultural state. Like a skilled force guiding an object's motion, leadership must actively steer the cultural change process, providing direction, modeling the desired behaviors, and ensuring consistency. Without this force, the organization may remain in its current cultural state. Just as Newton's first law highlights the need for an external force to change an object's state of motion, cultural change in an enterprise requires intentional and sustained efforts to redirect the ingrained cultural beliefs and behaviors towards the new state.

In this digital age, a remarkable transformation is underway by the unifying force of openness, collaboration, and community. This is the essence of Open Source Culture, a phenomenon that extends far beyond the realms of software development to influence businesses, industries, and our very way of life. Enterprises need to embrace open source culture so that they can benefit from this movement while making sure open source stays sustainable. For an enterprise used to building software in a proprietary way or only using open source software but not contributing back, this would require a significant cultural change. It would require for them to understand why and how they need to contribute back to open source in order to keep it sustainable. In order to bring a systemic cultural change such that the entire enterprise can benefit, an "external force," usually the leadership in the company, needs to understand the benefits of open source culture and then set up mechanisms to move to the new desired state.

This book is meant for executives that desire to innovate faster, deliver more value for their customers, and keep their employees happy. This book is relevant for executives in any company, independent of their size, geography, and years of existence. This expectation stems from the fact that in today's digital age, virtually every company, regardless of its primary business focus, incorporates technology as a fundamental component of its operations. Whether it's for communication, data management, customer engagement, or other functions, technology has become integral to modern business practices. A large part of this technology stack is usually open source. Many companies, even those traditionally not perceived as technology-centric, utilize open source technologies in their software development, infrastructure management, and other technological aspects. Reading this book will give them proven techniques to foster open source culture and deliver on the values promised to their shareholders, customers, and employees. The executives will be able to strike a balance between business imperatives and open source ethos. This book can become a guide that enterprises can adopt to improve open source culture within their company.

This book starts with explaining the open source culture and its key pillars. This book helps you understand the principles of openness, transparency, and shared innovation. It talks about why the open source culture must be tied to business imperatives to be sustainable. It helps you understand what systems, processes, and tools can be used to bring that cultural change within your enterprise. Exclusive stories demonstrating how other enterprises have implemented cultural change to leverage open source successfully would be quite appealing to the reader. I hope that they will read these stories multiple times and find something unique every time based on their current working environment. Independent of where readers are in their open source journey, they will gain new knowledge, skills, and perspectives that can be applied in their work setting.

Newton's second law of motion states, "The acceleration of an object depends on the mass of the object and the amount of force applied." The rate of change in open source culture is analogous to acceleration in Newton's second law. The external force applied, which primarily comes from leadership commitment, correlates with the acceleration of cultural change. Increasing the force behind open source principles, such as collaboration, transparency, and contribution, accelerates the cultural shift. Leadership support and active community participation act as accelerators in propelling the organization toward a more open and collaborative culture.

To wrap it up, Newton's third law states, "For every action, there is an equal and opposite reaction." The actions taken to promote openness and collaboration within an enterprise are visible and noticed by the wider community. It often generates positive reactions, fostering a culture of reciprocity and mutual contribution. Open source developers are often attracted to companies that have a healthy open source culture. Conversely, resistance or opposition to change can trigger reactions that need to be addressed strategically. Employees who contribute to open source and work in an enterprise that does not have a healthy open source culture may feel unwelcome and look for greener pastures. I'm speaking this from personal experience too.

Why Open Source Culture Matters!

Let's hear it from some industry leaders on the relevance of open source culture.

Open source is at the heart of Aiven. We are passionate about open source projects driven by communities of developers from diverse organizations and backgrounds, all working as one. Open source fosters an innovation culture through collaboration, shared ownership, and transparency to drive technological progress and build solutions that benefit all. We founded Aiven to make these technologies accessible to everyone, from individual developers to enterprises. This remains at our core as we continue to play our part in the community.

—Oskari Saarenmaa, Chief Executive Officer, Aiven Oy

At Bloomberg, our "open source first" culture enables us to make use of the best software solutions while also fostering a spirit of philanthropy within our collaborative community of engineers who contribute to extend these projects' capabilities. This accelerates time to market, fuels innovation, and ultimately benefits the broader digital world we all share.

—Shawn Edwards, Chief Technology Officer, Bloomberg

Embracing open source software and fostering an open source culture is pivotal for innovation and growth in today's digital landscape. By leveraging the collective intelligence and collaboration inherent in open source communities, BlackRock can not only accelerate technological advancement but also cultivate a spirit of transparency, inclusivity, and continuous improvement. As a fiduciary to our clients, this approach empowers BlackRock to deliver modern cutting-edge solutions, adapt swiftly to change, and drive sustainable success for our clients.

—Lance Braunstein, Senior Managing Director, Head of Aladdin
Engineering at BlackRock

It's difficult to be a successful technology infrastructure company without understanding and supporting open source software. Open source is crucial not only because many of the applications running on multicloud infrastructure are open source based, but it also plays an increasingly important role in building modern IT platforms. Additionally, community collaboration within open source projects brings together the best technical minds and ideas from diverse companies, fostering powerful innovations that no single entity can achieve alone. If you lean into open source, participate, contribute, and become part of the evolution of open technology, you get a front-row seat in moving the technology ecosystem forward.

—John Roese, Global Chief Technology Officer, Dell Technologies

Open source has been the driving force behind the resurgence and ongoing resilience of Docker. We have a deep OSS culture that both produces for and consumes from the community. This is an extremely well thought out approach which directly yields ROI for our business in community engagement, revenue, and improved developer productivity.

—Scott Johnston, Chief Executive Officer, Docker

Enterprises that foster an open source culture help ensure the production and consumption of open source is streamlined and actively encouraged. Such a culture brings awareness across different levels of the enterprise and direct business benefits. While many enterprises give back to open source as a way to be a good corporate citizen, the most sophisticated enterprises understand that giving back to open source can positively impact their bottom line. They can gain more productive value out of using open source, enhance their ability to recruit top talent, and gain deeper insights into cutting-edge technologies like artificial intelligence/machine learning and cloud infrastructure.

—Frank Nagle, Assistant Professor, Harvard Business School

For a quarter century, IBM has been contributing to numerous open source projects throughout many communities. IBM is a trusted partner to both grow open source ecosystems and add key features that ensure open source projects are enterprise-ready. IBM has seen numerous benefits from open source, such as increased speed of innovation and the creation of larger market opportunities, and also providing clients interoperability and freedom from vendor lock-in. Key to IBM's success is its emphasis on creating an open source culture and prioritizing the importance of understanding open source etiquette and how to become a responsible open source contributor.

—Brad Topol, Distinguished Engineer and Director of Open Technologies, IBM

Infosys has an open source first strategy and is both an active consumer and contributor of open source software. We have implemented some of the world's largest population-scale platforms using open source and have realized significant business value. By strategically integrating open source software, we believe the pace of innovation can be further accelerated and evolved in a sustainable manner. Through our Open Source Program Office, we are enabling a culture of continuous learning, collaboration, reuse, and scaled adoption across the developer community at Infosys and our clients and partners.

—Mohammed Rafee Tarafdar, Chief Technology Officer, Infosys

All modern software is built using open source. At the Linux Foundation, we ask ourselves three simple questions every day: Does the work we do in open source positively impact society? Does this work require collaboration among many parties? Can we create a positive feedback loop of upstream collective development, downstream use, and mutual reinvestment upstream? Open Source Culture is the detailed playbook for how industry can participate in open source development for their own good and the good of others at the same time.

—Jim Zemlin, Executive Director, Linux Foundation

At Microsoft, open source culture is integral to our innovation. Developers expect platform openness, and we are proud of the .NET and VS Code projects being cross-platform. As we build products and services, open source allows us to accelerate time to market by adopting industry standard tools (React, TypeScript, Kubernetes, eslint, and plenty more) – something that also helps attract talent. Together as an industry, we come together to create more secure, reliable, and scalable solutions. It's not just about sharing code, it's about empowering developers to drive change, contribute to meaningful projects, and shape the future of technology together.

—Jeff Wilcox, Manager, Open Source Program Office, Microsoft

Red Hat's commitment to open source has been a part of our company's culture since day one. Everything we do, from creating enterprise-class software to running our day-to-day operations, is done by putting collaboration first. Our culture is steeped in open source best practices, because we know that innovation flourishes when diverse talents are given a chance to collaborate with fewer barriers to impede progress. We believe that true collaboration benefits not only our efforts but also the work of anyone participating in open source projects. That's why we guide our customers and partners to use open source to receive the benefits of innovation through collaboration.

—Chris Wright, Chief Technology Officer, Red Hat

It is vital to be clear and organized when it comes to handling products and open source projects together. The rationale to initiate them is different at its core, and so is their life cycle management: from growth to stability and transitioning to another state when necessary, none of that works the same for products and projects even though they share the same technology. Having said that, it's equally critical to make sure that there are no two completely different teams working on them. From a people standpoint, it should not be segregated but joint with everyone involved in both.

—Thomas Di Giacomo, Chief Technology and Product Officer, SUSE LLC

Open Source and Banyan Tree

My dad always says that when you grow up, be like a banyan tree, not like a palm tree. While palm trees are resilient and deeply rooted, they stand tall and offer little to those around them. They don't provide shade, and a falling coconut can cause serious harm. He equates this with being self-centered – strong but unkind, offering little support to others, and sometimes even causing harm.

In contrast, a banyan tree spreads its branches wide, offering shelter and comfort to anyone beneath it. Its roots grow deep and wide, symbolizing not just strength but also a willingness to share that strength with others. The banyan tree embodies kindness, generosity, and the importance of creating a nurturing environment for those around you. My dad encouraged me to be like the banyan tree – strong and resilient, but also supportive and caring, creating a space where everyone can thrive.

Open source is like a banyan tree. Just as a banyan tree grows strong and expansive, spreading its branches wide to offer shelter and support, open source software creates an environment where collaboration and community thrive. The banyan's deep, interconnected roots symbolize the shared knowledge and interconnectedness that define the open source community.

In open source, everyone is welcome to contribute, learn, and benefit from the collective effort, much like how the banyan tree provides shade and protection to all who seek refuge beneath it. It fosters a culture of openness, transparency, and mutual growth, where ideas can be freely exchanged and innovations can flourish.

Just as the banyan tree's branches continue to grow and extend their reach, open source projects evolve and expand with contributions from people all around the world. The more people contribute, the stronger and more resilient the ecosystem becomes. This open exchange of ideas across a diverse, inclusive community creates a level playing field where everyone can participate.

By being like a banyan tree, open source embodies inclusivity, generosity, and long-term sustainability, creating a thriving community that benefits everyone involved. It's not just about building something strong and resilient; it's about creating an environment where everyone can grow and succeed together.

Foreword

While it may sound a bit far-fetched, I believe that in a sense that the ancient Greeks helped lay the foundation for open source software.

I admit to a degree of personal bias. I have been a lifelong student of history, and in recent years I have spent numerous vacations at archaeology projects in Greece, run by the preeminent archaeologist John Camp. "My own view," John says, "is that nothing has changed since antiquity except the technology."

To be fair, that is a pretty big caveat because technology has changed so much. But what his observation points to is the enduring effect of culture, which has been in an intimate dance with technology for centuries. And some believe technology has not been the one calling the tune.

The broader truth behind the popular maxim that "culture eats strategy for breakfast" is that culture eats basically everything – it emerges as the dominant factor in almost every human endeavor, whether or not we recognize it as such.

The cultural achievement for which ancient Greece is most famous is a system of government that radically expanded access to the political system – they crowdsourced political power. It not only gave them a more stable government, but it went hand in hand with a broader flourishing of Greek civilization.

Like Athenian democracy, the genius of open source is that it builds on a broad foundation, the fact that people working in concert can achieve what no individual can. I have worked with some very smart people (and still do!), and I have stood in awe of their insights and innovations. However, the path from insight to practical technology is complex, and no one travels that long road alone.

I am grateful for the many people who have traveled with me on my career path. Some were part of my early experience in networking where we helped implement TCP/IP and other protocols on ARPANet, the precursor to the Internet. It became clear to us back then that collaboration was the key to getting the throughput, reliability, and scalability we needed. This led to my efforts co-founding an open source Internet software consortium. That experience, along with developing an open source version of the Solaris operating system years later, showed me the potential of the open source model to unleash innovation. As I have said elsewhere, support for open source, open standards, and open competition creates an environment where innovation thrives.

What that support for open source looks like in practical terms is active engagement with the open source community: furthering the work of organizations like the Linux Foundation and the Open Source Software Foundation, upstream development of the Linux kernel, and contributing to open source projects like PyTorch and TensorFlow. Thirty years after my initial foray into open source, I find myself in the enviable and truly humbling position of guiding the efforts of Intel's 19,000 software developers, and I cannot imagine a more effective means of realizing their human potential than embracing the open source community and an open software development model.

Today, I am inspired and motivated by the vision Intel's CEO, Pat Gelsinger, articulated in his Open Letter to the Open Ecosystem: "Innovation thrives in an open, democratized environment where people can connect, communicate, and respond together to new stimuli." Pat said he believes that "our collective future – our collective potential – is unlocked when we enable openness, choice, and trust among us." I very much believe in that, and I know that Arun Gupta does also.

When I first met Arun, it was abundantly clear to me that we shared a common vision, that open source is critical to unlocking the highest possible potential for developers and our industry. Over the course of our time working together, I have learned a tremendous amount from Arun. The insights, explanations, and case studies he curated for this book are valuable contributions to the vitality of the open source community, with critical points I believe everyone can learn from.

Greg Lavender, Chief Technology Officer, Intel Corporation

CHAPTER 1

Open Source Culture

The phrase "Software is eating the world," coined by Marc Andreessen in 2011, captures the seismic shift that software brought to nearly every industry at that time. This statement reflected the reality that software is no longer just a tool for niche applications but has become the backbone of modern economies, driving unprecedented growth and innovation. Industries like finance, healthcare, manufacturing, entertainment, and even agriculture have been transformed by software, enabling them to operate more efficiently, innovate rapidly, and scale globally. The essence of Andreessen's observation is that software is not just a component of business; it is increasingly the core of business itself.

A decade later, in 2022, Jim Zemlin, Executive Director of the Linux Foundation, highlighted that most of this transformative software is open source. Open source software, characterized by its collaborative development model and transparent code, has become the foundation for much of the world's software infrastructure. This shift towards open source reflects a broader trend of democratization in technology, where individuals and organizations across the globe can contribute to and benefit from cutting-edge software. The widespread adoption of open source has enabled rapid innovation, as developers can build on existing code, share improvements, and collaborate across organizational and geographical boundaries. Open source is no longer just a niche movement; it is a driving force behind the software that powers our world.

A. Gupta, *Fostering Open Source Culture*, https://doi.org/10.1007/979-8-8688-0977-4_1

An open source culture in an enterprise sustains innovation and underlines the importance of this collaborative model in driving continuous technological advancement. Open source is more than just a way to develop software; it is a cultural shift that fosters innovation through transparency, collaboration, and inclusivity. This culture enables a diverse range of contributors to address complex problems, share solutions, and iterate rapidly, leading to more robust and innovative technologies. The flow from Andreessen's recognition of software's dominance to the assertion of open source's role in sustaining innovation illustrates how the open source model has become essential to the future of global technology. It empowers a new era of collaborative innovation that is poised to shape the next wave of technological breakthroughs.

Software is eating the world.	Most of that software is open source.	Open source culture sustains innovation.
– Marc Andreessen, Co-founder and Partner, Andreessen Horowitz, 2011	– Jim Zemlin, Executive Director, Linux Foundation, 2022	– Arun Gupta, VP/GM Developer Programs, Intel, 2024

Impact of Open Source

Open source technology has become a ubiquitous force, playing a pivotal role in a wide array of industries that range from the sophisticated realm of satellites to the intricate world of medical devices, the dynamic field of automobiles, the precision of surgical procedures, the transformative landscape of education, the optimization of agriculture practices, the sustainable energy sector, the immersive world of gaming, the intricate processes of manufacturing, and beyond. Its versatile applications demonstrate the adaptability and scalability of open source solutions across diverse domains.

GitHub's Octoverse 2022 report mentioned that 90% of companies use open source. OpenLogic 2024 State of Open Source report shows 95% of the respondents are either increased or maintained their use of open source in 2023. The World of Open Source: Global Spotlight 2023 shows that on a global average, 90% of organizations surveyed use open source at a moderate, significant, or widespread level. These numbers are staggering and only show the growing relevance of open source across the industry.

As the backbone of the digital economy, open source technology serves as the underlying framework for countless digital innovations and solutions. Its impact is not confined to a single sector but resonates across various domains, leaving an indelible mark on technology, business practices, collaboration models, and the very essence of innovation.

In the technological landscape, open source acts as an enabler of progress, fostering collaborative innovation that transcends traditional boundaries. It empowers developers and organizations to collectively contribute to and improve upon existing software, resulting in a continuous cycle of enhancement and evolution. This collaborative ethos has led to breakthroughs in areas such as artificial intelligence, cloud computing, data analytics, and more.

From a business perspective, the economic value delivered by open source is substantial. Organizations can allocate resources more efficiently and focus on customizing solutions to meet their specific needs by providing access to high-quality software solutions at reduced or no cost. The flexibility of open source technology contributes to business agility, enabling companies to adapt swiftly to changing market demands and technological advancements.

Collaboration lies at the heart of open source, creating vibrant communities where developers, businesses, and individuals come together to share knowledge, solve problems, and drive collective progress. This collaborative spirit fosters networking, mentorship, and a culture of continuous learning, amplifying the impact of open source beyond the realm of technology into a broader community dynamic.

Innovation, spurred by the open source model, extends far beyond the digital realm, influencing the physical world through applications in healthcare, agriculture, and manufacturing. Open source principles of transparency, accessibility, and adaptability have transformed industries by promoting interoperability, breaking down silos, and accelerating the pace of technological advancement.

Let us take an example of a dynamic open source project – Kubernetes. It has 85K+ developers from 5000+ companies and 4M+ contributions on GitHub and exemplifies the vibrancy in open source. Beyond its conventional web and e-commerce use cases, Kubernetes excels in mission-critical applications. For instance, it enables real-time video analytics in smart city surveillance, streamlines DNA sequencing analysis in genomics projects like the Genomic Data Commons, manages rendering for animated films, and orchestrates machine learning models for self-driving car object recognition. Open source enables diverse community-driven innovation that surpasses the capabilities of any single corporate entity.

In open source projects, like Kubernetes, the primary responsibility lies with maintainers and contributors. These are individuals or a group of people that lead projects, manage code, and foster collaboration, playing a vital role in both project success and community growth. They oversee everything from code review to decision-making and community engagement. Without maintainers and contributors, open source software would quickly become outdated, insecure, and frankly irrelevant. These developers are driven by a combination of intrinsic and extrinsic motivations. While some are financially compensated by enterprises for their work, others are primarily motivated by personal passion, skill development, recognition, and the satisfaction of contributing to a community-driven ecosystem.

Open source is pervasive in various industries, yet a recent Linux Foundation report on Open Source Maintainers reveals concerning statistics. Only 38% of maintainers feel well-supported by their employers

4

for open source work, and just 39% believe their organizations highly value open source contributions. This is surprising considering the critical role open source plays for enterprises. Additionally, the report reveals that only 35% of projects have a robust pipeline of new contributors, raising questions about their sustainability as they expand in scope and complexity. These findings underscore the importance of supporting maintainers and contributors and creating a culture in the company that supports them to ensure the continued reliability and growth of open source initiatives.

Give and Take Philosophy

Would guests go to a potluck dinner and not bring a dish? Would neighbors go to a communal garden and not help with planting or taking out weeds? Would readers go to a community library where they only take books for reading but never donate any? Open source is a potluck, a communal garden, and a community library. The resources available in the community are utilized while also contributing to benefit the community as a whole.

Contributing to open source is a mutually beneficial endeavor between the individual, the organizations, if applicable, that allow these individuals to contribute, and the open source community. For an individual, it fosters personal and professional growth, promotes collaboration, and empowers you to make a positive impact on the software that powers our digital world. It provides numerous benefits to enterprises, such as skills development, innovation to cost savings, and recruitment and retention. The open source community definitely benefits with improved overall quality of the project, diversity of bugs and patches, and broader adoption. Whether you're driven by a desire to learn, give back, or connect with a global community, open source offers a wealth of opportunities for those willing to get involved.

Relying solely on consuming open source software without actively participating in its development and contribution is an unsustainable practice. Open source thrives on a collaborative ecosystem where individuals and organizations give as much as they take. Sometimes how much the organizations give and take may vary, but the "only take" is definitely not the ethos of open source. Here are some reasons why "give and take" is a sustainable approach:

- **Collaborative Ecosystem** – It nurtures a collaborative ecosystem where individuals and organizations actively engage in sharing knowledge, expertise, and resources. This collective effort results in a vibrant community that collaboratively addresses challenges, leading to the sustained growth and development of open source projects.

- **Principle of Equitable** – By giving back to the open source community, contributors ensure a balanced exchange of resources. This equilibrium prevents overconsumption of open source software while maintaining the sustainability of projects. In essence, it creates a fair and mutually beneficial relationship between users and creators.

- **Continuous Improvement** – Open source projects thrive on continuous improvement. This approach means that issues and shortcomings are not just identified but actively addressed through contributions. This feedback loop leads to iterative enhancements, making the software more reliable, secure, and feature-rich over time.

- **Community Engagement** – Actively contributing fosters strong community engagement. Contributors are more likely to engage in discussions, offer support to others, and participate in decision-making processes. This engagement strengthens the bonds within the open source community and ensures that projects receive the support and input they need to thrive.

- **Skills Development** – It provides individuals with opportunities to develop a wide range of skills, including coding, communication, project management, and leadership. These skills contribute to personal growth and professional development, making contributors more versatile and valuable in various contexts.

- **Adaptability** – Open source projects often need to adapt to evolving technology trends and user requirements. This approach ensures that the community remains flexible and responsive to changing needs. Contributors can quickly address emerging challenges and explore innovative solutions, ensuring the relevance of open source software.

- **Ethical Responsibility** – Embracing this approach aligns with ethical principles of reciprocity and fairness. It acknowledges the communal spirit of open source, emphasizing that those who benefit from open source software should contribute back to sustain the ecosystem and support the creators and maintainers.

- **Long-Term Sustainability** – Open source projects
  depend on ongoing support and contributions. This
  approach helps maintain the long-term sustainability
  of projects, reducing the risk of stagnation or
  abandonment. This ensures that open source software
  remains viable for years to come.

- **Innovation Catalyst** – The diversity of contributions
  in an open source ecosystem serves as a catalyst
  for innovation Different perspectives, ideas, and
  talents come together to push the boundaries of what
  open source software can achieve. This continuous
  innovation keeps open source projects at the forefront
  of technology.

- **Broad Impact** – This approach extends the impact of
  open source software to a broad user and developer
  base. When contributions are made to improve open
  source projects, these enhancements benefit not only
  the contributors but also countless others who rely
  on the software, promoting a virtuous cycle of value
  creation.

Incorporating these principles into open source practices not only
ensures the sustainability of projects but also fosters a thriving and
inclusive community that continues to push the boundaries of innovation
and collaboration in the digital world.

On the other side, an "only take" approach in open source, where
individuals or organizations solely consume open source software without
giving back, can have several downsides:

- **Dependency Without Support** – When you only consume open source software without contributing, you become heavily dependent on the work of others. If a project you rely on doesn't receive adequate support, it may become outdated, buggy, or even abandoned, leaving you with potentially critical vulnerabilities and compatibility issues.

- **Limited Customization** – When you don't actively engage with open source projects, you limit your ability to customize and tailor the software to your unique requirements. Contributing allows you to have a say in the software's direction.

- **Missed Opportunities for Improvement** – Open source software benefits from the collective expertise of its community. By not contributing, you miss the chance to shape the software to better meet your specific needs and to improve its functionality and reliability for everyone.

- **Lack of Community Wisdom** – Open source thrives on project documentation, participating in community discussions, mentorship, and gradually building expertise in relevant areas. Keeping your patches and fixes internal to your organization limits your ability to participate in this crowdsourced community knowledge.

- **Accumulation of Technical Debt** – Prolonged use of open source software without contributing can lead to the accumulation of technical debt as outdated or unpatched components become more challenging and costly to manage.

- **Staffing for Internal Forks** – Creating and maintaining internal forks of open source projects can require additional Full-Time Equivalents (FTEs) for development, bug fixes, security updates, and customization. This allocation of resources may divert valuable manpower, in addition to the compute resources needed, from other critical organizational priorities.

- **Risk of Fragmentation** – If everyone adopted a passive approach to open source, it could lead to fragmentation in the ecosystem. Different users may create their own forks or custom versions of projects to meet their needs, resulting in a lack of standardization and increased complexity.

- **Reduced Motivation for Developers** – Developers who contribute to open source projects are often motivated by a sense of purpose, learning opportunities, and recognition. If users only consume without contributing, it can demotivate these contributors, potentially leading to fewer high-quality open source projects.

- **Ethical Considerations** – The open source community operates on principles of reciprocity and collaboration. Consuming without contributing can be seen as taking advantage of this goodwill and not giving back to the community that enables your work. It violates the fundamental principle of fairness.

- **Legal and Licensing Issues** – Some open source licenses require reciprocity. If you use open source software without contributing as required by the license, you might face legal consequences.

- **Negative Community Impact** – The open source community values collaboration and reciprocity. An "only take" approach can be seen as taking advantage of the community's goodwill and may lead to negative perceptions within the community.

- **Community Building** – Open source communities thrive when users actively participate. By contributing, you help build a stronger, more vibrant community, which benefits everyone involved.

To ensure the sustainability and continued success of open source software, it's essential to adopt a more balanced approach. This involves not only consuming open source software but also actively participating in its development, whether through code contributions, bug reports, documentation, financial support, or community engagement. By doing so, you contribute to the longevity, quality, and vibrancy of the open source ecosystem.

Why Is Culture Important?

The phrase "Culture eats strategy for breakfast" is often attributed to management guru Peter Drucker. The essence of the saying is that no matter how well-crafted a business strategy may be, it will ultimately be overshadowed and rendered ineffective if the organizational culture does not support it. In other words, organizational culture holds a more powerful and influential position in determining the success or failure of an organization's plans and strategies. Even the most brilliant strategy cannot overcome a toxic or dysfunctional culture that hampers teamwork, stifles innovation, or fails to align with the organization's goals.

Strategy outlines the "what" and "why" of an organization's direction and is typically developed by leadership. Culture defines "how things are done" within the organization and often evolves over time. Strategy is deliberate and purposeful. Culture is organic, deeply ingrained, and emerges from the collective beliefs and behaviors of employees. Strategy is communicated through formal documents, presentations, and directives from leadership. Culture is primarily communicated through everyday interactions, stories, symbols, and rituals within the organization. Strategy must align with the organization's culture to be effective. A strategy that contradicts the prevailing culture may face resistance and implementation challenges. A strong alignment ensures that employees' behaviors and attitudes support the strategic goals.

Imagine strategy as the engine and culture as the fuel. Just as an engine is the powerhouse of a vehicle, the strategy is the powerhouse of an organization. It provides direction, sets goals, and outlines the steps required to achieve those goals. Like an engine, a well-crafted strategy propels the organization toward its objectives. Culture, on the other hand, refers to the shared values, beliefs, behaviors, and norms that define how people within the organization interact and work together. Culture is what motivates and empowers employees to perform their roles effectively. It shapes their attitudes, decision-making, and the way they approach their work. Culture provides the energy, enthusiasm, and commitment needed to power the strategy engine.

Just as an engine can't function without fuel, a well-devised strategy alone can't achieve success without the support and alignment of the organization's culture. The quality and suitability of the fuel (culture) directly impact the performance of the engine (strategy). If the culture is positive, aligned with the strategy, and fosters collaboration, it will provide the necessary energy to drive the organization forward efficiently. Conversely, if there's a disconnect between the culture and strategy, it's akin to using the wrong type of fuel for an engine. The organization may experience inefficiencies, resistance to change, and a lack of motivation among employees. Just as an engine requires regular maintenance and care to ensure optimal performance, an organization needs ongoing attention to maintain a healthy culture and adapt the strategy as needed.

"Culture is the control mechanism that fills in the blank when policy and procedures don't talk about what needs to be done" – says Jay Barney, professor at the University of Utah's Eccles School of Business in https://hbr.org/podcast/2023/09/if-you-want-culture-change-create-new-stories. This statement highlights the role of organizational culture in guiding employee behavior and decision-making when formal policies and procedures are not explicitly defined for a particular situation. It operates as an implicit "control mechanism" because it influences how individuals behave, make choices, and respond to various situations within the workplace. For example, if a company's culture places a strong emphasis on customer satisfaction and empowerment, an employee facing an unusual customer request may decide to go above and beyond to resolve the issue creatively, even if there is no specific policy outlining how to handle such requests.

It is unequivocal that there is a tight correlation between strategy and culture. It emphasizes that while strategy provides the direction and objectives, culture provides the energy and commitment needed to execute the strategy effectively. Together, they enable the organization to move forward, achieve its goals, and navigate challenges successfully.

Let's talk next about what does it mean to have an open source culture.

Open Source Culture

The Linux Foundation's report on Measuring Economic Value of Open Source highlights cost savings, faster development speed, and open standards and interoperability as the top benefits for the adoption of open source. These all can very well be part of the strategy for a company. But as we discussed in the previous chapter, is having a strategy enough? There is a clear need for the underlying culture so that it can provide fuel to the engine of strategy.

Imagine a company's culture as a garden. In a traditional, closed culture, it's like having a walled garden with limited growth opportunities. The organization relies solely on its internal resources, and innovation is confined to a narrow space and constrained by the budget and diversity available within the company. On the other hand, an open source culture is like cultivating an open garden where diverse seeds, ideas, and practices are welcomed. External contributors (partners, customers, and the wider industry) are invited to collaborate and share their insights. This open approach allows for a rich mix of perspectives and innovations to flourish. Just as a garden thrives when it's open to a variety of plants, an open source culture within a company encourages creativity, adaptability, and continuous growth, ultimately leading to a more vibrant and resilient organization.

Fostering an open source culture within an organization yields a myriad of benefits that extend beyond the realms of software development. Embracing open source principles promotes a culture of collaboration, encouraging teams to work transparently and share knowledge. This not only accelerates problem-solving but also enhances overall productivity. An open source culture sparks innovation by providing a platform for creative exploration and diverse perspectives, ensuring that the organization remains adaptive in a rapidly evolving technological landscape. Furthermore, it establishes a talent magnet, attracting skilled individuals who are drawn to the ethos of shared ownership and meritocracy. Engaging with open source practices also fortifies the organization against technological obsolescence, as it leverages and contributes to cutting-edge solutions. In today's digital era, embracing an open source culture isn't just beneficial; it's imperative for long-term success and driving relentless innovation.

The reluctance to adopt an open source culture within an organization poses significant dangers in today's dynamic business landscape. Foremost among these risks is the potential for stagnation and technological obsolescence. Without embracing open source practices, organizations may find themselves isolated from the rapid advancements and collaborative innovations characteristic of the broader industry. Additionally, the lack of transparency and shared ownership inherent in an open source culture can lead to siloed work environments, hindering effective collaboration and impeding the flow of knowledge. This isolation not only stifles creativity but also diminishes the organization's ability to attract top talent, as professionals increasingly seek workplaces that embody a culture of openness and collaborative problem-solving. Ultimately, failing to adopt an open source culture jeopardizes an organization's resilience, competitiveness, and capacity for continuous improvement in the fast-paced world of modern business and technology.

Fostering an open source culture in a company involves embracing the open source ethos within the company. Let's learn about these ethos and what they mean.

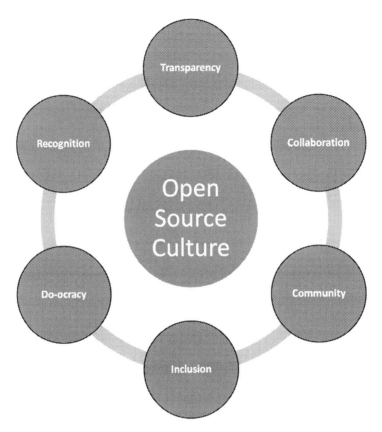

Figure 1-1. *Ethos of Open Source Culture*

Transparency

Transparency is the bedrock of an open source culture. It is a foundational principle within the ethos of open source, emphasizing openness and accessibility in all aspects of software development. At its core, transparency involves making the source code of a project openly available for inspection, modification, and distribution. This accessibility not only fosters trust within the community but also enables developers to examine and understand the inner workings of a software application.

The transparent nature of open source projects extends beyond code to include open discussions, decision-making processes, and documentation, ensuring that contributors and users alike have visibility into the project's evolution.

To ensure transparency, open source projects actively discourage the reliance on tribal knowledge – knowledge held by a select few within a team or community. The ethos encourages contributors to document their work comprehensively, making it part of the institutional knowledge accessible to everyone. This shift ensures that all project-related information is openly available, reducing dependency on specific individuals or closed circles of knowledge. Institutional transparency not only fosters a more inclusive and collaborative environment but also facilitates onboarding for new contributors. By maintaining clear documentation and open communication channels, open source projects embody the principle of transparency, reinforcing the collaborative nature of the community and enabling a diverse range of individuals to participate meaningfully.

Transparency in open source extends to the governance structures of projects. Open source governance often includes clear processes for code contribution, going up the contribution ladder, and conflict resolution. This transparency helps maintain a healthy and collaborative community by providing clear guidelines on how contributions are evaluated and integrated into the project and how disagreements are addressed. Many open source projects adopt transparent decision-making processes, often involving community voting or consensus-building mechanisms. This democratic approach ensures that decisions are made collectively, reflecting the diverse perspectives and needs of the community.

Collaboration

Collaboration in an open source culture means actively working together, often in a transparent and inclusive manner, to achieve shared goals and create innovative solutions. At its core, open source culture recognizes that no single entity possesses all the expertise needed to tackle today's complex challenges. Collaboration serves as the means to leverage the collective wisdom, skills, and experiences of a diverse group of contributors, both within and outside the organization. This collaborative approach accelerates problem-solving and leads to the rapid generation of innovative solutions that can keep the enterprise competitive and agile.

It emphasizes teamwork, knowledge sharing, and cross-functional cooperation. In an open source enterprise, employees are encouraged to work together, breaking down silos and fostering an environment where diverse skills and expertise can merge to drive innovation. Collaboration extends not only within the organization but also beyond its boundaries, with a willingness to partner and co-create with external stakeholders and open source communities.

Additionally, collaboration aligns with the core values of open source culture, emphasizing openness, transparency, and community. By actively engaging with external stakeholders, such as customers, partners, and open source communities, organizations demonstrate their commitment to these values. Collaboration nurtures a sense of belonging to a larger community, both within and outside the enterprise, fostering a culture where diverse voices and ideas are heard and valued. Ultimately, collaboration is the catalyst that propels open source culture forward, enabling organizations to thrive in today's ever-evolving business landscape.

Fostering a collaborative culture can attract a steady stream of new contributors, ensuring the ongoing success of these projects in a continually changing environment.

Community Engagement

Community engagement is at the heart of the open source ethos, embodying the principles of collaboration, inclusivity, and shared ownership. In open source, a vibrant and engaged community is essential for the success and sustainability of projects. Community engagement goes beyond mere participation; it involves active collaboration, communication, and a collective commitment to the project's goals. This ethos is rooted in the belief that diverse perspectives and contributions lead to stronger, more innovative solutions.

Open source projects foster community engagement through various channels, including forums, mailing lists, and collaborative platforms like GitHub. These spaces provide a forum for discussions, knowledge sharing, and collaborative decision-making. Engaging with the community extends to code contributions, bug reporting, and offering feedback. By actively involving individuals with diverse backgrounds and expertise, open source projects harness the power of collective intelligence, ensuring that the development process benefits from a wide range of skills and insights.

Open source events play a pivotal role in strengthening community engagement for both maintainers and contributors. These events, ranging from conferences and meetups to hackathons and workshops, provide a physical or virtual space for the community to come together, fostering connections and deepening collaboration. For maintainers, these events offer an opportunity to showcase the project's progress, share insights, and gather valuable feedback directly from contributors. Additionally, it allows maintainers to recognize and appreciate the efforts of contributors, reinforcing a sense of community and shared accomplishment. The social aspect of these events promotes camaraderie, turning virtual connections into real relationships. Such gatherings contribute significantly to building a sense of belonging within the open source community, encouraging sustained engagement and fostering a shared commitment to the project's success.

The open source ethos also emphasizes the importance of mentorship and the onboarding of new contributors. Seasoned community members often take on mentorship roles, guiding newcomers through the project's intricacies and providing support as they navigate the development process. This commitment to mentorship creates a welcoming environment and contributes to the sustainability of the open source ecosystem by ensuring a continuous influx of fresh perspectives and talent.

Inclusion

Inclusion reflects a commitment to creating an environment where individuals of diverse backgrounds, perspectives, and skill sets feel welcome and valued. At its core, open source inclusivity ensures that the doors to collaboration are wide open, inviting contributors from different cultures, experiences, and levels of expertise to actively participate. This commitment is not only ethical but also practical, recognizing that a diverse and inclusive community leads to stronger, more resilient projects with a broader range of insights and approaches.

Open source inclusion extends beyond mere access to code repositories. It encompasses initiatives and practices that actively seek to minimize barriers to entry, providing clear documentation, mentorship programs, and support networks for contributors of all levels. By fostering a culture that celebrates diversity, open source projects benefit from a rich tapestry of ideas, innovation, and problem-solving approaches. Inclusivity, therefore, is not just a virtue; it is a strategic imperative that ensures the sustainability and adaptability of open source endeavors in a rapidly evolving technological landscape.

Moreover, the commitment to inclusion in open source is reflected in governance structures that prioritize fair representation and decision-making processes that consider diverse perspectives. This ensures that the direction of a project is not determined by a narrow set of voices but reflects the collective wisdom of a global community. In summary, inclusivity in open source is not merely an aspiration; it is an ongoing commitment to building a community where everyone has the opportunity to contribute, learn, and thrive, ultimately leading to more robust and innovative software solutions.

Do-ocracy

A do-ocracy is a governance model where individuals are empowered to make decisions and contribute based on their demonstrated actions and contributions. The term "do-ocracy" is derived from the idea that those who "do" the work, take initiative, and actively contribute have a greater say or influence in decision-making processes.

It is rooted in the principles of meritocracy; this model posits that individuals who engage substantively and contribute meaningfully hold a greater sway in shaping the trajectory of a project. In this decentralized approach, decision-making is not confined to a predetermined hierarchy or formal roles; rather, it emerges organically from the collective actions of community members. The do-ocracy model is dynamic, allowing the project to adapt to changing needs, with decisions driven by those who actively involve themselves in the project's development.

Within the do-ocracy framework, there's a pronounced emphasis on initiative. Individuals are not merely encouraged but empowered to take proactive roles, propose modifications, and contribute without waiting for explicit approval. This ethos not only accelerates the pace of development but also fosters a culture where innovation and responsiveness thrive. In this environment, the recognition and respect accorded to contributors are directly proportional to the tangible impact of their work, creating a sense of ownership and shared responsibility within the open source community.

While do-ocracy is a powerful model, its effectiveness often lies in a balanced integration with other governance structures. Combining do-ocracy with elements that ensure inclusivity and prevent the concentration of decision-making power among a select few is crucial. Striking this balance is integral to maintaining a collaborative and diverse open source community where the principles of meritocracy coexist harmoniously with the broader ethos of accessibility and inclusivity.

Recognition

Recognition for open source in an enterprise entails acknowledging and celebrating the contributions, efforts, and achievements of individuals and teams who actively participate in open source initiatives and communities. This recognition can take various forms, including verbal praise, awards, certificates, promotions, or special events dedicated to honoring these contributions. It signifies the individual's or organization's appreciation for the valuable work done in the open source realm and the alignment of these efforts with the company's goals and values.

Recognition is a fundamental principle of open source culture in an enterprise. It involves creating incentives and mechanisms that motivate developers to continue their open source contributions. It involves providing education and support to managers and leadership, enabling them to manage open source contributors effectively. This serves as a potent motivator, boosting employees' morale and commitment by acknowledging their contributions in company meetings, newsletters, and all-hands. This recognition aligns with the meritocratic nature of open source culture, where excellence is rewarded regardless of hierarchy or tenure. It also helps bolster the influx of new contributors, enabling these open source projects to thrive in an ever-evolving landscape.

Recognition plays a pivotal role in attracting and retaining top talent, making the organization an appealing destination for individuals who seek appreciation and acknowledgment for their work. Moreover, it fosters a positive workplace culture, encouraging positive interactions, collaboration, and dedication among employees. It also encompasses simplifying open source consumption and contribution by streamlining and automating processes, documenting playbooks, and more.

In addition to motivating employees, recognition promotes a sense of ownership and accountability, as contributors see their efforts making a difference and being celebrated. It strengthens collaboration by acknowledging teamwork and knowledge sharing, essential components of open source culture. Furthermore, recognition enhances employee engagement and well-being, contributing to higher job satisfaction and overall contentment. Lastly, it showcases the organization's core values by reinforcing the importance of openness, collaboration, and innovation. In essence, recognition is a linchpin in fostering a thriving open source culture that empowers employees and fuels an environment of continuous growth and innovation.

Why Companies May Not Contribute to Open Source?

Organizations may be hesitant to contribute to open source for various reasons, and these concerns can vary depending on the nature of the business, industry, and internal policies. Some of the common reasons are:

- **Intellectual Property Concerns** – Companies may worry about the protection of their intellectual property when contributing to open source. Concerns may include potential conflicts with existing patents, trade secrets, or proprietary technologies.

- **Legal and Compliance Issues** – Fear of legal complications, including misunderstandings about open source licenses and compliance requirements, can deter companies from contributing. Ensuring adherence to licenses and understanding the legal implications of contributions are crucial considerations.

- **Lack of In-House Expertise** – Companies may hesitate that they lack in-house expertise in open source practices, tools, and community engagement. The learning curve can be perceived as steep, and the company may be concerned about making mistakes or facing challenges in the open source ecosystem.

- **Competitive Advantage** – Some companies view their software as a proprietary advantage. Sharing code with the open source community could be perceived as giving away a competitive edge, especially if the company relies on unique technologies or features.

- **Security Concerns** – Security considerations may be a significant factor. Companies might worry about exposing vulnerabilities or sensitive information when opening their code to public scrutiny. Security-conscious organizations may be cautious about the potential risks.

- **Resource Constraints** – Contributing to open source requires time, effort, and resources. Some companies, especially smaller ones or those with limited development resources, may be hesitant due to concerns about diverting valuable personnel from core business activities.

- **Reputation Management** – Fear of negative reactions or criticism from the open source community can be a deterrent. Companies may worry about reputational risks if their contributions are not well-received or if they are perceived as insufficient.

- **Uncertain ROI** – Companies may question the return on investment (ROI) of contributing to open source. The benefits of community collaboration, improved software quality, and enhanced brand reputation may not be immediately apparent or measurable. They may not be able to clearly articulate the "why."

- **Lack of Internal Support** – Without strong internal support from leadership or key stakeholders, employees may be hesitant to engage in open source activities. Lack of understanding or commitment from higher levels of management can hinder open source initiatives.

- **Regulatory Compliance** – Industries with strict regulatory requirements, such as finance or healthcare, may face challenges in contributing to open source while maintaining compliance with industry-specific regulations.

- **Control Over Development Roadmap** – Companies may be concerned about relinquishing control over the development roadmap. Open source projects often involve collaborative decision-making, and companies may worry about their ability to shape the direction of a project.

- **Cultural Resistance** – Organizational culture can play a significant role. Companies with a traditionally closed development culture may face internal resistance to the idea of contributing to open source, requiring a shift in mindset.

Summary

This chapter explained the relevance of open source culture and an introduction to the ethos of open source culture. It also explained how give and take philosophy is essential for sustainability and the continued success of open source software. The chapter concluded with some typical reasons why companies may not contribute to open source. There are clear benefits to contributing to open source and are explained in the next chapter. It explains different reasons why companies contribute to open source, as it serves as the foundation for the strategic intent of the open source initiative. Different philosophies of engagement in open source and common business models around open source are explained next. There are lots of interesting ways in which enterprises foster an open source culture. The next chapter is also loaded with case studies from a wide range of enterprises on what they did to bring a cultural change in order to make open source sustainable for their business.

CHAPTER 2

Business Alignment

The sustainability of open source within an enterprise relies on its integration with the core business functions; without this connection, it is not viable for the long term. This integration represents a strategic imperative that extends beyond mere technological considerations. When open source is effectively integrated into the core business functions, it functions as more than just a set of tools; it becomes a transformative force that aligns with the strategic goals of the enterprise. This goal could help you build and deliver products faster, provide choice and interoperability to your customers, innovate at a faster cadence, and improve operational efficiency. By leveraging open source solutions in tandem with core business processes, organizations can tap into the collective intelligence of a broader community, fostering collaboration and driving continuous improvement.

For example, what would you choose for a hyperscaler-agnostic compute platform to run your microservices-based application? Kubernetes is the compute platform with 85K+ committers across 5000 organizations. The source code available is only a starting point for such projects. The *intellectual knowledge* as opposed to the intellectual property that comes with open source projects is a key reason for their popularity. This intellectual knowledge, or IK for short, comes in the form of being able to see the discussion that has happened in pull requests. This discussion is immensely helpful as it enables you to understand the internals of the design, what it does, and why it does it that way. This in turn makes you a more effective programmer and leverages the project in a more successful way. IK comes from the blogs, stackoverflow Q&A, conference talks, tips, and tricks on what works and does not work. The popularity of these projects and usage by other large enterprises of similar scale brings a diversity of views that would not be possible if a project is closed source.

Companies can groom their engineers to be maintainers in open source projects. Alternatively, they can hire maintainers of existing open source projects. Usually, it could take several months, if not years, depending upon the project to become a maintainer. The maintainers will work for an enterprise only if they know they'll be allowed to continue their contributions to open source. They usually look at other open source influencers working at the company and how their activities have changed after joining the company.

Additionally, it may help you hire and retain talent and help employee morale as they get to work on tough problems in a global community. This integration ensures that open source technologies become intrinsic to the operational fabric of the enterprise, contributing to its overarching objectives and enhancing its capacity for innovation, efficiency, and adaptability.

This symbiotic relationship positions open source as a dynamic and adaptive resource that not only addresses immediate technological needs but also fortifies the enterprise against the challenges of an ever-evolving business landscape. Conversely, the absence of integration between open source and core business functions poses a significant risk to the long-term viability of such initiatives. Without this essential connection, open source solutions may become detached entities that lack the necessary support and alignment with the organization's broader strategic objectives.

The Why

As organizations embark on their open source journey, whether as their first-ever endeavor, or a new team within the organization, or a new project within a team, the most important question that needs to be answered is "why." The "why" serves as the foundation for the strategic intent of the open source initiative. It clarifies whether the organization is pursuing open source for reasons such as faster innovation, cost savings, community collaboration, talent acquisition, or strategic positioning. This strategic intent provides a roadmap for the journey ahead.

Defining the "why" provides clarity of purpose. It articulates the specific goals, objectives, and expected outcomes of the initiative. This clarity helps guide decision-making, resource allocation, and overall strategic planning. It enables organizations to establish measurable outcomes and key performance indicators (KPIs). This, in turn, allows for the assessment of the initiative's success and impact. Whether it's increased community engagement, enhanced software quality, or talent acquisition, clear goals provide benchmarks for success.

Understanding the "why" ensures that the open source initiative aligns with the broader goals and mission of the organization. This alignment is crucial for ensuring that the resources invested in the open source journey contribute directly to the organization's strategic objectives. It allows organizations to anticipate potential challenges and risks associated with their open source journey. This foresight enables proactive risk mitigation strategies, ensuring a more resilient and successful implementation.

The "why" for each organization, team, or project could be different. Let's look at some of the most common "why"s.

Figure 2-1. *The "Why" Enterprises Contribute to Open Source*

Faster Innovation

- **Accelerating Development**: Open source stands
  on the shoulder of giants. It provides robust and
  well-established solutions to common problems.
  Organizations can leverage these existing solutions as
  a foundation for their own projects, saving time and

effort compared to developing everything from scratch. By building upon existing open source solutions and collaborating with the community, organizations can significantly reduce development time and associated costs. This approach minimizes the need to reinvent the wheel, enabling teams to focus on unique aspects of their projects rather than recreating foundational elements.

- **Global Collaboration**: Solving global problems requires the engineering resources of more than a company. Instead of depending solely on a single company's capabilities, open source projects facilitate the collective contribution of diverse talents and expertise from a global community. This collaborative model brings together contributors with varied backgrounds, experiences, and perspectives, enriching problem-solving approaches. The diversity within this global collaboration introduces a broad range of solutions that may not be achievable within the constraints of a single organization.

- **Thought Leadership**: Participating in open source projects can significantly contribute to establishing thought leadership. Actively contributing to open source projects allows individuals and organizations to showcase their expertise in specific domains. Through practical contributions, such as code contributions, bug fixes, or architectural improvements, participants demonstrate a deep understanding of the subject matter. It also provides a platform to share insights, best practices, and innovative solutions with a wider audience. This knowledge sharing contributes to thought leadership by positioning individuals or organizations as go-to sources for valuable information. Engaging in open source can open doors to speaking opportunities where individuals can share their experiences, insights, and knowledge with a broader audience. This public presence further establishes thought leadership.

Sustainable Codebase

- **Code Quality**: Open source projects thrive on the power of collaboration, welcoming developers from diverse backgrounds to contribute to codebases. This collective approach elevates code quality as multiple perspectives converge to review, analyze, and enhance the code. The result is a robust and well-structured codebase, marked by improved readability, maintainability, and adherence to best practices. In this dynamic environment, diversity becomes a driving force, ensuring a thorough examination of code architecture and promoting a culture of excellence. The collaborative scrutiny not only enhances the immediate functionality of the code but also prioritizes long-term sustainability. By fostering continuous refinement, open source projects stand as a testament to the collective brilliance of a global developer community committed to advancing the art and science of software development.

Eric S. Raymond, in his book *The Cathedral and the Bazaar*," coined Linus's law, the idea that "given enough eyeballs, all bugs are shallow." It was created in honor of Linus Torvalds, creator and the lead developer of Linux kernel. This law emphasizes the power of community-driven collaboration and peer review in finding and fixing software bugs and security vulnerabilities. It highlights the importance of distributed peer review. The law suggests that with a sufficiently large and diverse group of developers and users examining a piece of software, problems and bugs are more likely to be identified and addressed quickly. The law also applies to security vulnerabilities. With a vast number of individuals scrutinizing the code for potential security threats, open source projects benefit from a proactive and collective approach to security.

While Linus's Law is a guiding principle in open source, it's important to note that the effectiveness of this model depends on the size and engagement of the community. A larger and more active community is generally better equipped to leverage the benefits of Linus's Law, ensuring a high level of scrutiny and rapid response to identified issues in the codebase.

- **Continuous Testing**: In the realm of open source development, maintaining a high standard of code quality is paramount. Continuous testing stands as a fundamental practice within open source projects, embodying a commitment to excellence and reliability. This rigorous testing process, often facilitated through continuous integration, plays a pivotal role in ensuring the robustness of the codebase.

Open source projects leverage continuous testing to create a dynamic and responsive testing environment. This involves the integration of automated testing procedures into the development pipeline. As new code contributions are made, these automated tests are systematically executed, enabling swift and thorough examination of the entire codebase. The collaborative nature of open source ensures that these tests reflect a diverse set of scenarios, contributing to a comprehensive quality assurance process.

The diversity of contributors in open source projects enriches the testing environment. With developers from various backgrounds and experiences, the testing process becomes more comprehensive, covering a wide array of use cases and potential edge scenarios. This collaborative testing approach significantly reduces the likelihood of introducing bugs or regressions into the codebase.

Continuous testing doesn't merely focus on identifying issues after they occur; it's a proactive measure aimed at preventing problems before they arise. By implementing automated tests that run consistently throughout the development lifecycle, open source projects establish a robust safety net. This helps catch and address issues in their early stages, minimizing the chances of defects making their way into the final product.

- **Improved Software Development Methodology**: Engaging with open source communities exposes organizations and its developers to best practices, coding standards, and innovative approaches to problem-solving. This exposure contributes to the improvement of internal software design and development processes within the organization. The open exchange of ideas encourages continuous learning and refinement of development practices. This collaborative model also allows for a continuous evolution of software as multiple contributors contribute their expertise, leading to a more dynamic and feature-rich codebase.

Cost Savings

- **Shared Maintenance**: Open source projects often involve a large and diverse community of developers. When organizations contribute to these projects, they actively participate in identifying and fixing bugs. The collaborative effort helps address issues more efficiently, distributing the maintenance workload among a broader group. The community-driven model also facilitates a faster response to emerging issues and a more dynamic update cycle. Beyond bug fixes, the community contributes to ongoing improvements and optimizations. This collaborative approach to development means that organizations benefit from the collective expertise of the open source community, leading to enhancements that might not have been possible with a solely internal development team.

- **Prevent Developer Burnouts**: Multiple developers contributing to an open source project prevents an excessive burden on individual developers or teams within the organization by avoiding overwhelming workloads and fostering a more sustainable development pace. Involvement in open source projects provides developers with opportunities to enhance their skills and learn from a diverse set of contributors. This variety in tasks and challenges can contribute to a more engaging and fulfilling work environment, reducing the monotony that can lead to burnout. This leads to lower churn among developers and a higher likelihood of them sticking around at the company.

- **Avoiding Vendor Lock-in**: Open source solutions offer organizations a valuable alternative to proprietary technologies, mitigating the risks associated with vendor lock-in. Dependency on a single vendor's proprietary ecosystem can result in challenges and high costs when attempting to transition to alternative solutions. Moreover, organizations may find themselves restricted by the innovation happening within the confines of a proprietary "walled garden." Embracing open source provides organizations with the autonomy to select from a diverse range of solutions, free from the constraints of a single vendor's choices. This independence empowers organizations to tailor decisions according to their specific requirements, circumventing limitations imposed by proprietary technologies. Unlike proprietary solutions, organizations leveraging open source are exempt from licensing fees, restrictions, or sudden price hikes dictated by a single vendor. Additionally, the flexibility to modify and customize open source software allows organizations to adapt swiftly to changing needs without being tethered to a vendor's timeline or priorities.

Strategic Initiatives

- **Strategic Alignment**: Organizations may contribute to open source projects that align with their strategic goals and initiatives. This can include projects that support industry standards or emerging technologies. By doing so, they ensure that their products or services are interoperable and compliant with widely accepted standards, enhancing compatibility and facilitating collaboration within the industry. Open source projects often pioneer or adopt emerging technologies. Organizations strategically contribute to projects related to these technologies to stay at the forefront of innovation. This strategic alignment enables them to integrate cutting-edge solutions into their own products or services.

- **Business Model**: Organizations strategically create open source projects to establish a presence in the developer community. By offering valuable tools, libraries, or frameworks, these organizations aim to capture the attention and loyalty of developers. This helps in building a dedicated user base and fostering a positive reputation within the developer community.

A classical way to monetize these open source projects is to provide supplementary services. This includes offering premium support packages, consulting services, and specialized training. Developers who rely on these open source projects are willing to pay for expert assistance, personalized guidance, and in-depth training, creating a revenue stream for the organization. Developers from organizations producing open source projects frequently engage in creating integrations with other complementary open source tools. This collaborative effort helps in establishing interoperability between different projects, creating a more cohesive and integrated ecosystem of open source solutions.

Compliance and Security

- **Transparent Security**: Security is a paramount concern in open source development. The collaborative nature of open source allows the community to collectively identify and address security vulnerabilities. Security experts and developers with diverse skill sets contribute to the detection and resolution of potential threats, enhancing the overall security posture of the software.

  Open source projects often maintain transparent and open discussions about security issues. Vulnerabilities are reported, discussed, and addressed openly within the community following published procedures. This transparency not only ensures prompt resolution but also facilitates knowledge sharing and the adoption of best practices for security measures. In the event of a security issue, the open source community can usually respond more swiftly. The distributed nature of the community means that a wide range of experts can contribute to resolving the issue in real time. This agility is crucial for addressing emerging security threats promptly and effectively.

- **Compliance Assurance**: Open source licenses come with distinct compliance requirements that organizations must carefully navigate. When organizations actively contribute to open source projects, it serves as a proactive measure to comprehend and adhere to the specific licensing terms associated with the utilized software. This engagement not only demonstrates a commitment to ethical and legal practices but also acts as a safeguard against potential legal complications that may arise from non-compliance. Contributing to open source projects, therefore, becomes a strategic approach for organizations to ensure a clear understanding of licensing obligations, mitigating the risk of legal issues and fostering a collaborative and compliant ecosystem.

Community Building

- **Networking**: Engaging in open source projects extends beyond code contributions; it serves as a gateway for organizations to establish valuable connections within a broader community of developers, users, and industry experts. This networking aspect of open source participation is instrumental in fostering relationships and cultivating partnerships. Understanding the community dynamics is a very critical element as that helps you engage with maintainers in a social setting. This helps them understand your perspective better and makes them more likely to help you address technical needs as well.

Open source participation provides a unique opportunity for organizations to build relationships within their industry. It allows them to connect with other entities – be they competitors, collaborators, or potential partners – who share a similar commitment to open source principles. This collaborative environment encourages the sharing of knowledge, resources, and solutions, fostering an atmosphere of mutual benefit. These relationships not only enrich the open source ecosystem but also offer organizations the chance to collaborate, innovate, and establish a lasting presence within their industry.

- **Talent Acquisition**: Participating in open source projects strategically positions organizations as attractive workplaces for maintainers – key contributors who play a pivotal role in shaping the strategic direction of a project. Beyond merely contributing code, maintainers hold significant influence over the project's vision, roadmap, and overall development trajectory. Organizations actively involved in open source not only benefit from the expertise these maintainers bring to their projects but also create an enticing environment for top talent. Open source participation signals a commitment to collaboration, transparency, and innovation, qualities that resonate with skilled maintainers seeking impactful and meaningful contributions. By aligning with and supporting maintainers, organizations not only enhance the development of the open source software but also directly address their business needs. This collaboration is mutually beneficial, as maintainers find a workplace that values and supports their contributions, while organizations gain access to highly skilled individuals who influence the trajectory of critical projects.

Market Visibility

- **Brand Recognition**: Engaging in open source projects presents organizations with a unique avenue to enhance their brand recognition and reputation. By actively contributing to open source initiatives, organizations showcase a commitment to values highly regarded in the tech industry – transparency, collaboration, and a sense of community.

  The act of contributing to open source extends beyond mere software development; it communicates a willingness to share knowledge, collaborate with a diverse community of developers, and actively contribute to the betterment of shared technologies. This commitment aligns with contemporary expectations of corporate responsibility and resonates with stakeholders who value organizations that go beyond proprietary interests.

Collaboration is a cornerstone of open source, and organizations contributing to this ecosystem signal their ability to work cohesively with others toward common goals. This collaborative spirit resonates positively, contributing to a sense of community both within the organization and among external stakeholders.

The values associated with open source engagement contribute to a positive brand image. Organizations that actively participate in open source not only gain recognition for their technical contributions but also for their broader commitment to fostering a collaborative and inclusive tech ecosystem. This recognition can lead to increased credibility, a positive reputation within the industry, and a competitive edge in attracting talent, customers, and partners.

- **Showcasing Expertise**: Participating actively in open source projects serves as a powerful platform for organizations to showcase their technical prowess in specific domains. Beyond being a venue for collaborative development, open source involvement becomes a public display of an organization's depth of expertise, innovation, and proficiency in specific technologies or industry niches.

Organizations contributing to open source projects have the opportunity to highlight their mastery of cutting-edge technologies, coding standards, and best practices. This demonstration of technical excellence serves as a live portfolio, allowing potential customers, partners, and the broader tech community to witness the organization's capabilities firsthand.

By contributing code, solving complex problems, and providing valuable insights within the open source realm, organizations establish themselves as thought leaders and authoritative voices in their chosen domains. This active engagement not only attracts attention from peers within the open source community but also resonates with external stakeholders seeking expertise in related technologies.

The visibility gained through open source contributions becomes a form of organic marketing, reaching an audience that values hands-on technical proficiency. This visibility extends beyond traditional marketing channels, attracting like-minded individuals and organizations who recognize and appreciate the demonstrated expertise.

Customization and Flexibility

- **Tailoring Solutions**: Active participation in open source projects provides organizations with a unique avenue for tailoring software solutions to meet their specific needs. This customization capability is a significant advantage, especially for industries characterized by distinctive requirements or stringent regulatory constraints.

  Open source projects offer a level of flexibility that proprietary solutions often struggle to match. By contributing to open source, organizations can not only consume but actively shape and customize software according to their unique specifications.

This adaptability becomes particularly valuable for industries where standard, off-the-shelf solutions may fall short of addressing specific workflows, compliance standards, or industry-specific challenges.

Industries with unique needs, such as healthcare, finance, or government, can leverage open source contributions to adapt software solutions to their specific regulatory frameworks. This flexibility allows organizations to navigate complex compliance requirements while benefiting from the continuous improvements and innovations driven by the broader open source community.

I encourage the readers to go through an exercise within their enterprise and define their "why." This should be clearly documented and agreed upon by the executive management.

Philosophies of Engagement in Open Source

A common philosophy in the context of open source is "corporate altruism." It refers to a company's voluntary commitment to contribute resources, expertise, or funding to open source projects without expecting immediate or direct financial benefits. This commitment may include code contributions, open sourcing internal tools or frameworks, financial support for open source initiatives, community engagement, and adherence to open source principles. Corporate altruism in open source is driven by a desire to give back to the community, promote transparency, and support the growth of a healthy and vibrant ecosystem, even if it may not directly serve the company's short-term interests. While corporate altruism can certainly have positive impacts on open source and a company's reputation, these challenges highlight the complexities involved in balancing altruistic motivations with corporate interests and practical constraints. Overcoming these obstacles often requires careful strategic planning, cultural shifts within organizations, and a deep understanding of the dynamics of the open source ecosystem.

For some enterprises, the philosophy of "enlightened self-interest" might have a better connection. It refers to the idea that companies can benefit themselves while also contributing to the common good of the open source community. It involves recognizing that supporting open source initiatives can align with a company's long-term strategic goals and ultimately yield positive outcomes for the company itself while also contributing to the collective advancement of technology and innovation. By aligning their interests with the principles of openness, collaboration, and community-driven development, companies can achieve both short-term gains and long-term sustainability.

A related philosophy is "scratch your own itch and help others with theirs." It is a foundational principle in the open source community, emphasizing both corporate utility and communal benefit. It suggests that developers should start by addressing their own needs and solving problems they encounter in their work or personal projects. When a developer encounters a challenge or a gap in existing software that affects their own workflow or goals, they're encouraged to take initiative and develop solutions to address those issues. Once developers have addressed their own needs and developed solutions, they're encouraged to share their work with the broader community. By making their code open source, documenting it, and potentially providing support and guidance, developers can help others who may encounter similar challenges or have related needs. It promotes a culture of self-reliance, innovation, and generosity within the open source community, where individuals contribute their skills and resources to collectively improve the quality and availability of software for everyone.

A common phrase in the open source community is "we stand on the shoulders of giants." It emphasizes the collaborative and iterative nature of software development. This embodies the idea of building upon the work of those who came before, leveraging existing tools, libraries, frameworks, and knowledge to create something new and innovative. Sometimes an existing project may serve a significant part of your needs. In that case, instead of starting from scratch, developers can contribute to existing open source projects by submitting code improvements, bug fixes, documentation updates, or other enhancements. This allows the developers to have a meaningful impact on the broader ecosystem while also benefiting from the feedback and support of the community. By leveraging these existing solutions, developers can save time and effort, avoid reinventing the wheel, and benefit from the collective wisdom and expertise embedded in those projects. In some cases, developers may "fork" or create a copy of an existing open source project to adapt it to their specific requirements or to pursue a different direction of development. By embracing and extending the work of those who came before, developers can accelerate innovation, foster a culture of knowledge sharing and collaboration, and collectively push the boundaries of what is possible in the world of open source software.

Another way to think about this is how "open source grows like a banyan tree." Open source embodies knowledge and experience of diverse and inclusive communities and enables ideas to spread and grow farther and faster than ever before. Banyan tree grows in the crevice of a host and has prop roots that start from the stem and grow down towards the ground. In open source, this correlates to providing a broad set of capabilities to users. Whether it is an operating system, databases, containers, CI/CD tools, and you name it. Anything you need can be obtained in open source or enhanced. In Banyan trees, frugivore birds disperse the seeds that give rise to prop roots, which then allow the tree to get grounded at multiple places. Prop roots also give a broader surface area and a rich set of nutrients to the tree. Open source is increasingly the same way, how different projects learn and build on each other. Git is an open source software. Its properties, such as its distributed nature, creating branches of code, and merging pull requests, change the way we build and enable the ideas to be propagated across the project. Many companies around the world have adopted Git as source code control and have unlocked innovation for their communities. In addition, open source licenses provide resilience and allow individuals and organizations to make their own paths. Open source projects exist because their ideas are propagated without coordinating with another party, through communities.

The Zen phrase "chop wood carry water" (CW^2) is used metaphorically in many contexts, including open source software development. It emphasizes the importance of performing essential, routine tasks with mindfulness and dedication, regardless of their perceived simplicity or complexity. While code is king in open source projects, there are plenty of routine and often unglamorous tasks that are crucial for the maintenance and improvement of a project. These tasks, though they may not be as celebrated as writing new features, are vital for the health and longevity of the project. These tasks include identifying, diagnosing, and fixing bugs in the codebase; reviewing and providing feedback on pull requests from other contributors; writing and updating documentation to ensure that it is accurate and helpful; writing, maintaining, and running tests; categorizing, prioritizing, and managing issues in the project's issue tracker; community support such as moderating channels, running events, and onboarding new users; refactoring code to enhance readability, maintainability, and performance; and updating dependencies to ensure compatibility and security. While these activities may seem unglamorous compared to developing new features, they are vital for maintaining project stability, enhancing user experience, onboarding new contributors, ensuring sustainability, fostering collaboration and trust, and maintaining security. By diligently attending to these routine responsibilities, open source projects remain functional, accessible, and resilient, ultimately ensuring their long-term success and growth.

Business Models

Once organizations define the purpose behind their engagement with open source, the "why," the next crucial step involves determining the most suitable business model. The alignment of a well-crafted business model with the collaborative nature of open source is paramount for creating sustainable revenue streams and ensuring long-term success. With this clarity of "why," organizations can then explore various business models tailored to leverage the collaborative ethos of open source.

Regardless of the chosen model, successful open source business strategies often involve finding the right balance between community engagement and revenue generation. By aligning the chosen model with the organization's overall objectives and the collaborative spirit of open source, businesses can unlock the full potential of their engagement with open source, fostering both innovation and financial sustainability.

Let's take a look at some common business models around open source.

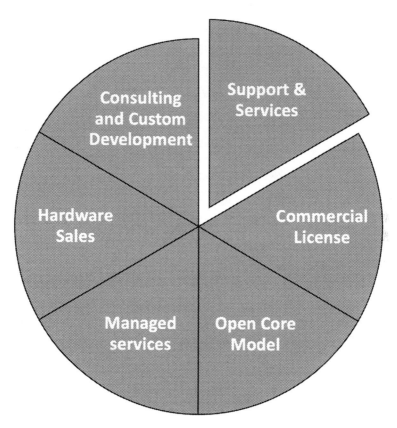

Figure 2-2. *Open Source Business Models*

Support and Services

Companies employing the support and services model offer assistance, troubleshooting, and training for open source software. Users pay for the expertise, timely support, and customized solutions provided by the company. This model thrives on the understanding that organizations often require professional assistance and reliable support when implementing and maintaining open source solutions in their infrastructure.

For example: A prominent example of the Support and Services model is Red Hat, a leading provider of open source solutions. Red Hat focuses on delivering enterprise-grade support and services for a range of open source software, including the widely used Linux operating system. In this model, organizations subscribing to Red Hat's services gain access to a suite of benefits. This includes expert technical support to address issues promptly, regular software updates and patches for enhanced security and stability, and comprehensive training programs to empower teams in effectively utilizing open source solutions.

Red Hat's success lies in recognizing that enterprises deploying open source software often encounter challenges that extend beyond the capabilities of the software itself. The need for timely assistance, reliable support, and customized solutions is crucial for organizations relying on open source in their infrastructure. By providing these essential services, Red Hat not only generates revenue but also ensures the seamless adoption and sustained success of open source solutions within the enterprise ecosystem. This model aligns with the collaborative ethos of open source, as the company actively engages with the community while offering specialized services that cater to the unique needs of businesses.

Commercial License

The commercial license model in open source involves providing a commercial (often proprietary) license for certain versions or features of an open source software product. It typically works where a version of the software is distributed under an open source license (e.g., Apache, GNU General Public License). This means that users have free access to the source code, can modify it, and can distribute their own versions. In parallel, the company or organization behind the open source project offers a commercial license for the same software. This commercial license may include proprietary features, advanced functionalities, or additional tools that are not available in the open source version. Commercial licenses often come with additional benefits, such as dedicated technical support, regular updates, and maintenance services. These services can be crucial for businesses relying on the software for critical operations.

This is also called *dual licensing* as the product is available under two separate licenses. Users can choose between the free open source version and a commercial version with added features. This allows companies to monetize their software by providing a clear path for those who need additional features and are willing to pay for them.

Open Core Model

For example: A noteworthy illustration of the subscription-based model is MongoDB, a widely used NoSQL database. MongoDB embraces an open source core, ensuring free access to its fundamental features for users. However, for businesses requiring additional capabilities, support, and advanced features, MongoDB offers an enterprise version.

Under this model, users can purchase the commercial license to MongoDB, unlocking a suite of premium features such as advanced security options, LDAP support, high availability and high throughput, and comprehensive technical support. The license fee not only sustains MongoDB's ongoing development efforts but also provides users with a reliable and feature-rich database solution backed by professional support.

This approach caters to businesses seeking an extra layer of value and support beyond the standard open source offering. By aligning revenue generation with the delivery of enhanced services, MongoDB strikes a balance between open source collaboration and the practical needs of enterprises.

The open core model offers a core version of the software as open source, with premium features available in a commercial version. The core, aligned with traditional open source principles, has open and accessible source code. Commercial offerings, including proprietary features, extend from this open source foundation. Users benefit from the open source version but can upgrade for exclusive functionalities.

A robust open source community is crucial, even as commercial offerings target a specialized audience. This model maintains a commitment to open source principles while ensuring sustainable funding. The core functionality remains open source, fostering transparency and community collaboration. This approach facilitates rapid scaling of the user base, with the free version attracting users who may later find value in premium features, contributing to revenue growth.

For example: GitLab, a web-based Git repository manager, provides an open source version with essential version control features. Two commercial versions, known as Premium and Ultra, are offered with advanced collaboration, better security and compliance, scalability, and other features.

Managed Services

Managed services involve delivering hosting, maintenance, and operational support for open source software, often within a cloud environment. Companies, such as hyperscalers, provide these services to ensure the seamless operation of the software, enabling organizations to reap the benefits without the day-to-day management burden. This allows customers to utilize open source projects without concerns about operational intricacies. Operating an open source project on a global scale involves setting up data centers worldwide, deploying the open source software, applying regular security patches, and implementing best practices for scalability and reliability. Hyperscalers handle these details, allowing customers to use a variety of open source projects without undifferentiated heavy lifting.

In certain cases, the company originating the open source project may offer its own managed service. While deployed on a hyperscaler, the operational aspects are owned by the company rather than the hyperscaler. Given the company's extensive involvement with maintainers on the project, they possess the deepest understanding of how to deploy the project at scale. This model establishes a reliable revenue stream for the company, appealing to businesses seeking additional value and support beyond the basic open source offering.

For example: Amazon Web Services (AWS) provides managed services for a variety of open source tools and databases, including offering Amazon Elastic Kubernetes Service (EKS) for efficient Kubernetes orchestration at scale. This service is accessible in all global regions of AWS, ensuring widespread availability. One of the core tenets of this service is upstream compatibility. This means that customers can seamlessly deploy open source Kubernetes applications across different regions. AWS assumes the responsibility for the complete lifecycle management of Kubernetes clusters, handling tasks such as setup, maintenance, and upgrades. This comprehensive management extends to the routine application of patches and addressing various operational aspects, relieving customers of these operational burdens yet able to enjoy the benefits of an open source project.

MongoDB, the company behind the namesake project, provides a managed service available on the three major hyperscalers. This service allows customers to leverage MongoDB's expertise in handling the operational aspects of their database solution.

Hardware Sales

This business model is tailored for hardware manufacturing companies, particularly silicon vendors. In this approach, the company actively contributes to open source projects relevant to their hardware products. The overarching goal is to ensure that all hardware features are fully integrated and enabled within the upstream open source software. Customers using the open source projects associated with the hardware experience enhanced satisfaction, as the contributions ensure that their hardware investment translates into superior performance and capabilities. The collaborative approach creates customer stickiness to the hardware vendor. They are inclined to stay loyal due to the optimized performance and integration achieved through open source contributions. This creates stickiness for the customers to that hardware vendor and creates a revenue stream for the hardware vendor to sustain open source development.

For example: Intel creates new silicon that is used in data centers, cloud, network, edge, or client devices. With each new iteration of silicon, Intel introduces a more advanced instruction set, enhancing processing speed and efficiency. They contribute to 300+ open source projects to ensure these newly introduced instructions are enabled in the most intuitive manner. By doing so, Intel aims to provide customers with a comprehensive and streamlined experience, allowing them to harness the maximum benefits of both the open source projects and the latest silicon technology. Customers, whether utilizing hyperscalers like AWS or employing a laptop purchased from a retail store, can leverage these open source projects. This results in a cohesive and optimized experience, where the combination of open source advancements and Intel's latest silicon delivers superior performance and functionality.

Consulting and Custom Development

The consulting and custom development model is a strategic approach where companies specialize in delivering tailored services, including consulting, customization, and bespoke solutions built upon open source software. This model centers around providing expertise to organizations that seek personalized implementations, configurations, and optimizations of open source solutions to meet their specific needs.

Companies in this model accumulate specialized knowledge and skills in open source technologies, positioning themselves as experts in delivering customized solutions. They hire maintainers for open source projects, which in turn allows them to build confidence with their customers. By providing personalized services and solutions, companies add significant value to the open source ecosystem. Clients benefit from tailored implementations that maximize the utility of open source software. And this creates a revenue stream for the companies.

For example: Many system integrators specialize in customizing open source solutions for clients.

While not exhaustive, these business models highlight the diverse approaches companies can adopt within the ever-evolving open source landscape. The continuous evolution of the open source ecosystem fosters innovation in business models, showcasing the potential for companies to capitalize on open source software, contribute to the community, and sustain their business operations.

Case Studies

Let's take a look at what and how some companies did to bring a cultural change in order to make open source sustainable with their business.

Aiven

Contributed by: Josep Prat, Open Source Engineering Director, Aiven Oy

Since the inception of Aiven, we have been regular consumers and producers of open source software. With a wealth of experience in the PostgreSQL development and consultancy, Aiven's founders had continually observed that many organizations were trying to address the challenge of configuring and managing their database services. To address this, instead of creating point solutions, they had a vision of developing a platform that could provide production-level services without any of the management overhead.

From that vision almost ten years ago, Aiven has evolved and innovated continuously and, today, provides X customers globally with a trusted Data and AI platform. Spanning across several data domains and solving our customers' biggest data challenges by using a myriad of open source technologies, we enable our customers to focus on innovation and driving value from their data.

Open source software is at the very core of Aiven, both as a consumer of open source software and a contributor to it. Our philosophy has always been to enrich the open source ecosystem with contributions and OS tools, enabling the wider community to embrace the new developments. This philosophy remains the same, with the whole company encouraged to contribute in the open.

Customers adopting the Aiven platform benefit from the variety of well-integrated services, enabling them to meet changing business demands with agility and scalability and achieve accelerated innovation. A lesser known fact is that Aiven is built and run on the Aiven solution itself, using the same mix of open source tools. The health and innovation of these open source tools are therefore not only important but they are mission-critical for both Aiven and its customers to scale and be agile.

As the company has grown, we realized that relying on occasional upstream contributions was simply not enough to ensure the level of sustainability and innovation required for the projects we and our customers rely on and in 2021 Aiven created its own Open Source Program Office (OSPO).

OSPOs differ from company to company, reflecting the needs of their organization. Similarly, Aiven's OSPO is engaged in important but routine projects needed by the company, such as Open Source compliance (for both consumption and production), as well as internal mentoring. These may be familiar standard OSPO practices, but Aiven's OSPO is special. It's mostly formed by Software Engineers whose purpose is to contribute to open source projects core to Aiven and its customers, regardless of who is the copyright holder of such projects. This means we help maintain Apache Kafka, Apache Flink, Apache Cassandra, MySQL, OpenSearch, and ClickHouse, among others.

It's important to state that Aiven doesn't contribute to open source projects because it's the "right thing to do," since that simply wouldn't be a sustainable business decision. The OSPO team exists to ensure sustainability, innovation, and business continuity for upstream projects our customers rely on.

The team makes sure that critical projects for Aiven and its customers are well maintained and have sufficient highly skilled support. The vast majority of OS projects need help in terms of contributors and maintainers, and this is where Aiven OSPO offers its support. By dedicating people to contribute to such projects, we help spread the maintenance burden. This is not only beneficial for Aiven and its customers but also for the entire community relying on their preferred OS tech.

Another objective of the team is to make sure innovation on critical open source projects doesn't stop. Dedicating contributors to a project long-term means they work on the bigger picture and collaborate with other members on the future of the project itself. By increasing the supporting base, we also ensure more diversity of contributions that are likely to appeal to the wider community than just a subset of it. Additionally, we always want to ensure the needs of the end users are heard so we keep a close loop with our customers to understand and define the future evolution of the project.

Last but not least, we ensure Aiven's business continuity given it heavily relies on open source projects. All essential software components of any company need to be actively maintained, companies usually define the impact radius of this software as the software they have the copyright to. Aiven goes one step further and also dedicates professionals to maintain open source projects whose copyright holder is a third party. Why is this important? For many reasons, one example being that we have seen numerous open source projects change license in the past, and we will see many more in the future. By having dedicated people working on such projects we can improve the odds of having a successful way forward, either with a forked project or an existing alternative.

Open source is not just important for Aiven, it is essential and at the core of its philosophy. We accomplish this, not just by having an Open Source Program Office, but by fostering an open source culture among all employees, not just our engineers. As a case in point, during 2023, almost 20% of all Aiven employees made 10 or more contributions to open source projects and 1/3 of all Aiven employees made at least one contribution.

Aiven engineers are empowered to contribute back as part of their role to the open source projects they rely on if they encounter any deficiency during their daily tasks. We regularly celebrate open source achievements of our team members via an internal newsletter.

But the biggest and most diverse contribution to open source culture at Aiven is the Plankton Program that was created for all Aiven employees who decide to work on any open source project during their free time. We want to celebrate these contributions, but we also want to recognize the effort put into it by compensating them economically for the hours they report back.

Aiven was built on the foundation of open source, and its future growth and success will be too.

Amazon

Contributed by: Nithya Ruff, Director, Open Source Program Office, Amazon

Background

Amazon has a number of distinct businesses, well known among them being Amazon Web Services (AWS) which is a developer-centric cloud services business, and the stores and devices side of Amazon, and its subsidiaries which includes a broad spectrum of areas such as Amazon. com, Prime Video, Amazon Music, and Whole Foods. Our open source strategy takes into account this diversity of uses, customer needs, and technology needs.

Amazon has a long history of building products and infrastructure on open source software. As far back as 2002, Amazon.com made news when it switched to Linux across its datacenter. Soon after, Amazon used Linux in the Amazon Kindle E-reader. From the start, Amazon's cloud services, including Amazon Elastic Compute Cloud (Amazon EC2) and Amazon Simple Storage Service (Amazon S3), have depended on the successful use of open source.

Why We Contribute

Today, the thoughtful use of open source continues to be widespread and encouraged both in the consumer business and the developer-facing AWS. We realize the importance of open source technologies to our infrastructure and products, and the open source teams at Amazon have worked hard to create policies and mechanisms that make it easy for builders or developers to participate in open source. They can contribute back patches and changes without seeking permissions and release Amazon-created works to open source with minimal reviews.

Our engineers routinely contribute in a number of different ways to sustain the communities we rely on. A subset of communities that we contribute to include the Cloud Native Computing Foundation (CNCF) at the Linux Foundation, and Apache Software Foundation, OpenJDK, Rust, Jupyter, PostgreSQL, and the Eclipse Software Defined Vehicles (SDV) community, among others. For example, multiple core maintainers of the PostgreSQL ecosystem work at AWS and spend their time sustaining and innovating in this ecosystem.

Amazon invests in working with open source communities for three main reasons: First, we use open source extensively as a company, whether in our infrastructure or in our products and services. Being customer obsessed, we acknowledge that open source enables us to provide the best possible customer experience at the best possible cost. Second, open source is important to our customers. AWS customers want the best operational experience to build and run open source workloads in the cloud. Customers also ask us to provide managed open source services to reduce the operational work at scale. The consumer side of Amazon cares deeply about choice, lower cost, and a great user experience, and our use of open source enables us to deliver on these customer needs. Third, given that much of the world's critical infrastructure is built on open source, we want to be a part of sustaining and securing it. This benefits our customers and partners, the world at large, and us.

Enabling Open Source Culture

Open source communities often have a different culture, cadence, and approach to development than what happens inside a company. It is the Amazon OSPO's role to create a bridge from the company to open source and back such that it is easier for builders to use and work with open source. This enables us to serve customer needs and balance it with the needs of the community around open source. Examples of how we do this are outlined below:

Raising Policy Awareness – The policy for the use of open source is low friction, well understood, and shared. Every builder goes through policy awareness training every other year. New builders go through open source training during their initial onboarding training.

Structuring Around the Business – Amazon has built a strong open source program with two components on purpose: One faces our internal builders and enables them to build successfully with open source and to work in communities that are important to us. And the other manages our outward-facing communications and engagement in communities. Together, these two organizations cover the areas that matter to Amazon and the communities we work in.

Investing in the Future and Acknowledging Champions – Another way we scale and build open source talent is through our open source champions program. As the OSPO cannot scale enough to serve the needs of the diverse and broad set of customers inside the company, we created the Open Source Champions program. Champions are experts who reside in the business, closest to their builders and leaders. Champions are recognized and commended through various recognition programs and help scale open source expertise across the company.

Sharing Best Practices – We use a number of different ways to build community, engage new open source contributors, and raise the skills of our builders in open source. We host Slack channels for open source enthusiasts and Champions, run a monthly webinar called the Open Source Practice Series, and hold regular office hours. A key part of scaling our efforts is including open source content in internal builder events and in re: Invent's open source track. As an example, Amazon's internal developer conference brings together thousands of on-site and virtual attendees. It includes keynotes by OSPO leaders and a whole open source track for builders to learn from.

Making Life Easier for Developers – We automate and build checks and balances into the developer workflow so that the developer does the right thing with little effort.

Recognizing Excellence – Acknowledging the good work and recognizing builders and teams for their work is something we do consistently. For example, recognizing builders who have built trust and achieved committer or governing board status in the community. Recognition for participating in open source contributions or leadership includes badges, shoutouts, feedback to the managers for performance, and promotions.

Summary

Open source collaboration is core and essential to how Amazon innovates. We use open source in our infrastructure, products, and services and know how important it is to our customers, partners, and the world. We empower Amazon builders to be full participants in open source innovation by using it safely to solve customer problems. We lead Amazon to contribute back to the global open source community as the world depends on sustaining this common good. We believe in supporting open source work and in serving our customers in solving hard problems using open source. Our open source strategy and program are aligned with our leadership principle of "Success and Scale bring broad responsibility."

BlackRock

Contributed by: Mike Bowen, Technical Fellow, BlackRock

Open source is a fundamental and growing part of BlackRock's culture, embedded in its engineering and development practices. BlackRock navigates a comprehensive range of open source engagements, including open source consumption, collaboration, contribution, and creation of open source software, which the firm recognizes as the four pillars of open source and is foundational to its efforts in the space. This comprehensive approach underwrites the organization's commitment to breaking down barriers between innovators through harnessing the power of open collaboration.

BlackRock's open source engagements are based on a clear understanding of the benefits of adopting its principles, showing the strategic benefits that come from open source participation. Primarily, the organization recognizes open source as a driver of faster innovation. BlackRock benefits from the shared knowledge of a large and diverse community of developers, which helps the firm to innovate faster, keep up with the ever-changing technology landscape, and serve its clients well.

Moreover, open source presents a compelling proposition for cost savings. By leveraging existing open source solutions and avoiding duplication of efforts, BlackRock can optimize its resource allocation, redirecting valuable time and talent towards areas of strategic importance. This not only enhances cost efficiency but enables the organization to allocate resources towards higher-value activities, fostering innovation and growth.

Collaboration is at the core of BlackRock's principles, leveraging the shared knowledge and innovation of diverse partners by participating in open source communities and promoting participation within the organization. This collaborative approach enhances the quality and scale of the software produced and helps to facilitate a culture of knowledge sharing and mutual support.

Furthermore, embracing open source serves as a powerful tool for talent acquisition and retention. In an increasingly competitive talent landscape, developers are drawn to organizations that embrace the values of open collaboration and innovation. Championing open source principles has helped BlackRock to attract top talent and fosters a sense of inclusion among its employees.

Open source contributes to reducing the mean time to delivery of business value to clients. By leveraging existing open source solutions and building on top of them, BlackRock can accelerate its development cycles, delivering value to clients more efficiently and effectively. The organization strongly believes that all simple and even some complex problems may have already been solved with open source. By leveraging high-quality solutions to build on top of, BlackRock seeks to provide more agility and higher velocity delivery of business value to their clients enhancing customer satisfaction and strengthening the organization's competitive positioning in the market.

The firm adopts a comprehensive strategy that involves different activities and measures to promote and enable a culture of open source within the organization. Internal events such as hackathons, both global and regional, open source days, educational workshops, and bringing in external open source experts serve as opportunities for employees to engage with open source technologies, experts, patterns, and practices, facilitating hands-on learning and collaboration. These events not only inform practical skills but also cultivate a sense of community and camaraderie among employees, fostering a culture of collaboration and innovation.

Moreover, recognition programs for contributors and authors of open source projects incentivize and reward participation, reinforcing the value placed on open source engagement within the organization. Education is prioritized through formal 1-2-1 sessions, training sessions, and resources that equip employees with the necessary skills and knowledge to engage effectively. This helps to empower them to contribute and collaborate meaningfully to open source projects and communities.

Additionally, policies and processes were established to govern the use of open source software and contributions back to the community. This helps to ensure compliance as a highly regulated organization and responsible stewardship of open source resources. Employee enablement is emphasized through providing access to tools, processes, platforms, and resources for participation in open source. Empowering employees to use a self-service approach to engagement, learning, and collaboration safely and within compliance.

In conclusion, BlackRock's adoption of open source culture reflects a strategic commitment to innovation, collaboration, and excellence. By fostering an ecosystem that facilitates and encourages open collaboration and contribution, the firm not only drives value creation and competitive advantage but also cultivates a culture of learning, growth, and innovation. Through its continued dedication to open source principles, BlackRock stands poised to lead and thrive in an increasingly interconnected and dynamic digital landscape.

Bloomberg

Contributed by: Alyssa Wright, Open Source Program Office, Office of the CTO, Bloomberg, Francesca Romano, Head of Global Operations, Corporate Philanthropy, Bloomberg

Cultivating a Culture of Contribution

Bloomberg's approach to open source is rooted in the belief that collaboration fuels innovation and that innovation drives impact; it is also rooted in our culture of giving back. For Bloomberg, open source isn't just a code repository; it's a vibrant community made better by diverse contributions, and it's a crucial asset to our business, the bedrock of a thriving global tech industry, **and** our shared digital world. As such, we don't just consume open source resources; we invest in their quality and longevity by actively participating in their development and building leaders who sustain this critical digital infrastructure.

Like many companies, Bloomberg supports open source foundations, creates upstream developer workflows, sponsors critical open source initiatives, and empowers our engineers to become leaders within open source communities. But uniquely, we have infused Bloomberg's culture of philanthropy into our open source strategy, creating a more scalable framework for sustaining open source by both attracting new and diverse talent and incentivizing ongoing contributions.

Sustaining Open Source: A Three-Pronged Strategic Approach

Product Alignment

As an "open source first" company, Bloomberg relies heavily on open source. In return, we invest in a varied portfolio of more than 20 open source foundations, strategically selected based on their commitment to creating a more technologically open and secure future, as well as their relevance to developing our core infrastructure and products. From the Apache Software Foundation and Ecma International to the OpenInfra Foundation and the Eclipse Foundation, we have supported many foundations that serve as cornerstones of sustainable open source governance. We also sponsor critical initiatives, such as our partnership with the Python Software Foundation (PSF) to fund a full-time Developer-in-Residence.

People Alignment

Beyond investing in technology, Bloomberg also invests in people. And by fostering a culture of code contribution and active community engagement, we simultaneously support the development of our own engineers and position Bloomberg as a trusted partner within the broader open source ecosystem.

- We developed a dedicated mentorship program for first-year college students that not only encourages a new generation of talent to contribute early and often to open source. This also provides those Bloomberg engineers who serve as their mentors with an opportunity to further develop as managers and leaders.

- We encourage our engineers to actively engage in external discussions, forums, and conferences related to open source communities in which we have a vested interest in their success. This provides them with an opportunity to strengthen their professional networks, foster strong relationships with key players across the industry, and become more established thought leaders within these communities.

- We cultivate a culture of open source through internal meetups and OSPO office hours, where we discuss open source trends and collaborate on solutions to key issues. Even our internal processes, built and continually refined over the last decade, prioritize an open source-style model of peer review and collaboration.

Philanthropy Alignment

Philanthropy and service are an integral part of Bloomberg's culture, centered around the core belief that giving back and supporting local communities creates lasting positive change. The key premise behind open source is no different. By strategically partnering to develop new programs and jointly fund initiatives, the Open Source Program Office (OSPO) and the Corporate Philanthropy teams have successfully amplified each other's impact and have truly cultivated a culture of open source contribution.

- The **Bloomberg Free and Open Source Software (FOSS) Contributor Fund** actively engages our engineers in the allocation of funding to open source projects. Each quarter, engineers can nominate and vote on the open source projects they think are most deserving of a corporate grant. This process helps surface and spread awareness of a wide range of innovative open source projects, provides the projects themselves with the capital they need to maintain or expand, and fosters a greater sense of ownership, responsibility, and pride within our internal open source community.

- **Open Source Dollars For Your Hours** recognizes code contribution as a form of volunteerism, and incentivizes it by allowing engineers to convert their hours spent contributing to open source projects into charitable dollars donated to nonprofits, creating a tangible link between their technical contributions and social good.

- Designed to be an accessible on-ramp for first-time open source contributors, our **Open Source Sustainability Series** matches teams of Bloomberg employees with projects hosted by our open source foundation partners. In parallel, it provides Bloomberg's engineers with valuable mentorship and leadership experience, encouraging and preparing them to become active participants and leaders within the wider open source community.

Open Source Sustainability Series Pilot

Launched as part of our skills-based volunteer program, the inaugural 2023 Open Source Sustainability Series intentionally moved away from a hackathon model to an extended – and more participatory – engagement. In close partnership with NumFOCUS, members of the Bloomberg Women in Technology (BWIT) community contributed to the Pandas library over the course of eight weeks. To ensure the program's success, both NumFOCUS and Bloomberg committed to providing dedicated mentors for the duration of the series, and leadership from both teams was closely involved in its planning and execution. This provided the support network so critical to building a cohesive and engaged community of diverse engineers, well-equipped and ready to give back to critical technology infrastructure that supports their work.

A Shared Future for Open Source

Bloomberg's open source culture leverages the company's innovative charitable giving programs and the expertise of its engineers. In turn, the company's employees gain valuable experience contributing to critical projects, fostering a further sense of purpose and professional fulfillment while simultaneously growing the community of open source contributors.

Ultimately, these collaborations contribute to a sustainable open source ecosystem that enables innovation, for the benefit of both businesses and the public good.

Sitting at the intersection of driving business value and doing good, this "open source first" approach creates a symbiotic relationship in which everyone benefits. Employees grow as leaders, core technologies are strengthened, and lasting social impact is created.

Canonical

Contributed by: Nicholas Dimotakis, VP of Global Field Engineering, Canonical, Gloria Quintanilla, Director of Communications, Canonical

Open source offers the world's innovation as code, but for most of its history, open source has lived in the domain of experts. Freely distributed operating systems like Ubuntu changed that paradigm, putting open source software in the hands of millions of people – experts, hobbyists, and end users alike. Canonical, the publisher of Ubuntu, has been on a mission to make open source accessible to the widest possible audience for over 20 years. In this short write-up, we will share how we foster an open source culture within our organization. We hope that by reading this, you will be inspired to adopt open source or scale its use within your organization too.

Open Source Is What We Do

Canonical is a product company and we touch almost every area of the modern technology stack – from the operating system to cloud platforms, containers, and data-intensive applications. Built with thousands of contributors, Ubuntu is an influential and well-known open source project. Besides spearheading the Ubuntu project, we develop and contribute to many others – from Netplan, which allows you to configure networking across Linux systems, to OpenStack, the powerful private cloud virtualization platform.

Most of our users and customers start their journey on Ubuntu, which is the world's most widely distributed Linux on the cloud. With 12 years of long-term support, Ubuntu gives you a reliable platform for innovation on any cloud – public, private, or bare metal.

If you want to orchestrate your bare metal servers like a cloud, you can do it very efficiently with MAAS, a hardware automation solution that helps you provision servers at speed. If you're building a private cloud, you can use our virtualization solutions, such as MicroCloud for low-touch, highly automated clouds and Canonical OpenStack for agile and large-scale data center operations. You can set up software-defined storage with our Ceph distribution, and if you're looking to build containerized applications, you can rely on our secure container offering and manage your containers using our supported Kubernetes distributions.

At the heart of our portfolio is Juju: an open source orchestration engine that enables you to deploy, integrate, and operate applications in a low-ops way on any infrastructure with a seamless admin experience across Kubernetes and VMs. Building on Juju's lifecycle management capabilities, we have built a portfolio of multi-cloud data and AI solutions in our distributions for Kafka, Spark, and Kubeflow, among others.

We sustain our business by offering commercial support, expanded security maintenance, and compliance tooling through a simple, per node subscription: Ubuntu Pro. Enterprises can also work with us to get fully managed offerings in their data center or the cloud of their choice.

To deliver the latest innovation in open source, we work very closely with both enterprise customers, partners, and open source communities. The open source ethos of transparency, equal access, and collaboration is fundamental to our company culture.

How We Foster an Open Source Culture

Just like we provide equal access to technology, we have built a company that provides equal work opportunities to people regardless of their location. We have more than 1,100 team members in over 70 countries from over 80 different nationalities. This broadens the scope of our reach and enables us to bring new ways of thinking to the organization.

However, managing a large, distributed workforce does not come without its challenges. For instance, ensuring everyone is informed about the latest developments and fostering a sense of belonging is more challenging when everyone works remotely. That is why we have instituted recurring in-person events where a large part of the company comes together at least two times a year. We call these events company sprints.

Canonical Sprints

Our sprints happen every 3–4 months. We host product sprints, where engineering, product, and marketing teams come together; and we host commercial sprints, where our finance, services, sales, support, product, and marketing review the state of the business. Sprints are the forums where we share how we build open source, how we support it, and how we bring it to market.

Hackathons

When we get the opportunity, we also host organization-wide hackathons during sprints to test the deployment, integration, and performance of our open source products. Hackathons serve as a great source of feedback for our engineering teams. Besides hackathons, we incentivize the use of open source internally to continuously develop best practices in open source development and adoption.

Producers and Consumers of Open Source

Most of our learnings come from our own use and implementation of open source technologies. We run our private cloud infrastructure on OpenStack, use open source databases like PostgreSQL, and rely on Kubernetes for container operations. Incentivizing open source adoption and testing internally is key for us.

Because we often deploy these technologies at customer sites, we also systematically gather learnings from the field. Our field engineering team often acts as the vector that provides best practices and feedback to the business, and this feedback is continuously channeled through business review meetings.

Together, these team rituals help us foster an open source culture.

Building Your Own Open Source Culture

At its heart, open source is the sharing of knowledge. If you're looking to bring open source to your organization, start sharing knowledge about it internally, then build an ecosystem around you to scale its use. Look for trusted partners who are also doing interesting things in open source so you can learn from each other and continuously strive towards excellence.

Dell

Contributed by: Barton George, Developer Community Manager, Dell Technologies

How a Technology Giant Created an Open Source Culture

Twenty years ago, the consensus at Dell Technologies was mostly "stay away from open source software." There were pockets of open source acceptance, but company-wide adoption didn't exist. The main concern was the risk of inadvertently giving away Intellectual Property Rights (IPR) and, possibly, proprietary advantage. Over time, those sentiments changed, and using open source software was embraced as part of Dell's development culture.

> **From Avoidance to Exploration**: As the concept of open source communities matured, the IT industry evolved and was no longer solely proprietary. Open source software became a significant component of IT infrastructure, and it was clear that participation in the open source community was crucial to innovation moving forward. Dell recognized open source now offered potential advantages. Leveraging the work of a community could provide cost savings as well as access to broader innovation and resources. With these developments, guidance within the company shifted from "stay away from open source" to "open source can be a tool, and we should explore it." This change in mindset signaled Dell's first step toward creating an open source culture.

> **Consumption and Integration**: As Dell developers explored open source software, they learned the intricacies of the various software licenses and the subsequent obligations to following community rules. Dell realized it could use open source software without unwittingly giving away IP and its competitive edge. This realization led to the next step in Dell's open source cultural evolution – the decision to allow product teams to include open source software in the systems it offered. By including open source software, Dell was able to skip the time-consuming creation of various components, move faster, and leverage the innovation of the community.

> **Contribution**: As Dell began incorporating open
> source software, both for internal systems and in its
> products, it realized it could modify or contribute
> code to the project to the benefit of customers
> and the open source community. By contributing
> resources, code, and expertise to the community, it
> could help shape the evolution of a technology and
> ultimately the industry.

Here are a few examples that illustrate the evolution of Dell's open
source culture and its community participation over the past 20 years:

- **Developing a Linux Laptop That "Just Works"**–
  "Project Sputnik" began in 2012 as an exploratory
  project to create a Linux-based developer laptop. To
  provide an offering that "just worked," Dell collaborated
  with the device driver manufacturers and Canonical,
  the provider of the included Linux distro, to write the
  drivers needed to deliver a flawless experience. These
  open source drivers were then upstreamed to the Linux
  kernel for all to use. Beyond the drivers, Dell provided
  the integration and certification required to create a
  standardized developer offering. Twelve years later
  this exploratory effort has become an entire portfolio
  of Linux-based systems. Dell's efforts mean consumers
  can buy Linux PCs off the shelf without having to do the
  heavy lifting of conversion.

- **Establishing the Cloud Foundry Foundation** – Dell
  led the establishment of the foundation, with its
  CTO serving as Chair of the Board. Dell contributed
  significant financial and technical resources with the
  goal of making Cloud Foundry the world's leading

platform-as-a-service, which it eventually became. At the time, the project was a significant step in the IT infrastructure stack, demonstrating the value of open source and community-driven development in shaping the future of technology.

- **Adding Persistent Storage to Kubernetes** – Kubernetes was not originally designed to support persistent storage, which meant organizations weren't able to use their existing data. Dell collaborated with the community to develop the Container Storage Interface (CSI), allowing enterprises to link their existing data to modern architectures. While this required considerable resources from Dell, the storage world now talks to the cloud native world, benefiting the broader industry.

- **Developer Relations** – In 2022, Dell's open source culture took another step forward when senior management approved the establishment of a developer relations team. The team was created to represent and advocate for the needs of developers within Dell and to influence product development. These team members actively contribute to community projects, speak at conferences, and organize community events. In 2024, a member of Dell's developer relations team led the latest Kubernetes release, a significant responsibility with high visibility in the community. Despite the activity not directly benefiting Dell or its offerings, the team member was granted permission to focus solely on delivering the release.

Establishment of an Open Source Culture: Over the past 20 years, Dell has progressively increased its involvement in open source. Today, not only are many of Dell's products based on open source, but the company has founded and led broad communities. Leveraging open source and contributing to its ongoing development are now part of the Dell Technologies development culture.

Docker

Contributed by: Andi Ramirez, Chief Marketing Officer, Docker

Docker could arguably be considered the most successful company to turn an Open Source culture into a thriving business. We developed the core of our business from open source by making Docker available to developers on their preferred desktop environment. Open source software is a vital part of how we build our products, both in the upstream projects like Moby Engine, which we distribute as Docker Engine, as well as the numerous open source libraries and programming languages used by our developers every day. Open source is also a key part of the value we provide to our customers: the Docker Official Images and Docker-Sponsored Open Source programs enable customers to consume open source software from Docker Hub with confidence.

Because of the value we get from open source software, Docker invests in the open source software ecosystem. Highlights include:

1. Membership in the Linux Foundation (and subsidiary organizations: Cloud Native Computing Foundation, Open Container Initiative, Open Source Security Foundation)

2. Engineering and infrastructure support for the upstream Moby Project

3. Developing first-party open source projects

4. Docker-Sponsored Open Source program, which provides free Docker Hub hosting, free Docker Team, and free Scout Team subscriptions to qualifying open source projects

5. Docker Official Images program, which provides a curated set of vetted open source software images freely available for download from Docker Hub

The primary WHY behind Docker's involvement in open source is the profound relationship we have built with the developer community. While we are a commercial enterprise, we have steadfastly maintained our open source roots, ensuring our projects and relationships thrive. This commitment has earned us the right to expand commercially where the value exchange is equitable. Beyond this, open source fosters an environment where innovation thrives and accelerates our productivity. By leveraging open source primitives, our teams can build bleeding-edge software solutions more efficiently. According to a 2024 Synopsys report, 96% of codebases for applications and services contain open source components, making up 76% of the codebase on average. This underscores the critical importance of open source in modern software development and aligns perfectly with industry trends.

Our vision is to continue to deepen this relationship between open source and commercial, to continue acting as the catalyst for open source innovation and leveraging that to drive commercial success. Thus creating a more integrated and collaborative technological landscape. By investing in open source, we unlock new possibilities, empower developers, and drive technological breakthroughs.

To keep this going, we must foster an open source culture internally. The most successful program within Docker to foster open source adoption, development, and thinking is our Hackathons. Held quarterly, these contests encourage everyone in our organization to build new and innovative ideas within a very short timeframe, which most often leads to the marriage of open source and our tools. They provide a unique environment where creativity and experimentation are encouraged, allowing employees to step outside their usual roles and explore new technologies and concepts. This often results in breakthrough ideas and solutions that might not emerge during regular work routines. The rapid prototyping and iterative nature of hackathons help to quickly identify viable projects that can be further developed and integrated into our product offerings.

With each Hackathon also comes the recognition. We leverage our global all-hands to share the most striking projects, award not only judged winners but fan favorites, and recognize the projects that have moved to more serious development phases.

One additional note on Hackathons is that they also act as a talent magnet, showcasing our innovative culture to potential recruits and positioning Docker as a forward-thinking, dynamic place to work. The excitement and energy generated during these events are palpable, making them a highlight of our company calendar and a testament to our commitment to pushing the boundaries of what's possible.

Fidelity Investments

Contributed by: Brian Warner, Director and Architect, OSPO, Fidelity Investments

Fidelity Investments was founded in 1946, was an early adopter of mainframe technologies, and has offered computer-based stock trading since 1984. Since then, Fidelity has made significant and sustained investments in infrastructure and must constantly balance the need to deploy new products quickly against the expectation that the source code will remain available and maintainable for many years.

Like every other company in the financial services industry, Fidelity is a major user of open source software. The broad availability of high-quality open source code has had a profound impact on how and where Fidelity deploys both new and legacy workloads. Overall, the industry sees open source usage in their software can range from 80% to 90% and above, and Fidelity has seen the same pattern.

Fidelity was founded in 1946, was an early adopter of mainframe technologies, and has offered computer-based stock trading since 1984. Since then, Fidelity has made significant and sustained investments in infrastructure and must constantly balance the need to deploy new products quickly against the expectation that the source code will remain available and maintainable for many years.

At the core, the primary reason to use open source is that it has a significant cost advantage over the non-open alternatives. Fidelity's model requires a substantial amount of in-house application development, implementing business and compliance workflows that are compatible with decades of historical business processes. As a result, Fidelity relies heavily upon open source frameworks and libraries so that we can apply our engineering focus to work that adds actual value to the firm. Access to the shared commons allows us to more efficiently develop applications which support our corporate mission.

As consumers, we also have strong incentives to play a supportive role in these communities by contributing back code, knowledge, and resources. The ability to support and positively influence helps us ensure we have access to code which supports our core business processes.

Like others in the financial industry, Fidelity's approach to external communities has been measured but has yielded significant dividends. At the core, Fidelity's success began with written policies that explicitly permitted open source-related activity. While policy may not be as important to non-regulated firms, within financial services it is an essential prerequisite.

The benefit of Fidelity's written policy is twofold. Regulated firms primarily create policies to support the audit process, but Fidelity also found that employees look to these policies for assurance that open source activity is allowed. Fidelity's OSPO invested time into creating auditable processes that govern how open source adoption and contribution should work. In doing so, this established explicit expectations that open source is a normal and expected part of the technology stack at Fidelity.

Fidelity's OSPO has refined these policies through the years to adapt to changes in the business. At a high level, they address how the OSPO reviews and approves the use of open source software, how employees should contribute back to public open source projects, and how to create new open source projects hosted by Fidelity.

A company's engineering culture forms around the tools and systems used by developers. Fidelity's OSPO used tools and automations to encourage adoption of open source code and mirror beneficial practices from the open source community. For example, the OSPO manages open source license policies and implements rules through SCA tools. Fidelity explicitly sets end-of-life policies to phase out older versions of open source code, and the OSPO encourages teams to track upstream versions of code whenever possible. Code scanning tools are configured to support shift-left methods, providing feedback to developers as early as possible when an application is failing policies.

Fidelity has also developed internal tools to support internal review and approval of contributions to public open source projects. These tools help keep internal mirrors of public open source projects up to date with upstream and ensure that contributions have been approved before being made public.

The final component is intentionally building culture through active encouragement by executive sponsors, and repetition of consistent processes until they become engrained. While recent hires often have direct prior experience with open source from university or other jobs, they may be more accustomed to unrestricted use and contribution and become frustrated by the presence of red tape. On the other hand, employees with longer tenure may be so enmeshed in internal processes that using externally developed code without a formal procurement agreement or contributing code to a public project may seem intimidating or too much work. Regardless of the reason, despite the hype about the benefits of using and contributing to open source, it's very easy to fall back to "maybe someday but not today," or worse, "let's circumvent the controls."

Fidelity's approach includes both executive and engineering-led engagement. Senior executives regularly communicate that open source software is a strategic imperative for Fidelity, without being overly prescriptive about what that means. As this message of support cascades through the organization, it empowers engineering teams with the flexibility to determine the extent to which they will use or contribute to open source in the context of their own goals. At the same time, engineers are strongly encouraged to make small contributions to exercise their understanding of the approval process. In doing so, Fidelity is encouraging contribution to become a routine part of business for its employees.

GitHub

Contribtued by: Jeff Luszcz, Staff Product Manager, GitHub OSPO

The importance of Open Source Consumption, Creation, and Maintenance at GitHub GitHub heavily depends on open source software to build and run our business. GitHub uses open source operating systems, databases, libraries, utilities, as well as end-user applications.

GitHub employees are encouraged to leverage open source software that enables them to perform their job effectively with the expectation that they are consuming this software in accordance with our policies. Understanding the license and security status of the software is an important aspect of using open source.

GitHub uses tools to enforce our license compliance policy to help us comply with the open source licenses we use, as well as help prevent the usage of software whose license is contrary to our policy. We track where these OSS dependencies are used and how these projects are distributed.

This enables us to perform actions like providing required Open Source License attributions in software we distribute as well as provide Software Bills of Materials (SBOMs) as needed.

We use security systems like GitHub's Dependabot to help us be alerted to new Open Source vulnerabilities/CVEs and patch our repositories as needed.

We monitor our dependencies and provide code contributions for improvements, bug fixes and security, and legal updates. We also provide financial contributions through GitHub Sponsors, GitHub Fund, and GitHub Accelerator, as well as significant in-kind donations of software licenses and hosting.

GitHub has an OSPO, Legal Team, and other teams who are able to help engineers navigate questions around open source consumption, licensing, security, and usage. Dedicated chat channels are monitored to provide communication channels for questions.

GitHub creates and maintains a significant number of Open Source projects. These projects fall into four main buckets:

- Applications and Utilities

- Libraries

- Examples and Documentation

- Experiments

Before a project can be released as open source at GitHub, the team must go through a checklist to confirm that the project conforms with our Open Source Release standards. This checklist guides a team through multiple important steps to make sure the repository is in clean, safe, and clear shape to release as open source. A project should be released under an MIT license (unless an ecosystem requires a different license), have our security scanning tools turned on, include important files such as a Code of Conduct, Security. md, and Contributing.md files. These files help the community understand the expectations and governance processes used in this open source project.

Additionally, our checklist and release policy provide guidance to the maintainer on how to get help, let others know about the new project, and how to improve their maintainer skills through video and text based training.

Each project has a clear owner, and projects which are no longer maintained or owned are clearly marked as "archived." This allows the source code to remain available to the community but communicates the project's status to potential users.

We work closely with our partners and open source users to accept contributions, requests for enhancement, and bug reports via the GitHub interface.

GitHub believes that Open Source is the bedrock of tech innovation and is committed to not only providing the home for its community of developers but also fostering space for a sustainable open source ecosystem.

Both at GitHub and beyond, the utility and usability of Open Source have made it the clear choice for building large applications using reusable building blocks of free, well-vetted, secure, and performant software. A developer can quickly bring in functionality and get started on the same day with an open source library without having to submit a purchase order, sign an NDA, or interact with a salesperson.

Additionally, creating open source projects allows us to receive improvements from the community, improve trust by allowing inspection of important functionality, as well as provide examples and best practices to accelerate others' activities.

Using open source allows GitHub to support open standards and interchange formats, as well as provide interfaces to expand our products to ecosystems or languages we might not otherwise be able to support.

By creating an environment where Open Source culture is nurtured and supported, GitHub is able to hire the best open source creators and maintainers as well as encourage existing developers to embrace open source through training and mentoring.

To cultivate an open source culture, GitHub's open source teams collaborate across the organization on several initiatives:

- Open Source Surveys: Conducted among GitHub employees to gauge engagement and identify improvement areas.

- Maintainers Discussions: Forums for open source maintainers to share challenges and insights.

- Newsletters and Communications: Regular updates to keep the community informed and engaged.

- Promotion and Recognition: Implementing leaderboards and gamification to recognize significant open source contributions.

- Training and Best Practices: By providing guidance and best practices, GitHub's OSPO helps teams learn how to use, create, share, and maintain open source.

Additionally, we have staff members who directly support open source projects both internal and external to GitHub. Employees are encouraged to create and maintain open source projects. Some employees directly contribute code to external open source projects, help with maintainer duties, and make non code contributions as well.

Significant effort is applied to creating materials, processes, and communities to support both the creation and consumption of open source. Dedicated chat channels exist to support communication around open source topics. Staff members, through both dedicated jobs and volunteer efforts, look for "paper cuts" and other impediments to using and maintaining open source at GitHub.

Funding and sponsoring open source is important to GitHub. Dedicated funds look to improve sustainable careers in open source, such as the GitHub Fund, which invests in early stage open source companies, and GitHub

Accelerator (`https://accelerator.github.com/`), which helps open source maintainers turn their projects into companies. Surveys of employees are used to identify important and up-and-coming open source projects and communities. Close relationships with maintainers through programs like GitHub Stars (`https://stars.github.com/program/`) help both sides work better together. All together, these activities help make GitHub a great environment to learn how to use as well as how to create open source.

Infosys

Contributed by: Naresh Duddu, AVP and Global Head of Open Source, Infosys Ltd

Infosys is a global leader in next-generation digital services and consulting. Over 300,000 of our people work to amplify human potential and create the next opportunity for people, businesses, and communities. We enable clients in more than 56 countries to navigate their digital transformation. With over four decades of experience in managing the systems and workings of global enterprises, we expertly steer clients as they navigate their digital transformation powered by cloud and AI. We enable them with an AI-first core, empower the business with agile digital at scale, and drive continuous improvement with always-on learning through the transfer of digital skills, expertise, and ideas from our innovation ecosystem. We are deeply committed to being a well-governed, environmentally sustainable organization where diverse talent thrives in an inclusive workplace.

Infosys has a longstanding commitment to open source software, actively participating as both a consumer and contributor. In 2016, we launched the "OSSMOSIS" program to promote enterprise-wide adoption and evangelization of open source. To further strengthen this commitment, we established the Open Source Program Office (OSPO) in 2022. The OSPO serves as a central governing body, streamlining policies, best practices, and processes for both open source consumption and contributions.

Consumption of Open Source

- Infosys has an "Open source first" policy and prioritizes open source technologies and standards for building solutions for in-house applications (such as Infosys intranet platform – InfyMe), client-facing IPs/ Platforms (such as Infosys Live Enterprise Application Development Platform, Infosys Live Enterprise Application Management Platform, Infosys Helix, etc.), and customer projects.

- Infosys ensures free and open source software (FOSS) usage complies with licensing requirements, customer compliance standards, contractual requirements, and internal policies.

- Infosys has an open source playbook for internal use, centrally accessible on the OSPO portal. This is tailored for in-house applications and utilizes Infosys intellectual property (IPs) in addition to open source.

- Project teams track all open source usage, including component name, version, download link, and license.

- Tools like SBOM, SCA, etc. are used to verify FOSS license and best practice compliance and guide project teams towards corrections.

Contribution to Open Source

- Infosys fosters a culture of active contribution to open source, encouraging employees to participate in both code and non-code contributions. We actively contribute substantial code back to open source projects on an ongoing basis. Some notable communities benefiting from our contributions include MOSIP and Backstage.

- Infosys endeavors to make its projects open source whenever possible. In the preceding year (CY23) alone, we open sourced ten projects, including a variety of third-party party connectors, application modernization utilities, etc., and published them on Infosys GitHub.

- To foster collaboration within the open source ecosystem, Infosys partners with leading open source vendors to contribute to their open source initiatives.

- To guarantee that contributions are devoid of any client-specific or confidential information, we have devised user-friendly workflows on the Infosys OSPO portal. These workflows enable contributors to declare specifics of their contributions, which are subsequently reviewed and approved by an expert panel in accordance with Infosys guidelines. This approach democratizes the contribution process, encouraging employees to participate without risk of potential errors.

- Infosys demonstrates its commitment through a dedicated team that actively works on contribution to open source communities.

Why Open Source?

- Infosys has embraced open source technologies to achieve a multitude of objectives.

- Infosys published key open source trends in the form of Infosys TechCompass in 2022. This vision document outlines the critical role open source is playing in various technology areas.

- Infosys recognizes the tremendous potential of open source that is leading innovation in almost all emerging technologies, such as cloud, AI, IOT, blockchain, etc.

- Beyond technological innovation, open source fosters a "collaborative spirit." We believe this collaborative approach promotes the development of secure, cost-effective, and innovative solutions, creating a win-win scenario for both Infosys and its clients. By fostering a collaborative open source culture, we encourage this spirit within Infosys, leading to the creation of superior, integrated solutions that address our clients' needs.

- Interoperability and flexibility are essential for IT solutions. Open source, by its very nature, promotes the use of open standards, minimizing vendor lock-in. Infosys champions the adoption of open standards for both our clients and employees.

- Open source results in better outcomes for our clients, with solutions being performant, agile, cost-effective, and portable. Any new development or modernization program inevitably uses open source technologies, and we collaborate with our clients to increase their success rate in implementing these programs.

- Open source communities allow us an opportunity to participate and shape the future of technology via contributions and feedback. Being an open ecosystem also allows us to position ourselves as a strategic technology player.

Fostering Open Source Culture

Infosys promotes open source culture through a three-pronged approach:

- **Consumption** – Prioritizing open source technologies over proprietary alternatives.

- **Contribution** – Actively giving back to open source communities.

- **InnerSourcing** – Fostering a collaborative spirit within the organization

To cultivate open source culture in our employees, Infosys deploys a comprehensive set of measures:

1. **Employee Enablement** – Infosys Education, Training, and Assessment team works closely with business units to identify key emerging open source technologies and invest heavily in building the required skillsets. We have created 200+ courses and 57 learning paths for various open source technologies and reward the employees who earn open source professional skill tags or certifications.

2. **Employee Engagement** – Infosys conducts a series of org-wide events focused on open source to foster collaboration, contribution, and knowledge sharing within the community. These events encourage employees from different units to collaborate on innovative use cases. For example, in the OpenHack, which was conducted in collaboration with our open source partners, employees from different units came together to build an innovative solution for sustainable IT. We also encouraged employees to join forces with industry experts from foundations

and partners to develop reference architectures, blogs, etc. These events provide an open forum for employees to come together and discuss the latest trends and features in open source.

3. **Incentivization** – OSPO conducts various open source events that carry attractive rewards to encourage participation. Projects that leverage open source technologies in an innovative fashion are recognized and celebrated. Exemplary cases of collaboration and client value delivery are also recognized and considered during appraisals. We also spotlight employees – whether it is for a new open source skill acquisition, project delivery, or any contribution.

Intel

Contributed by: Melissa Evers, Vice President, Intel Corporation

The vision of Intel Corporation is to create world-changing technology that improves the lives of every person on the planet. Intel is at the forefront of developing new technologies, products, and solutions as building blocks for an increasingly smart and connected world across a broad spectrum of markets. Providing a ubiquitous computing platform that is available on laptops, data centers, cloud, network, and edge, they are a leading developer of process technology and a major manufacturer of semiconductors. Intel is the company that literally puts silicon in Silicon Valley.

And it is impossible to separate Intel's vision and who they are from their approach to the Open Ecosystem. "Fostering an open ecosystem is the foundation of our approach at Intel," says Greg Lavender, CTO of Intel. Technology history has borne out that open almost always wins in the long term vs. proprietary vertical markets. Proven out by trends from Geoffrey Moore's Crossing the Chasm and Martin Casado's 2019 analysis to Wardley Mapping, an open ecosystem not only establishes a level playing field allowing "the best solution to win," but it also provides an open platform on which innovation can be built – one generation of developers leveraging on the prior art of the previous developers. In turn, this enables developers to innovate with completely new use cases, like advances in microservice architectures or edge computing. Whether it be the rise of the x86 Linux-based datacenter or the advent of software defined networking, open source development provides the foundations and building blocks empowering various entities, Intel included, to disrupt existing markets and cultivate new ones. It is also the fastest path for global adoption, scale, and ubiquity of technology. An open ecosystem approach facilitates a global community to come together, collaborate, and address global challenges, fostering innovation. Ultimately, it promotes choice and interoperability for customers, characterized by extensibility and ubiquity – and it is on that choice that technology competition is born.

While open source development is de facto for many institutions today, it is worth noting that this was not always the case. While it is clear to see why a horizontal platform provider, such as Intel, would be benefited by open, neutral ecosystems in which to compete, why did the rest of the ecosystem predominantly shift to open source codebases?

1. **The Power of Community** – When developers across companies are working together to solve a problem, they can run faster than any one company's assets or developers in the long run.

2. **Controlling Their Destiny** – Technology moves fast, and software evolves faster. When a company puts code into production, they want to have assurances that they can maintain that code for as long as THEY need – not the length of their maintenance contract, or the length of their suppliers' existence.

3. **Security** – As the saying goes, "sunlight is the best disinfectant" – having whole communities, researchers, and hackers working hard to improve code security will over the long haul deliver the most secure outcomes.

Roger Martin said, "Strategy is what you do, not what you say." Intel's software development is the embodiment of our strategy. Intel's products are integral to a wide range of applications, including public cloud infrastructure, data centers, networking equipment, edge devices, and client devices such as traditional PCs and laptops. As Intel's customers extensively utilize open source software, Intel contributes to hundreds of open source projects, ensuring compatibility with the latest silicon advancements and product features. The following diagram demonstrates the customer value cycle that's catalyzed through the upstream enablement of new product capabilities. This upstream software is then enabled in downstream distribution by working with partners. Customers consume these distributions and provide further feedback on the contributions in respective upstream communities. This strategic involvement allows Intel to share platform value through open source and scale rapidly, reinforcing their dedication to delivering cutting-edge solutions to their user base.

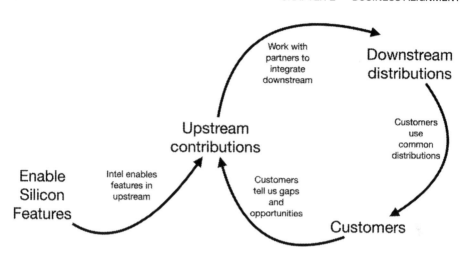

Figure 2-3. *Intel's Open Source Strategy Flywheel*

Intel lives its strategy through investments in 300+ community-managed open source projects like OpenJDK, Kubernetes, PyTorch, Linux Kernel, and many others. The company has 1000+ open source projects at github.com/intel and is part of 800+ open source foundations and standards bodies. Intel invests because not only is it a differentiator but also key to the way they build and expand markets.

Beyond ensuring seamless integration of Intel silicon features into open source software, the company upholds over three decades of legacy through exemplary community engagement. With tens of open source projects launched and contributed to neutral governance foundations, like the Linux Foundation, or many employees earning maintainer status in respective projects, Intel embodies the community's notion of "Chop Wood and Carry Water." For example, as of 1H'24, Intel stands out as the sole silicon vendor with maintainers in PyTorch's CPU module. This unique position enables them not only to implement features for Intel silicon but also to review and incorporate patches from other CPU vendors, an honor as this position is earned by creating an equitable field for others to compete in. But embrace of open source is not only how Intel engages externally – it is also core to the expectations set for each developer, embodied through their Open Ecosystem Pledge to

- Develop in the open.

- Invest in open software communities.

- Drive open, industry-shaping standards.

- Enable our developers and partners with choice and collaboration.

- Surround our hardware with open software.

With this commitment, combined with the support of internal conferences and events to build Intel's internal open culture and embracing Intel core values, Intel strives to be inclusive in its approach and supports community efforts while embracing diversity and differences because they make everyone better.

And so, Intel's vision, to improve the lives of every person on this planet, is inherently and only achieved through open ecosystem development. While Intel has known this for decades, Generative AI has brought the world's consciousness to this reality as well. Dialogue internationally around the critical importance of Open AI – open software AI development – has reached a fervor that is hard to miss. Whether it is communities like the AI Alliance, efforts like the Unified Acceleration Foundation's work to deliver SYCL 2020 and oneAPI implementations, or pioneering work such as the Model Openness Framework, the economic future of free and fair competition rests on the shoulders of open AI development globally. As Pat Gelsinger shared in his 2021 public "Open Letter to an Open Ecosystem," Intel firmly believes, validated by technology's last 40 years of advancement, that openness is not a choice; the challenges we face as a planet are too great, the consequences of the few with power over the many too vast, open development is the only way.

Red Hat

Contributed by: Brian Proffitt, Sr Manager, Open Source Program Office, Red Hat, Inc.

Open source is central to who we are at Red Hat, as we believe that open unlocks the world's potential. Open means better software, and open means making the world a better place.

On the surface, Red Hat is an enterprise software company organized around the belief that open unlocks the world's potential. Everything we do is shaped by our principles of Freedom, Community, and Sustainability.

Freedom

Red Hat is committed to enriching the open source commons with the software we create, extend, or acquire.

- Red Hat has pledged that we will never use our patents offensively against free and open source software, and we also deter, defend against, and resolve patent threats to free and open source software.

- Red Hat seeks to influence the legal and regulatory framework under which open source operates to maintain its accessibility and viability for the open source community.

Community

Red Hat is committed to being a catalyst in communities of customers, contributors, and partners, creating better technology the open source way.

- Red Hat associates collaborate – openly and iteratively – with customers, contributors, competitors, and partners to seek the best ideas and integrate them into upstream source repositories, making the improvements more accessible to everyone.

- Red Hat's Open Source Participation Guidelines empower every Red Hat associate to contribute to any free and open source project they wish, and our Code of Ethics gives us leave to place the interests of these projects above those of the company.

- When we work with communities, we recognize that only by encouraging and including diverse perspectives in our work can we be certain we've identified the best ideas.

Sustainability

Red Hat is committed to ensuring that the open source software codebases that our customers, partners, and community rely on continue to be developed, maintained, and supported over time, and that Red Hat itself persists as an engine for open source innovation.

- Red Hat takes community-built code and hardens its security, adds features, and makes it enterprise-ready and scalable. We push these improvements back out to the original project to benefit the community as a whole.

- Red Hat funds the development of these freely licensed and openly developed components by assembling them into integrated products, pairing them with support, certifications, expertise, and delivery services, and selling these products via subscription.

- Red Hat strives to positively impact the ecosystem of projects, foundations, and standards that produce and support free and open source software by funding them, providing infrastructure services, and helping with maintenance, mentoring, and governance.

Sun Microsystems

Contributed by: Simon Phipps, Open Source Initiative, formerly Sun's Chief Open Source Officer and Danese Cooper, Founder/Director InnerSource Commons Foundation, formerly Sun Chief Open Source Evangelist

Sun Microsystems was one of the corporate pioneers of open source, after founding their flagship operating system product, Solaris, on a proprietary fork of the Open Source BSD Unix variant written by Sun chief scientist, Bill Joy during his PhD studies at the University of California, Berkeley. In 1994, Sun experimented with publishing Java source code under a license that allowed almost all the freedoms that would be later called open source, but without redistribution rights to avoid it being "embraced and extended" by competitors. As Open Source gained momentum, both of these projects came under pressure from the community to go all the way to true Open Source.

Starting in 1998, Sun established the first Open Source Program Office (OSPO) and went on to create several important open source projects including Apache TomCat (Java Servelet engine), NetBeans (an IDE for Java), OpenOffice.org, GlassFish (the reference implementation of Java Enterprise Edition specification), OpenSolaris and OpenJDK (the reference implementation of the Java language specification), as well as the identity middleware that went on to become ForgeRock, an experiment in open silicon called OpenSparc and much more.

97

In 2004, MySQL, the most popular open source relational database, was acquired by Sun. Four years later, Sun was acquired by proprietary software vendor Oracle, which proceeded to offload or abandon most of Sun's incredible open source portfolio.

Sun Microsystems embraced the philosophy that freely available open source projects would capture the mindshare of developers. This approach hinged on fostering an environment that was open, collaborative, and transparent in its development processes. The accumulation of mindshare, fueled by the positive aspects of openness and collaboration, became a strategic advantage for Sun.

Most of Sun's open source projects included selling supported commercial versions of the same software with value-added components and professional services to optimize software running in a customer's environment, and training on how to use the software.

While its big vision revolved around cultivating markets where its products could flourish, Sun's plan was to make money on hardware as well as growing business around the complexity of the adopted software. It saw a business opportunity in the sale of appliances and personal devices that used a Java-based thin client and were backed by Sun servers. Their market share is also derived from the strategic positioning of open source software, specifically optimized for Sun's hardware and software ecosystem. This alignment enhanced the appeal of Sun's solutions in the market, contributing to the company's overall market share growth.

Transforming Sun from a closed source company to an open source company required a decade of people, processes, tools, and sometimes difficult culture change across the company, especially recognizing and engaging with the true community beyond just customers – a key role for Sun's OSPO.

As a company, Sun was motivated to embrace open source due, in part, to competition from various proprietary vendors at the time. Sun very successfully used open source as a market disruptor, open sourcing certain technologies as a strategic move to position itself as a more transparent, collaborative, and community-oriented company, distinguishing its approach from that of some of its competitors.

OpenOffice.org, for instance, was a zero-cost alternative to Microsoft Office launched shortly after Sun and Netscape jointly filed anti-trust claims against Microsoft's business practices. The project successfully forced Microsoft to standardize and open their file formats, ending more than a decade of milking their installed base for costly upgrades through proprietary file format tweaks. Another such disruptive move was the creation of Apache Tomcat, which successfully halted mass adoption of Microsoft's Active Server Pages.

The legacy of Sun Microsystems in open source history underscores the enduring impact of their philosophy on the dynamics of the software industry.

SUSE

Contributed by: Alan Clark, Director, Emerging Standards and Open Source, SUSE LLC

About SUSE

Since 1993, SUSE has been a pioneer in open source technology, offering customers secure solutions to their business and technology needs. Today, SUSE's mission is to bring the infinite potential of open source to the enterprise. SUSE is a global leader in innovative, reliable, and secure enterprise open source solutions, including Linux, Cloud Native, Edge, and AI solutions. More than 60% of the Fortune 500 rely on SUSE to power their mission-critical workloads, enabling them to innovate everywhere – from the data center to the cloud, to the edge, and beyond. SUSE puts the "open" back in open source, collaborating with partners and communities to give customers the agility to tackle innovation challenges today and the freedom to evolve their strategy and solutions tomorrow.

SUSE and Open Source

SUSE's uniqueness lies in its commitment to providing enterprise-ready open source software, supported and serviced to meet the demanding and ever-changing requirements of large enterprises. Over the years, enterprises have grown more familiar with open source, yet it's important to continually educate stakeholders about its intricacies. Open source is not just about free software; it involves licensing, support, and security considerations, including ensuring everything works securely and being able to fully trust the open source code. Moreover, there is a distinct difference between merely using open source technologies and commercializing products that incorporate open source components. SUSE places significant emphasis on educating its ecosystem, both internally and externally, to foster a joint understanding of the capabilities and benefits of open source in enterprise contexts.

By embracing open source, SUSE accelerates innovation, upholds company values through transparency and collaboration, and creates a common language between employees, customers, and partners. This approach ensures that SUSE's customers are better served and positioned to innovate effectively.

Sustaining Open Source

While open source can be cost-effective and a source of innovation, it's very important to also recognize that innovation needs to be sustained and made secure and manageable for enterprise use. This highlights the distinction between merely taking open source from GitHub versus working with trusted and experienced partners, like SUSE, to leverage open source effectively.

Additionally, while open source offers many advantages, it doesn't inherently ensure security or the safety of your supply chain – regardless of whether the industry is retail, healthcare, or any other sector. Community distributions are different from enterprise distributions in that enterprise distributions deliver tested and secured solutions. To guarantee these aspects, collaboration with partners and vendors is essential, as direct support or security from the open source community isn't guaranteed. Moreover, in certain cases, such as selling to regulatory bodies like the US Federal Government or Department of Defense, certifications are mandatory. Open source projects alone cannot obtain these certifications; they must be products backed by a company to meet regulatory requirements. This underscores the importance of compliance in regulated industries, where adherence to regulations is paramount.

How Open Is Open: Beware of Vendor Lock In

Adopting open source provides a sense of freedom by offering various choices. You can either manage the intellectual property or technology independently or transition between different service providers. Just as with proprietary solutions, there's still a risk of becoming locked into an open source ecosystem.

To best safeguard against vendor lock-in, organizations will want to check the level of openness of their software. For example, how many contributors are there, does the project have a formal governance board, and where do those folks work? Technically, when assessing open source technology, it's crucial to consider whether it's solely supported by one company, as this could indicate a risk of vendor lock-in. Even a highly successful, popular, and widely used open source technology backed

by only one company could lead to situations where customer choice is
not an option. Ensuring there's involvement from multiple companies
contributing to or supporting the chosen open source technology is
essential.

Long-Term Support in Open Source

Surprises are inevitable. Take Kubernetes, for example. It sees a new
version from the community every three or four months currently, with
support for three concurrent versions. This means every nine months,
you're outside the community support window. For enterprises, updating
core infrastructure software along with the community releases is often
impractical. The lifecycle management and release cadence of mainstream
open source may move too swiftly to be practical for enterprises.

It's crucial to be proactive and consider long-term management and
support of your open source technology. While it's tempting to implement
something from the Internet immediately, you must anticipate how to
sustain it over time. Communities often progress to newer versions, leaving
older ones unsupported. Hence, it's vital to contemplate the lifecycle of
your technology and implement management tools for updates. These tools
usually come from vendors offering long-term support. As an enterprise, it's
essential to acknowledge the power of open source while also recognizing
the need for control and structure. Without proper planning, the real value
of open source adoption may never be truly realized.

Fostering Open Source Internally

SUSE is deeply committed to fostering an internal culture rooted in open
source principles. We outline these principles and practices in a formal,
publicly available open source policy. We achieve this through various
initiatives, including Hack Week, where employees worldwide collaborate

on open source projects without interruption. Additionally, our transparent open source policy, publicly available on our website, reflects our dedication to openness and clarity.

Participation in programs like Google Summer of Code further demonstrates our commitment to giving back to the wider community. We integrate open source education into onboarding processes and nurture practitioner communities to encourage collaboration and knowledge sharing.

Our Open Source Employee Network serves as a central hub for education and collaboration, empowering employees to actively engage in the open source ecosystem. By cultivating a deep understanding and appreciation for open source within our organization, we enable our team to contribute their talents effectively and advocate for the greater good.

Additionally, SUSE values acknowledging colleagues' hard work and contributions in open source. SUSE's Annual Technology & Product Awards have been established to celebrate the excellence, passion, and commitment demonstrated by our teams.

SUSE's comprehensive approach to fostering an open source culture serves as a best practice for other organizations aiming to leverage open source principles. Through initiatives like Hack Week, transparent policies, continuous education, and recognition programs, SUSE creates an environment where innovation thrives, and collaboration is paramount. By aligning business goals with open source values, SUSE demonstrates that fostering an open source culture internally can lead to significant benefits for the organization and its stakeholders.

Summary

This chapter explained the different "why" companies contribute to open source. Different philosophies of engagement in open source and common business models around open source are explained next. A large part of the chapter consists of case studies from a wide range of enterprises on what they did to foster an open source culture in order to make open source sustainable with their business. The next chapter talks about the Open Source Program Office (OSPO) and its role within an enterprise. Like this chapter, there are lots of interesting OSPO case studies from different enterprises in the next chapter. They explain the origin of OSPO, where the OSPO sits in the organization, and what it does to foster open source culture.

CHAPTER 3

Open Source Program Office

The Open Source Program Office, commonly known as the OSPO, is a dedicated team within an organization with the primary purpose of managing and promoting open source software and culture. OSPOs play a crucial role in helping organizations navigate the complexities of open source, adopt best practices, remove friction from consumption and production of open source projects, and maximize the benefits of open source participation.

The Linux Foundation Research report, A Deep Dive in OSPO, is a comprehensive guide that examines the OSPO. It provides a five-stage maturity model that helps organizations assess their OSPO and identify the elements that need to be implemented to advance the maturity. It explores how enterprises structure OSPOs and emphasizes that there is NORA (No One Right Answer). The guide also talks about minimal staffing needed for their operation and how it can evolve over time. The OSPO roles and responsibilities, and the challenges that are faced in open source enterprise adoption, conclude the report.

The Linux Foundation's research on The Business Value of the OSPO breaks the value of the OSPO in two distinct phases: OSPO creation and OSPO maturation. The report says the value from the first phase is "cleaning up the mess of open source, recovering from years of ad hoc approaches to consuming and contributing to open source." The benefits in the second phase build upon the first phase, and this is where culture and education take a primary seat. The report also calls out how OSPOs wear different hats of counselor, facilitator, and ensure OSPOs sustainability.

Let's take a look at the primary role and responsibilities of an OSPO.

Role of OSPO

As mentioned before, the OSPO plays a multifaceted and pivotal role within an organization, serving as a strategic catalyst for fostering and sustaining an open source culture. At its core, an OSPO is instrumental in orchestrating various functions and initiatives that collectively contribute to the integration of open source principles and practices into the fabric of the organization. Let's take a look at different roles.

Figure 3-1. *Role of Open Source Program Office*

Effective Governance

The OSPO develops and enforces a set of policies and governance structures that dictate how the organization engages with open source. This includes guidelines on contributing, licensing, and compliance to ensure a standardized and organized approach. Well-defined policies set the groundwork for consistent and aligned open source practices.

This role provides a well-defined framework, encompassing the assessment and management of legal and compliance aspects, respect for open source licenses, tracking obligations, and due diligence to prevent legal issues. It also involves conducting thorough license reviews for all open source components used, tracking dependencies, and mitigating any legal risks associated with the organization's use and contributions to open source projects. This commitment to maintaining a clear and responsible approach to open source minimizes risks and establishes a secure foundation for its adoption within the organization.

As a result of these measures, the organization significantly reduces the risk of encountering legal issues related to open source licenses. They possess a clear roadmap for responsible and ethical open source software usage, regularly updated through audits and policy enhancements. This not only mitigates risks but also fosters trust within the open source community and among potential customers who highly value the organization's commitment to legal and ethical software practices.

Strategic Alignment

The OSPO takes a strategic approach to open source by aligning it with the organization's broader business objectives. It formulates a comprehensive plan for adopting open source solutions and contributing to them that complement these goals. This strategy requires a deep understanding of the organization's unique needs and how open source can address them. Oftentimes, there are multiple business units within an organization.

The needs and processes of each of these units could be vastly different. OSPO collaborates with different business units across the company to ensure their business needs are clearly understood, the usage of open source is clearly understood, and it is seamlessly integrated as part of that. Any process bottlenecks are streamlined, and tools are created to automate the process and eliminate friction. This constant process and tool improvement enables a faster adoption of open source. This strategic alignment enables the organization to harness the full potential of open source as a driving force behind its success.

Community Engagement

Effective engagement with external open source communities is vital for the organization's success in open source endeavors. The OSPO may serve as a facilitator, encouraging active participation and collaboration among employees with external communities. It may take care of the membership dues, submit the paperwork, and sign the contracts for joining these external communities. This allows the business units to focus on engineering collaboration and establishes OSPO as the center-of-excellence for this facilitation. This bridge connects the organization to the wider open source ecosystem, enabling employees to connect, engage in discussions, and contribute their expertise to open source projects. This collaborative effort fosters the development of shared solutions, strengthens the organization's bonds with the open source community, and nurtures a culture of open collaboration and knowledge sharing. By connecting the organization's talent with external communities, the OSPO enhances innovation, accelerates development, and expands the organization's footprint within the open source landscape.

Training and Advocacy

The OSPO plays a pivotal role in educating and advocating for open source best practices to the organization. It conducts comprehensive and regular training sessions and educational programs to ensure that everyone is well informed about the benefits and challenges of open source. It may author playbooks that serve as a strategic resource that outlines best practices, processes, and guidelines for various aspects of open source engagement within the organization.

OSPOs serve as educators for senior leadership within the organization. It helps them understand the strategic significance, benefits, and potential risks associated with open source adoption. It educates the leaders about market trends, case studies, and risk mitigation. They work with leaders to create incentive plans so that engineers are motivated to contribute to open source. Their role is instrumental in ensuring that senior leaders make informed decisions about incorporating open source into the company's strategic vision.

The OSPO actively encourages the organization to give back to the open source community, often by following those practices within the company. This includes contributing code, expertise, and resources to open source projects. These contributions encompass various areas, from coding and documentation to sharing best practices. Simultaneously, the OSPO develops and maintains a repository of valuable resources. These resources include playbooks, templates, and tools designed to support teams and projects within the organization as they adopt open source practices. They may consider sharing their internal processes outside the company so that others can adopt and even open source their internal tools. By providing readily available resources, the OSPO simplifies the integration of open source into the organization's projects, ensuring seamless collaboration and effective contribution to the open source community.

Impact Measurement

Management guru Peter Drucker said, "If you can't measure it, you can't improve it." The OSPO not only serves as a passionate center of competency for open source within the organization but also aggressively tracks the measurable impact of open source contributions through a combination of qualitative and quantitative metrics. Advocacy is essential for promoting the adoption of open source across the organization. The OSPO communicates the advantages of open source solutions, both internally and externally, to build awareness and support.

OSPOs may track contribution metrics, acceptance rate of these contributions by the open source community, and if needed, what needs to be done to improve the acceptance rate. They track adoption of open source projects within the company and external contributors to projects started by the company. They may conduct surveys or gather feedback from developers within the organization to gauge their satisfaction with open source tools and practices. Community Health and Analytics in Open Source Software (CHAOSS) is a Linux Foundation project and provides an extensive range of metrics, models, and software to measure the health of the open source community.

Additionally, it monitors and measures the concrete impact of open source initiatives on the organization's bottom line, innovation efforts, and overall strategic goals. This data-driven approach helps demonstrate the value of open source within the organization.

TODO Group

Contributed by: Ana Jiménez Santamaría, Senior Project Manager, Open Source Office, Linux Foundation

The TODO Group, an open collaboration project hosted at the Linux Foundation, serves as a backup channel and a resource hub for companies to manage and integrate open source operations and culture across team units effectively.

Officially established in 2014, it now represents a global community of practitioners and experts dedicated to fostering best practices and strategies for managing Open Source through Open Source Program Offices (OSPOs), ensuring alignment with C-level and business objectives. This organization facilitates knowledge sharing and collaboration among its contributors, which include companies across various industries (software, automotive, hardware, retail, finance, etc.), academic institutions, non-profit organizations, and public administrations.

Getting Started with TODO Group Resources

The TODO Group has developed a wide variety of resources to help open source strategists and managers working at companies. Below are some of them:

Open Source Guides for the Enterprise: These guides have been developed and used by open source leaders from large to medium companies. These guides leverage best practices for running an open source program office or starting an open source project in your organization. The guide on outbound open source, which provides a framework to contribute and release open source projects, is particularly recommended for large, medium, and small enterprises.

OSPO Definition: The TODO Group's definition of the OSPO, developed collaboratively by a wide range of subject matter experts involved in open source strategy and integration in different organizations, acts as a living document, allowing the community to contribute to its improvement and updates over the years.

111

OSPO Landscape: This open source project maps the OSPO Ecosystem, including adopter organizations and tooling used by OSPO teams and open source professionals within organizations.

OSPO Book: A body of knowledge for organizations to gain a better understanding of the OSPO's role in day-to-day operations, its integration with business units' tasks, and alignment with C-level goals. It has been developed openly by a group of contributors with deep knowledge in open source strategy, community, metrics, and management.

Networking Spaces: Among the working groups focused on developing specific initiatives, the TODO Group community organizes a range of events, including OSPO tracks at conferences, webinars, and local meetups, to facilitate networking and knowledge sharing among open source practitioners.

1. OSPOCon Tracks at OSSummit: Sessions with industry leaders and experts who share insights and experiences related to open source management and strategy.

2. OSPOlogyLive and Local Meetups in Europe, LATAM, China, and Japan: Roundtable discussions and panel sessions on various aspects of OSPO operations, from compliance and security to business strategy and community engagement. OSPOlogyLive is in collaboration with organizations such as OpenSSF, InnerSource Commons, OpenChain, LF APAC OSPO SIG, LF Energy, Foundation for Public Code, CNCF, and more.

3. Networking Sessions (Touchpoint calls): Monthly calls for practitioners to connect, share ideas, and collaborate.

The list of resources goes on, and interested individuals can check the full list of outputs developed by the community at TODO Group's resource section, check future meetings in the meetings and calendar page, and get involved in the community through the get started page.

Case Studies

Let's explore how OSPOs brought about a cultural change in different enterprises.

Blackrock

Contributed by: Mike Bowen, Technical Fellow, BlackRock

The genesis of the BlackRock Open Source Program Office (OSPO) was a key milestone in BlackRock's open source journey. It represents a strategic response to the evolving technological landscape and the growing significance of open source in driving innovation, collaboration, and value creation.

The decision to open source Argo Events and subsequently donate it to the Argo project was marked as a pivotal moment in the formation of BlackRock's Open Source Program Office. By donating the Argo Events IP to the open source community and contributing it to the Argo project, BlackRock demonstrated its commitment to fostering collaboration, innovation, transparency, and open standards-based development. Using the open source cloud events specification from the Cloud Native Compute Foundation (CNCF) to create a cloud native solution and architecture based on event-driven principles and standards. This strategic move not only empowered developers and other organizations to leverage and build upon Argo Events but also underscored BlackRock's belief in the power of open collaboration and community-driven development.

113

Furthermore, the decision to establish an OSPO was driven by the recognition of the strategic importance of open source initiatives and the need for a centralized function to oversee and coordinate these efforts effectively across a globally spanned and diverse organization. Therefore, the genesis of OSPO can be traced back to the transformative act of collaborating, writing, and donating Argo Events to the open source Argo project. Creating a strong culture of openness, collaboration, and innovation at BlackRock and with the communities we support and partner with.

OSPO was established with a clear mandate and purpose to serve as a centralized hub for overseeing and coordinating the organization's open source initiatives. This centralization of responsibility ensures consistency and alignment of open source efforts across different departments and teams to maximize impact and minimize duplication of efforts.

At the heart of OSPO's mission lies a commitment to facilitating and promoting open source adoption, enablement, contribution, and compliance within BlackRock. By providing guidance, support, and resources, the OSPO empowers teams and individuals to leverage the power of open source to drive innovation and excellence in their respective domains safely and within compliance.

The executive sponsors of the OSPO are Lance Braunstein, head of Aladdin Engineering, and Matthew Kamen, COO of Aladdin Engineering. They both play a pivotal role in championing the adoption and integration of open source principles and practices throughout the firm. Their leadership and advocacy serve to underscore the strategic importance of open source and instill a culture of openness, diversity, collaboration, and innovation at all levels of the organization.

The OSPO's placement within the Aladdin Engineering organization underscores its close alignment with BlackRock's engineering wing, software development processes, and teams. This strategic positioning enables easier integration of open source practices into BlackRock's product development lifecycle, ensuring that open source considerations are advocated for from the outset and throughout the software development process.

To foster open source culture within BlackRock, the OSPO undertakes a range of roles and responsibilities. These include developing and communicating open source policies, guidelines, and best practices to ensure clarity and consistency in open source adoption and usage. Moreover, the OSPO provides resources to employees on open source technologies, tools, and practices, equipping them with the skills and knowledge needed to engage effectively with open source projects.

Additionally, the OSPO plays a crucial role in facilitating the identification and evaluation of open source projects relevant to the organization's needs, helping teams make informed decisions about which projects to adopt, collaborate on, or contribute to. Furthermore, the OSPO manages relationships with external open source communities, non-profits, projects, and partners, fostering collaboration and synergy between BlackRock and the broader open source ecosystem.

Compliance with open source licenses and regulations is another key responsibility of the OSPO given the highly regulated nature of BlackRock's business, ensuring that the organization adheres to legal and ethical standards in its use and contribution to open source projects. By providing guidance and oversight in this area through partnerships with Technology Risk, Information Security, and the Legal and Compliance Intellectual Property Council, the OSPO helps mitigate risks and safeguards the organization's reputation and integrity.

Promoting a culture of collaboration and contribution to open source projects both internally and externally is central to the OSPO's mission. Through initiatives such as open source days, open hacks, workshops, and community engagement events, the OSPO fosters a sense of belonging and ownership among employees, empowering them to actively participate in open source initiatives and make meaningful contributions to the wider community.

In conclusion, the OSPO plays a pivotal role in shaping and nurturing BlackRock's open source culture, driving value creation, innovation, and collaboration across the organization. By providing guidance, support, and resources, the OSPO empowers teams and individuals to leverage the power of open source to achieve their goals and aspirations, propelling the organization towards greater success and impact in an increasingly interconnected and dynamic digital landscape and ultimately delivering best-in-class solutions to its clients to facilitate a better financial future.

City of Paris

Contributed by: Philippe Bareille, Open Source Program Officer, City of Paris

History of OSPO

The City of Paris began developing its digital services platform, Lutece, in 2001 at the request of the city executive. The following year, the Paris Council voted to make the source code available to the public, making it the French administration's first open source project. On one hand, we developed our infrastructure on open systems and developed an "open source first" policy, and on the other side, we got involved in many other open source initiatives amongst which the digital workplace for alumni, parents, and teachers from primary to high school. It was decided in 2018 to formalize the city's open source policy and grow a sustainable community around our flagship project Lutece.

To achieve total transparency and share our developments with other local authorities, it was essential to incorporate open source practices into our business practices, such as cultivating internal teams, adopting best practices, contributing to related projects, taking HR and legal aspects into account, organizing and taking part in hackathons, and providing all documentation enabling users to use the Lutece platform, access the source code, and contribute to it if necessary: "public money, public code," as the Free Software Foundation Europe campaign puts it. Even though this whole culture was well established, it was necessary to write down the objectives concretely.

In addition, it was essential to make any Lutece deployment easier, to foster distribution, and therefore dedicate more time to it. Communication also needed to be unified, homogeneous, and more sustained.

Finally, we needed to identify a "single point of contact" for business teams looking for open source solutions in their work, to act as a link between the community and development teams, and who could evangelize the benefits of using open source within the organization.

The reflection was initiated during the open source symposium organized in June 2019 in Paris, bringing together the biggest players in the ecosystem. The experimentation began in 2019 at a time when we knew of no other OSPO in the public sector in France or abroad. We therefore had to surround ourselves with professionals to define the missions, scope, etc., and implement them in our City context. With the help of the OW2 association, we helped incorporate the public sector dimension into the *Good Governance Initiative.*

Primary Purpose of OSPO

By adopting a few best practices from the ecosystem, the main objectives of the City of Paris' OSPO are made of two major components:

- **Technical**: Assume our role as an open source software editor: open up our ticketing tool to external users, clarify sprint roadmaps for each project, clarify our repositories, and internationalize our tool for better distribution abroad, in collaboration with members of the European public OSPO network.

- **Community**: Firstly, we foster partnerships with other OSPOs, universities, and public service players that have the same tooling needs, improving communication in favor of the projects we use, and contributing to these projects.

Secondly, we allocated the required official time to promote and disseminate our Lutece digital services platform and reduce the technical work involved in deploying it for testing and future adoption via the CiteLibre solution, white-labeling solutions based on Lutece, communicating with and animating communities of functional and technical users, and volunteer translators.

As a local authority, our decision-makers are elected representatives and deputy mayors, who have strongly supported the initiative. The City of Paris IT department is run by Néjia Lanouar, who has also defended the legitimacy of such an initiative.

The OSPO was created and is currently based at the Direction des Systèmes d'Information et du Numérique de la Ville de Paris (Information Systems and Digital Department), with one person in charge of governance and promotion, who relies on operational teams in the departments, especially for the creation of the white label and processes around the replication of the solution.

Naturally, the environment is mainly technical (engineering), but we make sure we surround ourselves with marketing and legal expertise to make our solution more accessible.

Open Source Culture

Our in-house development teams are strongly committed to the genericity and reusability of all our developments, and our architects and developers ensure the best possible modularity to enable us to reuse our developments internally as much as possible for new projects.

With the creation of OSPO, we have designed an internal and external communication strategy for our open source developments, using our communication tools such as our newsletter, blog, and wiki with Lutece, to enhance the value of our platform, improve knowledge of it among project and business teams, and create a feeling of support for this shared project.

GitHub

Contributed by: Ashley Wolf, Director, Open Source Programs, GitHub

Open Source at the Home of Open Source

Since launching in 2008, open source has been a core part of GitHub's DNA. As a critical part of our business and our community, we believe in not only hosting it but actively participating in, improving, and helping lead it. Our goal is to set an example of how to do open source well. Our platform now supports over 100M developers, including more than 90% of Fortune 100. We recognize that we not only have to serve the needs of GitHub's staff to help them be successful with open source, but we have a responsibility to help other organizations be successful in open source on GitHub.

The drive to create an OSPO at GitHub stemmed from a need for structured stewardship over GitHub's growing number of open source projects and initiatives. Following Microsoft's acquisition of GitHub in 2018, the need for a formal office to manage open source became more apparent. The acquisition not only expanded GitHub's reach but also its responsibilities to the broader developer community and its corporate users.

Why did we create an OSPO?

1. We need to be purposeful stewards and maintainers for our projects that we share with the world. We need to be a shining example of how to do open source well. The GitHub OSPO formally started in 2021. Prior to this, we had ad hoc initiatives and

support structures in place to assist GitHub staff with their open source efforts, but it wasn't enough. At that time, we were creating a ton of open source projects like Atom, a hackable text editor with millions of users, and GitHub Desktop, a GUI for Git, and GitHubHubot, a customizable chatbot, but we needed to have more robust structures and an organized approach around open source. We wanted to be sure the open source that we created and put a spotlight on was supported, healthy, and active.

2. We're a developer-first company, and we need to continue building a strong community of developers, starting with our employees. We celebrate and encourage the open source work we do, as well as manage and monitor the open source ecosystem we participate in.

3. We can help companies become more open. GitHub customers all over the world ask for our guidance and best practices for managing open source and InnerSource (open source inside the enterprise). In parallel with organizing our internal open source program, we also come up with new ways to help and work with other OSPOs around the world. Examples of this work include

   - Offering services and product features that benefit OSPOs

   - Conducting case studies on enterprise open source management workflows

   - Publishing best practice guides for managing open source and InnerSource at scale

Mission and Vision

The GitHub Open Source Program Office looks after GitHub's open source communities and ecosystem, as well as the standards, policies, and tools required to maintain, create, and contribute to open source projects. We maintain over 1,000 open source projects, including some well-known projects like npm, GitHub CLI, GitHub desktop, and dependabot-core.

We help with

- Open Source compliance and license management

- Best practice sharing with customers and other OSPOs

- Support for open source contribution, release, and usage

- Open source and OSPO training

- Sponsoring Open Source

- Open source tooling

Customers often ask about our OSPO and how we manage our open source ecosystem. Not only do we need to provide tools and best practices for ourselves, we also need to be an example for companies that are starting OSPOs or using open source at scale.

Activities/Initiatives the GitHub OSPO Helps With

- Durable open source ownership, making sure OSS projects have owners, and also sunsetting inactive projects

- Setting up process and checklists and guidance for employees for Open Sourcing new projects, including AI reviews

- Open source dependency health and management

- Compliance and security tooling

- Reviews for open source

- Strategic open source efforts

- Sponsoring open source

GitHub's commitment to open source through OSPO has not only supported internal projects and upskilling open source education at GitHub but also served as a model for other companies. The visibility of OSPO's work has led to increased inquiries from customers interested in establishing or enhancing their open source strategies. By providing tools, practices, and examples, GitHub OSPO helps other organizations to navigate the complexities of open source management.

OSPO's Role and Organizational Placement

The OSPO sits in the Developer Relations team as part of the Operations organization. The Developer Relations organization's mission is to welcome new members, teach people about software development, and build programs to make GitHub the home for software developers and help enterprises (including GitHub!) work well with open source software.

The Future of OSPO at GitHub

As GitHub continues to evolve, so too will its OSPO. The office is committed to adapting its strategies to meet the changing needs of the open source community and GitHub's business objectives. By maintaining a focus on education, compliance, and community engagement, GitHub's OSPO aims to sustain and grow its leadership in the open source world, ensuring that the company not only hosts but also significantly contributes to the open source ecosystem.

To cultivate an open source culture, GitHub's OSPO collaborates with many teams across the organization on several initiatives:

- Open Source Surveys: Conducted among GitHub employees to gauge engagement and identify improvement areas.

- Maintainers Discussions: Forums for open source maintainers to share challenges and insights.

- Newsletters and Communications: Regular updates to keep the community informed and engaged.

- Promotion and Recognition: Implementing leaderboards and gamification to recognize significant open source contributions.

- Training and Best Practices: By providing guidance and best practices, GitHub's OSPO helps teams learn how to use, create, share, and maintain open source.

Lastly, one of the most important actions the OSPO does is to make connections between the various Open Source stakeholders at GitHub. By connecting disparate roles like Developers, Engineering, IT, Legal, Business, Sales, Security, and Open Source maintainers, the OSPO is able to make sure the important parts of Open Source Culture are communicated and maintained.

Infosys

Contributed by: Naresh Duddu, AVP and Global Head of Open Source, Infosys Ltd

Infosys has a longstanding commitment to open source software, actively leveraging it across our internal operations and client projects. Our open source software stack underpins core internal platforms like InfyMe

(Infosys' intranet platform), Code Store (Infosys internal innersourcing platform), etc. These internal applications cater to 300K+ Infosys employees.

All Infosys IPs – such as Infosys Live Enterprise Application Development Platform, Infosys Live Enterprise Application Management Platform, Infosys Helix, etc. – are built on an open source foundation.

Infosys contributes to open source communities consistently and partners with 40+ open source vendors.

Infosys has an **Open Source First** strategy. To drive systematic curation, consumption, incubation, and contribution to the open source ecosystem both internally and externally, Infosys established an Open Source Program Office in **Q3 2022**, under the executive sponsorship of Infosys CTO – Rafee Tarafdar.

The OSPO aims to establish Infosys as a thought leader in open source through a strategic and efficient approach.

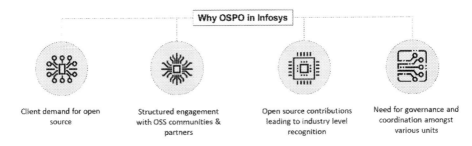

Figure 3-2. *OSPO in Infosys*

OSPO functions as a central hub and spoke system within Infosys, coordinating all the open source activities and strategies across multiple units. This includes multiple teams such as marketing, legal, security, and industry verticals. OSPO consolidates efforts from diverse units and enhances visibility for open source initiatives across the organization and external platforms. OSPO centralizes governance, increases engagement with foundations, ensures compliance, and supports developer contributions.

The key objectives of Infosys OSPO are covered in the charter below.

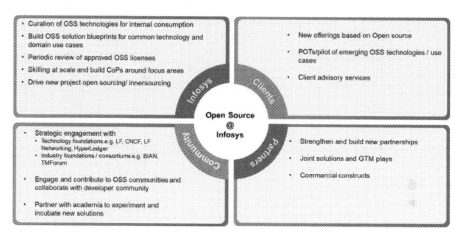

Figure 3-3. *Open Source at Infosys*

Infosys OSPO philosophy has three main pillars:

- **Connect** – Establish deeper connects and partnerships with Open Source Foundations and vendors. Infosys is a member of multiple foundations – e.g., Platinum membership at Linux Foundation for Networking (LFN) and Cloud Native Computing Foundation (CNCF) and has strong partnerships with 40+ open source vendors. These connections enable us to gain early insights into emerging developments within the open source domain, facilitating the creation of pertinent, innovative, and secure solutions for our clients' transformation endeavors.

- **Collaborate** – Work with all the service lines and subsidiaries to drive "innersourcing" culture within the organization and drive greater collaboration between the engineering teams to drive reuse and re-bundling of our assets. Enhance collaboration with open source communities, partners, and contributors worldwide to cultivate profound technical proficiency within key open source endeavors, thereby advancing our engineering prowess.

- **Scale** – Scale both the contribution and consumption to open source projects securely. Strategize, enable, and drive rapid expertise in emerging open source projects to become the trusted and respected open source experts for our clients.

The OSPO spearheads Infosys' initiatives to position itself as an industry leader and foster a dynamic open source culture within the organization through a multifaceted approach.

Strategy and Best Practices

1) Launch of OSPO Portal served as a centralized hub for all open source activities accessible to all employees. Consolidating policies, strategies, and SOPs in one location, it offers user-friendly approval processes for open source contributions and consumption.

2) Promotion of internal collaboration/innersourcing culture, Infosys joined TODO (Talk Openly Develop Openly) foundation to promote the creation and sharing of knowledge, best practices, tools, and other ways to run a successful and effective OSPO.

3) Curation and publication of open source trends through Infosys TechCompass and periodic open source newsletters.

4) Became the first GSI in 2019 to comply with OpenChain2.0 for enforcing open source best practices, license obligations, and security standards. This helps build trust with clients and users and continuously improve vis-à-vis open source adoption.

5) Pledged commitment in 2020 to GPL Co-operation that gives licensees a fair chance to correct violations before their licenses are terminated.

Governance Process Simplification

1) Worked with security and legal to simplify the processes around contribution and consumption.

2) Enforcing adherence to Infosys FOSS policy.

3) Creation of automated scan process to check for security, quality, and license compliance risks for projects using open source.

4) Defined process to setup a containerized open source development environment and quick starts.

Employee Enablement

1) Working in collaboration with the internal training team and open source partners to enrich enablement content, including open source skill tags and curated learning paths.

2) Leveraging foundation-specific training and certifications to empower employees in developing competencies in emerging open source technologies.

3) Coordinating with technology officers across various service lines to establish mentorship groups dedicated to open source, aimed at providing guidance to beginners.

4) Inviting industry leaders to deliver tech talks on emerging industry trends and key open source projects.

5) Motivating employees through rewards and recognition for their voluntary participation in open source activities, including contributions, knowledge sharing, and the development of reference architectures.

Events and Hackathons

1) Encouraging employees to actively participate in key foundation events by presenting papers, publishing blogs, etc.

2) Governing the relationship with foundations and coordinating with foundations on participation in various activities.

3) Organizing numerous organization-wide events to facilitate collaboration, contributions, and knowledge acquisition for employees, offering insights into some of the most prominent communities within the open source ecosystem, and fostering real-world software development and domain expertise.

4) Engaging with open source partners to build joint solutions, papers, etc.

5) Conducting hackathons with open source partners.

Success Stories (CY23)

Contributions:

1. Increased the overall open source contributor count to double the previous number.

2. Volume of contributions to various open source projects grew more than three times.

3. Open sourced ten projects, with 40+ active GitHub repositories.

4. Focused contributions to Backstage (one of the top ten contributor companies) and MOSIP.

Enablement:

1. 75K+ engineers trained each year, with 62K+ certifications on open source.

2. 200+ courses across 57 learning paths on the internal training portal (Lex).

Engagement:

1. Conducted 10+ open source events including CodeCon (internal contribution campaign), Hacktoberfest, Hackathons, etc.

2. Active participation in org-wide initiatives, e.g., TechZooka (annual tech fest), TechCohere community, etc.

3. Participation in open source events (KubeCon Europe, ONESummit, etc.)

Intel

Contributed by: Jessica Marz, Director, Open Source Program Office, Intel Corporation

Operationally, what we now call Intel's Open Source Program Office (OSPO) dates to before 2007; being evolutionary in nature, an exact origin story has not been precisely documented. My belief is that a convergence of factors gave rise to it, but there are two that seem particularly compelling (read: likely). The first is that someone did something that wasn't respectful of a third-party intellectual property right, and that this "escape" was discovered. The second is that someone lacking familiarity with the cultural norms of free and open source software acted in a way that did not comport with community expectations. Neither scenario makes for a good impression, with consequences that could range from reputational harm to legal damages. To mitigate against future incursions, the beginning of the OSPO took shape in partnership between Intel's software development organizations and Legal department, with sponsorship from executive leadership (who, presumably, had been on the receiving end of feedback from unhappy external constituents related to the unfortunate missteps mentioned previously and did not want the experiences repeated).

OSPO Purpose and Objectives

The key functions of Intel's OSPO can be roughly divided into governance, education, and advocacy.

In terms of governance, the OSPO helps establish corporate-wide policies and practices around the consumption and production of "open source material," which we currently define as work offered by a creator under free/libre, open source, "free culture," or similar licensing or permission regimes. The definition will probably continue to be refined, but hopefully you get the gist: whether something is in scope for us is determined by the terms under which it is made available to the market, with "open source" used as a sort of shorthand to signify a general ethos of sharing and communality. The bulk of our work has historically been in the software space, but we are also regularly involved with hardware. Our team's governance activities also include centralized administration of certain outward-facing distribution channels, e.g., Intel's external GitHub presence.

Effective governance isn't possible without education, so a significant portion of the OSPO's work revolves around providing training to the thousands of developers and other employees who interact with open source software. It's definitely an ongoing challenge to reach out to a large audience comprised of people with varying levels of interest in the subject matter, but we leverage a combination of minimally required web-based instruction with a robust collection of self-serve resources to provide deeper dives into myriad related topics. In addition, members of the OSPO make themselves available to provide personalized, intact-team training to organizations across the company, as well as hosting drop-in "office hours" and actively engaging with constituents using internal enterprise community tools such as message boards and wikis.

Much of the work our OSPO does in the education space can't really be separated from advocacy. We endeavor to go beyond merely informing employees about company rules or procedures that need to be followed by seeking to impart an understanding and appreciation of the history and ethos surrounding the free and open source software movement(s). Helping to connect the dots, if you will, between themselves now standing on the shoulders of giants and how the work they are doing can enable continued discovery and innovation for generations to come. Advocating for open source means championing a culture of transparency, collaboration, and shared progress – more about that later.

Organizational Placement

Structurally, the OSPO currently resides within Intel's central software engineering organization. We recruit, nurture, and support a network of ambassadors and allies across Intel's hardware product engineering units, because they each produce software, too! We also maintain strong ties with the Legal and Security departments to address compliance issues and promote secure software development best practices.

Fostering Open Source Culture

To cultivate an open source culture within Intel, the OSPO really tries to role-model community best practices in its operations. For example, the internal project review board follows a community governance model where decisions are made collaboratively by employees who have been recognized over time for their consistent, significant contributions to the project review process. Anyone wishing to become involved in the board is welcome to attend and observe; sustained, meaningful participation often leads to an invitation to become something akin to a "maintainer" or "core contributor." The OSPO approval workflow uses the convention of needing a thumbs up from two reviewers and no unresolved objections. In a similar vein, the OSPO's documentation is maintained in GitHub and contributions are invited from any employee in the form of Pull Requests (PRs) or Issues. When it comes to discussing major changes to policies or practices, a Request for Comment (RFC) system is used. In these ways, the OSPO demonstrates some of what developers can expect to encounter when they participate in external free and open source communities; the goal is to reinforce principles of transparency, collaboration, and inclusivity so that they carry these best practices with them into the ecosystem.

Conclusion

Intel's OSPO plays a key role in building a strong open source culture within the company. It models best practices in community governance and collaboration, setting an example for internal teams, helping Intel employees not only follow community standards but also understand and appreciate the deeper values of the free and open source movements. This approach not only reduces risks but also empowers Intel employees to make meaningful contributions to the greater global shared community. Go open!

Johns Hopkins University

Contributed by: Bill Branan, Hodson Director, Digital Research and Curation Center and Open Source Programs Office and Megan Forbes, Program Manager, Open Source Programs Office, Johns Hopkins University

The Johns Hopkins University Open Source Programs Office (OSPO) was established in 2019 as the first academic OSPO in the United States. Five years on, the OSPO serves as a central resource for the Hopkins community by building awareness of the value and impact of open source software; providing resources, tools, and engineering support to promote the use of open source within the university's academic community; supporting the participation of faculty, staff, and students in open source through educational programs, information sharing, and guidance on best practices; and facilitating the translation of open source software into products and services that generate social impact in addition to commercial success.

The OSPO is anchored in the Johns Hopkins Sheridan Libraries, reinforcing the OSPO's role as a central resource for the entire university community. By residing in the Libraries, which has a long history of promoting open access and serving as a hub of learning, innovation, and collaboration, the OSPO can effectively engage with faculty, students, and staff across all schools and disciplines. This organizational structure allows the OSPO to foster cross-campus partnerships and initiatives without being perceived as tied to any specific school or department.

The OSPO's commitment to openness, learning, and collaboration mirrors the principles and goals set forth by the university's highest leadership and strategic priorities. The Ten for One framework, which guides Hopkins' vision through 2030, emphasizes investing in cross-university programs, providing support services that nurture research, creativity, and teaching, and reinforcing faith in expertise via leadership in open scholarship and open educational resources. Johns Hopkins President Ronald J. Daniels currently serves as co-chair of the HELIOS Open initiative, a cohort of colleges and universities committed to collective action to advance open scholarship within and across their campuses. The OSPO, as a central driver of open source initiatives on campus, plays a crucial role in realizing this vision.

To foster open source culture at Hopkins, the OSPO has undertaken various initiatives and experiments. In 2023, the OSPO launched FOSSProF, the Free and Open Source Project Fund. The program provides funding, execution support, and community-building opportunities to open source projects across the university. FOSSProF received an enthusiastic response, with proposals from six academic divisions requesting nearly $500,000 in funding support, demonstrating the growing interest and engagement in open source initiatives at Hopkins.

The OSPO's commitment to fostering open source culture and providing immersive experiences for students is exemplified by its support of Semesters of Code, a computer science course at the Johns Hopkins Whiting School of Engineering taught in fall 2022. Aligned with the university's Ten for One strategic framework, which emphasizes creating a preeminent undergraduate experience that connects students with leading faculty and research programs, Semesters of Code offered students the opportunity to engage with real-world open source projects. The course, taught by Microsoft executive Stephen Walli, combined lectures on a range of software-related topics with hands-on participation in open source initiatives. Students worked on projects such as the Public Access Submission System (PASS), OpenCRAVAT (an NIH-funded project at Hopkins), Semester.ly (a Hopkins student project), Lutece (an international project), and Microsoft PowerShell. By collaborating with mentors from these projects, students gained invaluable experience in software engineering, community engagement, and open source best practices.

The OSPO also plays a crucial role in supporting existing open source projects on campus, helping them to become more sustainable and embrace open source culture. Simply making code open source is necessary but not sufficient; to foster a thriving open source ecosystem, projects must also prioritize community engagement, transparent practices, and effective governance. The OSPO has worked closely with initiatives like SciServer, OceanSpy, and Econ-ARK to help them develop strategies for building and maintaining active, engaged communities around their projects and implementing transparent governance models that ensure decision-making processes are open, inclusive, and accountable to the community. The OSPO also manages the campus-wide GitHub Enterprise account, ensuring that the critical work of sharing code is supported, and curates the Campus Open Source Catalog, a continuously growing collection of projects developed or contributed to by faculty, staff, and students on campus. By emphasizing the importance of these practices, the OSPO helps open source projects at Hopkins grow into collaborative, community-driven endeavors.

As a service organization dedicated to supporting the mission of Johns Hopkins University, the OSPO will continue to leverage its network and expertise to drive the adoption and success of open source across the institution's research, education, and translation activities. Through its ongoing commitment to collaboration, innovation, and community-building, the OSPO will play a vital role in shaping the future of academic open source software and solidifying Johns Hopkins' position as a leader in this transformative field.

Mercedes-Benz

Contributed by: Dr. Wolfgang Gehring, FOSS Ambassador and OSPO Lead, Mercedes-Benz Tech Innovation GmbH

Starting the OSPO

At Mercedes-Benz, we have been using FOSS for around 20 years. Back then, we didn't see the full potential of Open Source yet, probably like most of our industry peers. The view was that it was something that our suppliers would use. Nevertheless, we internally looked at the role of FOSS more closely in around 2016, and that resulted in a FOSS strategy that was passed by the Board of Management in 2018. Thus, the FOSS Center of Competence (CoC) was founded. The FOSS CoC now comprises experts from our Enterprise IT, R&D, Legal Department, and two of our tech subsidiaries: Mercedes-Benz Tech Innovation and MBition. At Mercedes-Benz Tech Innovation, we have an appropriately named Open Source Program Office (OSPO) consisting of colleagues with technological backgrounds, legal and compliance expertise, and skilled community managers.

We think that our employees are very – excuse the pun – open towards FOSS. One of the reasons why Mercedes-Benz has given itself an Open and InnerSource strategy was the fact that it was demanded by more and more of our employees. The realization that FOSS is necessary, beneficial for all parties, and absolutely essential for software work was also partly a grassroots movement within the company.

Primary Purpose

The primary purpose of our FOSS CoC/OSPO is to support our organization and all of our colleagues to engage in Open Source activities and to do so in a safe and legally compliant way. Everybody in software development is doing FOSS these days, but if you really want to make full use of it in your company, you need an OSPO. Otherwise, everybody is doing FOSS somehow, but not in a concerted and synchronized way. That can create risks, and you are certainly also not tapping into the full potential of FOSS.

Fostering Open Source

We are working hard on becoming a player and a good citizen of the worldwide Open Source community. So we contribute back to Open Source projects as best as we can, e.g., bug-fixes and other code- and non-code contributions. We still have some work to do in this regard, admittedly, but we strive to get better and better – learning by doing, just the Open Source spirit.

We give talks at Open Source conventions to report on our experience and to hopefully serve as example, for other companies that are struggling with the adoption of Open Source into their daily work.

Mercedes-Benz is also a member of several Open Source foundations, either directly or through our tech subsidiaries: We are, for example, a strategic member of the Eclipse Foundation as well as the Software Defined Vehicle Working Group; we are members of the Linux Foundation, the Cloud Native Computing Foundation, KDE; and we have recently joined the Green Software Foundation. We believe that these foundations are doing a tremendous job and invaluable work for the advancement of FOSS.

Another way is sponsoring: We sponsor selected Open Source conferences such as FOSS Backstage, EclipseCon, KubeCon/Cloud Native Con Europe, as well as the InnerSource Commons. In particular, though, we sponsor FOSS projects financially – which actually goes beyond just giving money, but also gives the creators of the software the recognition they deserve. It helps to ensure that the software we use will still be around tomorrow. We believe that sponsoring is a great way to drive FOSS forward altogether, specifically to make it more sustainable so that maintainers of crucial parts of today's software infrastructure don't have to do this when they come home from their day jobs. This allows them to concentrate on what they do best: Crafting exceptional software.

Finally, one of the key pillars of our Open Source efforts is our Mercedes-Benz FOSS Manifesto. It is a set of guidelines and core values which explicitly sends our employees on their Open Source mission, knowing well that they are fully supported by the company. The fact that the Manifesto was signed by the CIO (and actually, welcomed by the Board of Management) shows that the FOSS strategy and an Open Source culture are supported, fostered, and even demanded by the highest management level. We think that the FOSS Manifesto will help us to modernize and transform our IT organization to drive forward the cultural change towards Open Source which will profoundly impact the way in which software is developed at the corporate level. We believe that if other companies follow suit and adopt similar guidelines, it could elevate Open Source to a whole new level in the corporate world across industries. Having said that, there are already quite a number of reputed tech companies that have followed our example and recently published their Open Source manifestos, a move we find absolutely amazing and indicative of their commitment to Open Source.

In software development, FOSS is like the air you breathe: You need it, and that's all there is to it! Open Source is the way to go. For individuals, companies, and even for administrations and governments, as we are experiencing more and more. FOSS gives us all a strong sense of "Together we are better!"

Red Hat

Contributed by: Brian Proffitt, Sr Manager, Open Source Program Office, Red Hat, Inc.

As more organizations realize the advantages of open source, many are looking for ways to integrate open source technologies and strategies into their own business practices. But they've learned that simply throwing developers into an open source project and hoping for the best isn't enough to *really* reap those advantages. Increasingly, organizations are *also* recognizing the need for building centralized open source programs offices (OSPOs) that nurture, guide, and align open source best practices with business strategy.

In fact, that work is so important that even a company like Red Hat, which lives and breathes the open source way, established an OSPO. But our OSPO operates much more differently from other corporate OSPOs.

So what does our OSPO do?

Inside Red Hat's OSPO

In some ways, Red Hat's OSPO operates the same way as any other organization's OSPO – except there are some aspects that don't fall within the scope of our specific mission.

Our OSPO started rather late in the history of Red Hat. What began as the Open Source and Standards team as an effort to consolidate resources for the many open source upstream communities Red Hat fosters did not align itself as an Open Source Program Office until the Spring of 2019. This rebranding to OSPO was done to align ourselves with industry teams showing up with the same name in other organizations. But even though we share the OSPO label, there are marked differences in how we operate.

Surprisingly to many, we don't focus on open source licensing and compliance. Red Hat started from open source and had a long head start on the rest of the industry, so our focus is more on providing education and resources to associates, not making licensing choices. This isn't to say that Red Hat blithely ignores legal risk and compliance – it's just not one of our OSPO's core responsibilities. Instead, Red Hat has a legal team who can focus on those open source issues that do crop up.

With regard to community participation, Red Hat's OSPO also operates differently than many other offices with a similar function. Because the health and success of the upstream projects with which we work are so important, our OSPO team spends *a lot* of effort making sure those projects' communities are working efficiently and well. To that end, we pursue what we refer to as "community building": helping new projects set up vibrant communities and assisting existing projects to keep their communities engaged.

This work will include high-level strategic planning for what a project's community will look like, such as, "Will it be a contributor-based or user-focused community?" "What will the governance of the project be?" Our team also plans and implements tactical-level aspects of community around the core value of onboarding best practices. Making sure onboarding new community members to a project for Red Hat is a critical piece of any successful project. It's a fairly straightforward set of questions that we apply to all projects for incoming community members:

- What does the project do?

- How do I get and use the project?

- How do I contribute changes to the project?

If those three questions can't be answered for potential users and contributors, then the barrier to entry for the project will be higher than is necessary. Red Hat's OSPO works with projects to ensure these onboarding practices are well implemented.

Another key difference in how our OSPO works is that we also help customers and partners with their open source journey, especially if they are getting started and just entering the open source ecosystem. We also work with them to advocate open source licenses and corporate stewardship and contribution. For our OSPO, distinguishing ourselves as thoughtful stewards with a stake in a healthy open ecosystem is critical and speaks to our position as an industry leader in open source communities and within Red Hat's Office of the CTO, of which we are a part. Our team also works with customers and partners to educate them on how open source projects can not only be beneficial to consume but also to participate in.

This also applies to conversations we have with our own leadership team. The knowledge base around open source in Red Hat is very deep, but as with most things in life, there is seldom only one solution to any situation. OSPO is part of ongoing and consultative conversations with business leads, executive decision makers, and line engineers in Red Hat to guide everyone to the best possible open source approach to any challenge.

Eyes on the Goal

All OSPOs need not look or function alike. But they all have one thing in common: helping to keep the goals of the business and its open source implementation complementary and aligned. By keeping their eye on that important mission, they will certainly benefit the organizations of which they are a part.

UC Santa Cruz

Contributed by: Stephanie Lieggi, Executive Director, Center for Research in Open Source Software, University of California, Santa Cruz

UC Santa Cruz has a long history with open source and open science, so it is only natural that one of the first university OSPOs would get its start there. UCSC researchers were a leading part of the publicly funded Human Genome Project and led the effort in the late 1990s and early 2000s to publish the human genome as an open source artifact. This team was able to publish just ahead of a privately funded group who would have patented the human genome; instead, UCSC researchers ensured that this knowledge was freely available to researchers throughout the world.

As the open source Genome Browser was taking off at UCSC, so too was the work of an entrepreneurial UCSC Ph.D. student, Sage Weil. As part of his dissertation project, Weil developed the open source storage project known as Ceph. After graduating, Weil built a start-up as the commercial arm around Ceph, which he sold to Red Hat in 2014 for $175 million. In 2015, Weil gifted UCSC – in particular, his advisors Scott Brandt and Carlos Maltzahn – with $3 million, meant to create programs that enabled other students to pursue a similar career path. The gift created an open source endowed chair and allowed for the establishment of the Center for Open Source Software (CROSS.) CROSS, a research center under the Baskin School of Engineering, aimed to bridge the gap between student work and successful open source projects. In this way, Weil's gift aimed to create a platform where students with innovative ideas could recreate the kind of success he experienced with Ceph. CROSS also engaged with industry partners interested in supporting open source development and research, bringing in $2.6 million in industry membership fees in its first six years.

CROSS's success highlighted how open source projects can be a powerful catalyst for bringing together industry and academic researchers – and enabling university research to have an increasing impact. In 2020, the CROSS leadership began working with other academic institutions promoting open source on their campuses and exploring the idea of developing an Open Source Program Office (OSPO) at UCSC. Although CROSS had many trappings of an OSPO, it lacked others, particularly a campuswide reach and ability to impact university open source policies.

In 2022, the Sloan Foundation provided CROSS a grant to pilot the creation of an OSPO at UCSC; this grant was followed by a second grant in 2024, which funded a network of OSPOs on additional campuses across the University of California system. The purpose of the UCSC OSPO, as well as the network of OSPOs throughout the UC system, is to increase the translation and impact – both socially and economically – of academic research, highlighting the importance of open source to this end. The UCSC OSPO, similar to many other academic OSPOs, aims to further advance the educational, research, and service missions of the school by leveraging open source methodologies and communities. This is accomplished through the initiation and support of specific activities related to workforce development, open source ecosystem building, and the creation of best practices. More specifically, these include

1. Support of existing UCSC open source projects through identification of resources and funding

2. Growing of open source communities through our postdoc-focused incubator program

3. Advising researchers on governance models and ways to collaborate with industry and communities

4. Creating coursework and workshops focused on teaching open source tools and methodologies

5. Providing a platform to match students with mentors within existing open source projects

Each of these activities works to promote and foster open source as guiding principles of the campus research enterprise. The UCSC OSPO also holds numerous public-facing events each year that highlight the open source work being done at UCSC and elsewhere in the UC system. The most prominent of these activities is the UCSC Open Source Symposium – which is a three-day hybrid event that brings together UC researchers, industry representatives, and members of numerous open source communities, spotlighting the ways in which open source amplifies the impact of academic-based research.

As part of a public university with the mission to educate and build a diverse workforce, the UCSC OSPO sees mentorship programs as integral to this work. Beginning in 2018, CROSS became a mentor organization for the Google Summer of Code (GSoC, offering mentees the chance to contribute to open source research projects.CROSS saw significant benefit to participating mentors as well, particularly in helping build diverse communities of contributors. Building upon the GSoC model, the UCSC OSPO developed the Open Source Research Experience (OSRE), which expanded their offerings to support new contributors both inside and beyond the UC system, and on a broader range of research projects. In an effort to further diversify the open source talent pipeline, the UCSC OSPO also launched the Catalyst Contributor program in 2023, which focuses on mentoring students from Historically Black Colleges and Universities (HBCUs). Catalyst students are provided workshop-style instruction, plus peer and mentor support that enables them to productively engage and contribute to an open source community of their choice. Founded in partnership with Norfolk State University, Contributor Catalyst will be expanding to another five HBCUs over the next three years.

The UCSC OSPO is currently part of CROSS – which sits in the Baskin School of Engineering. However, its final home within the university remains under discussion, particularly as to what will maximize campuswide impact in the long term. Many academic OSPOs sit in either the Office of Research or the University Library, in large part due to the campus-wide reach of these entities. Understanding this need, the UCSC OSPO is working with campus-wide organizations such as the Center for Innovation and Entrepreneurial Development (CIED) and the Innovation & Business Engagement Hub (IBE) to strategize where it should sit moving forward.

Toyota

Contributed by: Masato Endo, Group Manager of Open Source Program Group, Toyota Motor Corporation

Toyota officially launched its OSPO in January 2024. This case study outlines Toyota's open source initiatives to date, the establishment of the OSPO, and the current activities being taken inside the company.

The History of Toyota's Open Source Activities

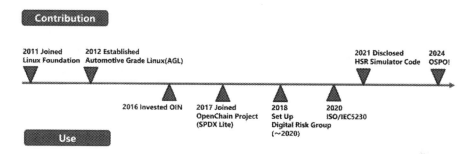

Figure 3-4. *History of Toyota's Open Source Activities*

Joining the Linux Foundation, AGL, and OIN

Toyota joined the Linux Foundation in 2011. It contributed to the establishment of Automotive Grade Linux (AGL) to promote the development of In-Vehicle Infotainment using an open source approach, acting as a Platinum Member of the project and delivering keynote speeches at key events such as the Automotive Linux Summit.

[SC1] Toyota also established or joined initiatives to ensure that open source is used appropriately by employees and in its supply chain. For example, Toyota is a Platinum member and maintains a board seat in the Open Invention Network, a patent licensing entity and community that enables companies around the world to use open source with confidence from the perspective of patents related to open source software.

Promotion of the OpenChain Project

Toyota is the first Japanese company and the first automotive company to participate in the OpenChain Project as a Platinum member, contributing significantly to its development and promotion. In 2017, together with Sony and Hitachi, Toyota launched the OpenChain Japan Work Group to create an environment where issues related to the use of open source in the supply chain can be discussed in Japanese. The community has grown rapidly, with over 200 members working within eight subgroups. An example being how one of the subgroups created a simplified version of the SPDX SBOM format and proposed it to the global community to ensure smaller companies or companies with limited resources could benefit from more professional software supply chain management. This proposal was approved as a sub-format of SPDX called SPDX Lite and became part of ISO/IEC 5962:2021.

To facilitate the sharing of best practices within the industry, Toyota also launched the OpenChain Automotive Work Group and has been organizing events in the US, Europe, Asia, and online as part of this activity.

Building Processes for Open Source Software Use and Contribution

Using the knowledge gained from engagement with the open source community, Toyota worked to establish internal rules and processes for open source software use and contribution. In 2018, they established a temporary organization at the head office, and others facilitated discussions to integrate open source management into existing software developing processes approaches and developed educational materials to support excellence across the organization.

In 2020, some departments met the requirements of OpenChain ISO/IEC 5230:2020, the International Standard for open source license compliance. This activity was aligned with the formal release of ISO/IEC 5230:2020, making Toyota the first company in the world to announce ISO/IEC 5230 certification.

How Was Toyota OSPO Established

Toyota has been working with the broader open source community to develop open source software and address challenges related to its adoption, management, and long-term sustainability. To further promote community activities among employees, a project team was formed in 2023 to establish an OSPO. The team conducted interviews with employees already involved in open source activities across the company to understand real-world challenges and expectations for support that could be offered by the OSPO.

Based on the interview results, the initial team defined the role the OSPO should play and the activities it should focus on inside the company. Consequently, the Open Source Program Group (TOYOTA OSPO) was established in January 2024, operating under the direct control of the President of the Advanced R&D and Engineering Company.

OSPO's Function

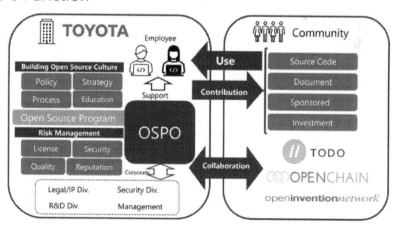

Figure 3-5. *Toyota OSPO's Function*

The Expected Role of OSPO

The role of TOYOTA OSPO is straightforward. It defines policies and processes and provides training programs to help employees use and contribute to open source. Additionally, the OSPO keeps employees informed about the latest trends in open source and responds promptly to their inquiries.

In collaboration with the IP and security departments, the OSPO also works on risk management. The OSPO engages with communities such as the Linux Foundation, the OpenChain Project, and the TODO Group to promote open innovation within the company and also across the automotive industry and beyond.

OSPO's 3 Key Activities

Figure 3-6. *Toyota OSPO's Key Activities*

OSPO's Three Key Activities

Toyota's OSPO is newly formed but already has a clear remit to focus on three key activities:

1. **Culture**: Establishing an open source culture cannot be achieved overnight. Therefore, members of the Toyota OSPO have been working to nurture an approach of productive open source engagement event before OSPO was formally established. Educational materials on open source have been

prepared for multiple purposes in support of this. For example, the Toyota OSPO prepared manuals for R&D, for application to products, and for contribution processes. In addition, it has created customized e-learning material for all employees. This material takes the form of a comic book to attract employees who are not normally familiar with software development. Even before the COVID pandemic, future members of the Toyota OSPO invited industry experts to conduct bootcamp-style training sessions. More recently, the Toyota OSPO collaboration with Woven, a cutting-edge software developer within the Toyota Group, has accelerated the cultivation of Toyota's open source culture. For example, Woven established the Safety-Critical Rust Consortium in 2024 with the Rust Foundation and others. Toyota and Woven regularly share information and foster collaboration with the community.

2. **Strategy**: OSPO has defined a strategic community focus for the company with respect to open source and is providing targeted support for engineer activities against these corporate goals. OSPO members are also actively involved in helping to focus community engagement internally and externally that facilitates and enhances overall open source benefit.

3. **Automation**: License compliance and security assurance are crucial when utilizing open source software. The OSPO is spearheading the automation of these tasks to help engineers maximize their

productivity of software development. As part of
this, the OSPO is introducing tools and internal
systems related specifically to open source with
a focus on streamlining processes related to its
management.

Summary

This chapter explained what OSPOs are and their role within an enterprise.
There is no one way to structure OSPO, and even the functionality can
differ. This variation is evident in case studies from different enterprises'
OSPOs. Each case study explains the origin of their OSPO, where does
OSPO sit in the organization, and what does it do to foster open source
culture.

The next chapter explains the relevance of internal events inside
the company and different types of internal events. There is a dedicated
section on hackathon with clear tips on how to organize one successfully.
Like previous chapters, the next chapter concludes with case studies
explaining how some companies did internal events to foster an open
source culture.

CHAPTER 4

Internal Events

Internal events are organized activities within a company designed to bring employees together for various purposes, such as team building, knowledge sharing, and professional development. These events play a multifaceted role in enhancing employee engagement, fostering a positive work culture, and contributing to the overall success and well-being of a company and its workforce. Internal events foster engagement through team building and social interactions, contributing to motivated and satisfied employees. Internal events promote continuous learning, professional growth, and the reinforcement of company values.

Such events are typically organized on a regular cadence, such as monthly, quarterly, or annually, ensuring that they become an integral part of the company's rhythm and culture. The word "internal" emphasizes that these events are exclusively for employees, creating a safe and controlled environment where they can freely exchange ideas, share experiences, and work collaboratively without external pressures. By regularly bringing employees together in this way, companies can reinforce their values, align teams with strategic goals, and foster a sense of belonging and shared purpose, all of which contribute to a more motivated and cohesive workforce.

Internal events with an open source focus play a pivotal role in fostering an open source culture within a company by providing a controlled and supportive environment for employees to engage with open source principles and practices. These events serve as powerful tools for instilling the principles of openness, collaboration, and community engagement in a safe environment. These events create opportunities for employees to experiment with open source tools, share their knowledge, and collaborate on projects in a setting that encourages learning and growth without the external pressures that might accompany public contributions.

As explained earlier, there are a large variety of reasons why organizations may not contribute to open source. Internal events offer a controlled and supportive space for employees, within the company's firewall, to interact with each other using open source principles. It allows the employees to make mistakes and recover gracefully without putting the company's reputation at risk. Sometimes, there is a "false hesitation" in the company's mind that if their employees contribute poor quality code, then the company's engineering reputation is at stake. Doing that in an internal event limits the exposure and provides a safe space for the employees to recover. Employees can practice public speaking in front of their colleagues as opposed to strangers. They learn the basic mechanisms of how to submit a Pull Request, do code reviews, and engage in deep technical discussions across multiple geographies. There is a lot less risk for a company's intellectual property to be leaked.

Benefits of Internal Events

Internal events gradually build confidence, address concerns, and prepare employees for public contributions to open source projects. This approach facilitates a guided transition toward embracing open source practices within the organization. Here are specific benefits from internal events:

- **Education and Awareness** – Internal events provide a controlled and supportive environment to educate employees about open source principles, practices, and the benefits of contributing to open source. Workshops, seminars, and training sessions can demystify misconceptions and increase awareness.

- **Risk Mitigation** – Companies may have concerns about the perceived risks of contributing to open source. Internal events offer an opportunity to address these concerns directly, discussing legal considerations, intellectual property protection, and strategies for mitigating potential risks.

- **Hands-On Training and Skill Development** – Conducting hands-on training sessions within the company allows employees to develop the necessary skills for open source contribution in a safe and controlled setting. This can include sessions on version control systems, collaborative coding practices, and project management tools.

- **In-House Open Source Projects** – Internal events can initiate in-house open source projects that start within the company. This allows employees to experience the collaborative nature of open source development within a familiar and secure environment before contributing externally.

- **Gradual Exposure** – Organize events that expose employees gradually to the external open source community. This can include attending industry conferences, participating in virtual meetups, or engaging with external contributors in a controlled setting, easing the transition to public contributions.

- **Cultivating a Collaborative Environment** – Internal events focused on open source practices help cultivate a collaborative environment within the company. Employees learn the value of sharing knowledge, receiving feedback, and working together, fostering a culture that aligns with open source collaboration.

- **Internal Code Reviews** – Conducting internal code reviews and feedback sessions replicates the collaborative aspects of open source development. This allows employees to experience the constructive feedback culture without the immediate exposure to external scrutiny.

- **Recognition and Rewards** – Recognize and reward employees for their contributions to in-house open source projects during internal events. Positive reinforcement builds confidence and encourages a mindset where contributions are acknowledged and celebrated.

- **Building Trust and Confidence** – Internal events play a crucial role in building trust and confidence among employees. Addressing fears, providing clear guidelines, and sharing success stories during events help employees feel more comfortable with the idea of contributing to open source.

- **Internal Open Source Community** – Establish an internal open source community within the company. Regular events, forums, and discussion groups can create a sense of belonging and encourage employees to share experiences, challenges, and insights related to open source practices.

- **Customized Training Programs** – Develop customized training programs that address specific concerns or challenges the company may have regarding open source contributions. Tailored sessions can focus on legal considerations, code quality, and community engagement strategies.

- **Showcasing Internal Success Stories** – Use internal events to showcase success stories of employees who have successfully contributed to open source projects. Real-world examples within the company provide tangible evidence of the positive outcomes of open source participation.

Internal events serve as catalysts for cultural transformation, offering a controlled and supportive space for employees to interact with open source principles. These events strategically address the multifaceted concerns organizations may have, fostering a nurturing environment.

Types of Internal Events

A wide range of internal events can be conducted within the company, each with a unique purpose. This is analogous to a well-rounded athlete who needs to follow a diverse training regiment. Internal events act as the varied workout routines designed to target specific aspects of an employee's engagement with open source principles. Much like a well-rounded athlete focuses on strength, endurance, and agility, different internal events play distinct roles in enhancing the organization's open source culture.

Let's take a look at different types of internal events that can be conducted inside the company to promote open source culture.

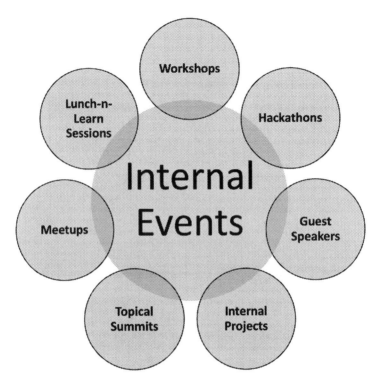

Figure 4-1. *Open Source-Focused Internal Events*

Workshops

Workshops are interactive sessions designed to provide employees with hands-on experience, skill development, and practical knowledge related to open source practices. Workshops within a company's open source culture are akin to the foundational weight training exercises that athletes engage in to build strength and endurance. These events serve as the cornerstone for empowering employees with the essential skills required for effective participation in open source endeavors. Employees can delve into the intricacies of version control systems, collaborative coding practices, and the utilization of tools commonly employed in open source development. These sessions provide hands-on experience, allowing participants to grasp the fundamentals and hone their proficiency in navigating the open source landscape.

Much like weight training targets specific muscle groups, these workshops focus on strengthening employees' capabilities, ensuring they are well-equipped to contribute meaningfully to open source projects. Participants gain proficiency in using popular platforms like GitHub, GitLab, or Bitbucket, learning how to efficiently manage code repositories, handle branching and merging, and collaborate seamlessly with fellow developers. Additionally, they delve into best practices for documentation, performing and receiving code reviews, and issue tracking, acquiring a comprehensive skill set that prepares them for the collaborative nature of open source development.

The interactive nature of these workshops encourages active engagement, fostering an environment where employees can ask questions, share insights, and troubleshoot challenges collaboratively. Moreover, the workshops can be tailored to address the specific needs and goals of the organization, ensuring that employees acquire the skills most relevant to their roles and the open source projects they intend to contribute to.

Overall, these workshops lay the foundation for a robust open source culture within the company, empowering employees with the proficiency and confidence needed to embark on their open source journey. Just as athletes build strength through consistent and targeted training, participants in these workshops develop the skills necessary to navigate the collaborative and dynamic world of open source development.

Hackathons

High-intensity interval training (HIIT) for athletes is intense bursts of exercise followed by a brief rest period. This allows athletes to achieve significant fitness benefits in a shorter amount of time compared to traditional, steady-state workouts. Hackathons and coding sprints are like HIIT for open source developers. They provide time boxed and concentrated bursts of engagement that push participants to deliver impactful contributions within short timeframes. These events serve as dynamic platforms to accelerate learning, foster collaboration, and simulate the fast-paced nature of open source development.

In the open source arena, hackathons are intensive coding sessions where employees come together to work collaboratively on specific projects or solve predefined challenges. Much like athletes pushing their limits during HIIT, participants in hackathons immerse themselves in focused and rapid development, aiming to produce tangible results within a limited time. These events encourage quick thinking, creativity, and the application of skills acquired during workshops and skill development initiatives.

Coding sprints, on the other hand, share similarities with short-distance sprints in athletics, emphasizing rapid and concentrated effort. These sprints often revolve around making significant contributions to open source projects, whether it's fixing bugs, implementing new features, or optimizing existing code. Participants work in a focused and time-boxed manner, mirroring the intensity of a sprint, with the goal of achieving meaningful outcomes by the end of the session.

Hackathons and coding sprints inject a burst of energy into the open source culture, providing employees with practical experience, fostering collaboration, and instilling a sense of achievement as they witness the tangible outcomes of their efforts within a short span.

Guest Speakers

Guest speaker sessions are like the mentorship and coaching that athletes receive from seasoned experts. These sessions provide employees with valuable insights, guidance, and real-world perspectives from experienced individuals in the open source community, typically outside the company. Much like athletes benefit from learning from those who have mastered their craft, participants in guest speaker sessions gain a deeper understanding of open source principles and best practices.

These speakers may have a rich history of contributing to significant open source projects, leading initiatives, or shaping industry standards. They may share their experiences in overcoming hurdles, navigating complex projects, and addressing common issues encountered in the open source landscape. They provide insights into emerging trends and innovations within the open source community. They may discuss cutting-edge technologies, evolving best practices, and the future direction of open source development. These sessions typically have Q&A and interactive discussions. It allows participants to pose questions, seek clarification on specific topics, and engage in meaningful discussions with the speaker, fostering a collaborative learning environment. Hearing success stories, learning from challenges, and understanding the impact of open source contributions can inspire employees to excel in their own endeavors.

Athletes benefit from exposure to diverse coaching styles, and guest speakers bring diverse perspectives to open source sessions. These individuals may come from different industries, backgrounds, or geographic locations, offering a broader view of the open source landscape. Guest speakers often have a global presence, connecting participants with the broader global open source community. This exposure helps employees recognize the worldwide impact of their contributions and understand the interconnected nature of open source development.

Guest speaker sessions contribute to the development of a robust open source culture by providing employees with mentorship, insights, and inspiration from accomplished individuals in the field. These sessions enrich the learning experience, enhance participants' understanding of open source practices, and encourage a sense of community within the organization's open source initiatives.

Internal Projects

Athletes build muscle memory through repetitive training and hone their skills through simulated game scenarios in practice. Just like that, internal open source projects serve as a training ground for employees. This controlled exposure allows employees to navigate the intricacies of collaborative coding, much like athletes simulating match situations to enhance their performance. The environment is intentionally crafted to be supportive, providing a safety net for learning and experimentation. As contributors engage with these internal open source projects, they develop a reflexive understanding of best practices, efficient workflows, and the nuances of collaborative coding. This preparatory step is crucial, fostering a level of familiarity and competence that empowers our teams to seamlessly transition into the dynamic and often unpredictable landscape of external open source contributions with confidence and skill. The goal is not just to instill knowledge but to cultivate a form of "open source muscle memory" that becomes second nature, enabling contributors to adapt, collaborate, and contribute effectively in the broader open source community.

There is more discussion about this topic in the InnerSource section.

Topical Summits

Topical summits offer a platform for deep dives into specific aspects of open source technology, methodologies, or industry trends. These events bring together like-minded individuals, experts, and enthusiasts to explore and collaborate on particular topics relevant to open source. These focused discussions enable participants to share specialized knowledge, insights, and best practices within a particular domain. This targeted knowledge sharing contributes to the continuous learning and upskilling of participants, fostering a culture of expertise and innovation. This is akin to an athlete going to a specialized training camp to enhance their skills in one particular area.

By concentrating on a specific topic, these summits create opportunities for networking and community building among individuals with shared interests. Attendees can connect with like-minded peers, industry leaders, and experts, fostering relationships that extend beyond the event. The sense of community developed in these focused gatherings enhances collaboration and encourages ongoing communication within the organization.

Given the specific focus areas, topical summits often attract participants from various departments and roles within the organization. This cross-functional integration facilitates a holistic understanding of open source practices across different teams. It breaks down silos, promotes knowledge exchange, and encourages a unified approach to open source development.

Summits can adopt a singular talk track, following a uniform agenda for all attendees. Alternatively, and more commonly, there may be multiple talk tracks, each focused on a subtopic. This approach accommodates a larger number of speakers, offering attendees flexibility to create a custom schedule based on their interests. Sessions from the summits are often recorded, enabling participants, or even non-participants, to catch up on discussions after the event concludes. These summits serve as fertile ground for curating talks that can later be submitted to external conferences. Additionally, they provide a secure space for employees to hone their speaking skills in front of colleagues before venturing into public conference presentations.

Summits can take various formats, including exclusively in-person, fully virtual, or a hybrid approach that combines both physical and remote participation. Virtual summits offer scalability, but the valuable hallway conversations unique to in-person events are often missed. To leverage the benefits of both, a hybrid strategy may involve hosting key portions, like keynotes, in-person at major sites, or organizing social gatherings at the end of the day to foster employee connections. This approach balances the advantages of virtual accessibility with the irreplaceable dynamics of face-to-face interactions.

During my tenure at Apple, we pioneered the first internal Kubernetes Summit, drawing a diverse audience of over 1000 individuals from across the company. This groundbreaking event successfully unified the entire cloud native community within Apple. Similarly, at Intel, my team organized an internal Open Ecosystem Summit, attracting a massive participation of over 2,500 employees. The summit encompassed keynotes, panel discussions, technical sessions, birds-of-a-feather gatherings, hackathons, and more, operating seamlessly across three different time zones for a globally inclusive experience. Both of these events had moments where attendees said, "I didn't know you were working on this." These experiences really helped break down silos within the company and thus promoting a culture of transparency, collaboration, and community engagement that are core pillars of open source culture.

Meetups

Organizing topical summits is a resource-intensive endeavor that involves considerable coordination among multiple teams, often leading to their annual occurrence. However, the open source landscape is dynamic, constantly evolving with the emergence of new tools, technologies, projects, and processes. Thus, it becomes crucial to maintain direct communication with developers on a regular basis to ensure their continuous engagement and keep them informed about the latest developments in the open source world. This is where the significance of internal meetups comes into play. Unlike the comprehensive and less frequent nature of summits, internal meetups offer a more agile and lightweight approach, enabling organizations to host them on a more frequent cadence. This flexibility ensures that developers stay consistently connected, well-informed, and actively involved in the fast-paced evolution of the open source world. Athletes rely on proper nutrition throughout the year for peak performance. These meetups provide the intellectual nourishment needed for employees throughout the year to understand, discuss, and share experiences related to open source.

The meetups would usually last 30 mins to an hour and are typically tailored to focus on specific open source topics. The meetup organizer, or possibly a set of volunteers, would actively seek input from various teams within the company to curate diverse and engaging content. Each meetup would be announced through various channels on a set day and time, fostering a sense of anticipation and participation. It always takes time, effort, and organizational perseverance to create a new meetup. However, the dividends would become apparent over time as you start building a healthy pipeline of speakers and the audience base steadily grows. The meetup topics and speakers become a fertile ground for the inception of more comprehensive and specialized topical summits.

It's a common practice to record these sessions as that significantly enhances accessibility. Those unable to attend live meetups can catch up at their convenience by accessing the recorded content. This flexibility ensures that the learning experience is not confined to a specific timeframe, accommodating the diverse schedules and commitments of participants.

Lunch-and-Learn Sessions

The term "lunch and learn" refers to a training or learning session that takes place during the lunchtime hours. The concept likely evolved as a response to the busy schedules of employees, offering a chance for professional development without disrupting the regular workflow. The idea is that employees can use their lunch break to engage in a learning session, often accompanied by a meal. The format typically involves bringing in a speaker, expert, or facilitator to present information on a specific topic while participants enjoy their lunch. It provides a relaxed and informal setting for knowledge-sharing, discussion, and skill-building.

These sessions, typically conducted during the lunch hour, serve as short but impactful opportunities for professional development. The brevity of these sessions, aligned with the lunch duration, allows for minimal disruption to the workday while maximizing the intake of valuable knowledge. Complementing meetups seamlessly, lunch-and-learn sessions serve as a flexible entry point, offering a more informal introduction before transitioning into a more structured meetup format.

These internal events, just like a comprehensive athletic training program, provide a holistic approach to building a robust and resilient open source culture, enhancing collaboration, skills, and a shared sense of achievement among employees.

Organizing Hackathons

Organizing a successful open source hackathon involves careful planning and execution to ensure a collaborative and productive event. The hackathons are usually led by a "core team," which plays a pivotal role in shaping the event's purpose, defining its scope, and managing logistical intricacies.

Here are some tips to help you organize a successful open source hackathon.

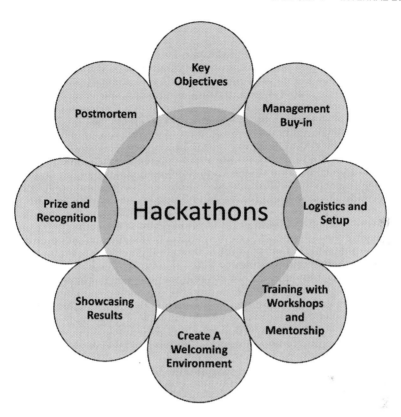

Figure 4-2. *Open Source Hackathons*

Key Objectives

The core team must first articulate a clear purpose for the hackathon. Whether it's addressing specific challenges, fostering innovation, or advancing open source projects, a well-defined purpose serves as the foundation for the event's success. The hackathon should contribute to the company's overall vision as this enables support from the management.

Hackathons are a great platform for a multitude of reasons. Some typical examples are onboarding new developers to a project, improving quality of tests and docs, and creating plugins that will extend the open source project to work with other tools. These are all critical tasks for an open source project's sustainability. Sharing that vision with the hackathon attendees will motivate them to contribute towards the cause.

Consider objectives related to employee engagement. Hackathons provide a unique opportunity for employees to connect, share ideas, and work together outside their usual roles. Fostering a sense of community and engagement can be a valuable objective. Encourage a spirit of experimentation and exploration. Set objectives that allow participants to explore new technologies, methodologies, or approaches. This can lead to unexpected innovations and breakthroughs.

Encourage cross-functional collaboration by setting objectives that promote teamwork and interaction among individuals from different departments. This can lead to the development of multidisciplinary solutions and a more interconnected organizational culture, usually much appreciated by the management.

A clearly defined objective and key results provide participants with direction, encouraging them to channel their skills and creativity toward solving problems or contributing to predefined projects. Establishing concrete objectives ensures that participants and organizers share a common understanding of what the hackathon aims to achieve. Additionally, having key results enables organizers to assess the outcomes at the end of the hackathon, providing a basis for evaluation and identification of areas for improvement. This structured approach enhances the overall effectiveness and impact of the hackathon.

Management Buy-In

Securing a buy-in from management for these hackathons is crucial for several reasons. This is one of the tasks that the core team needs to take care of before the detailed planning starts. Firstly, obtaining buy-in from leadership and key stakeholders helps allocate necessary resources, both in terms of budget and support, ensuring that the hackathon receives the attention it deserves. Ultimately, people are going to be working on this hackathon during the work time using work resources. This support facilitates the organization of a well-planned event with adequate infrastructure, mentorship, and promotional activities.

Secondly, buy-in from leadership lends credibility to the hackathon, signaling its importance and relevance to the company's overall goals. When leadership actively endorses and promotes the event, it encourages wider participation from employees and boosts morale. It creates a good incentive structure for the employees and their management to recognize them. Employees are more likely to engage enthusiastically when they see the hackathon as a recognized and endorsed initiative rather than just a grassroots effort. This incentive mechanism is critical for a wider employee participation.

Thirdly, obtaining buy-in facilitates the integration of the hackathon into the company's strategic objectives. Aligning the goals of the hackathon with broader company initiatives ensures that the event contributes meaningfully to the organization's growth, innovation, and skill development. It becomes a valuable tool for achieving specific objectives, whether related to product development, employee engagement, or fostering a culture of innovation.

Logistics and Setup

For an in-person hackathon, you need to ensure there is a physical space for attendees to sit together. The classroom-style seating maximizes the capacity in a room and provides enough flexibility for people to create their own groups. Usually, an auditorium or large conference room would be required for opening and closing talks. For virtual hackathons, you may like to use a platform such as DevPost or HackerEarth. Such platforms provide an end-to-end experience from serving your landing page for the hackathon to the distribution of awards to the winners.

For internal hackathons, employees would usually bring their own laptops. Ensure that they have access to the necessary resources, including code repositories, documentation, and communication channels. Facilitate access to cloud resources ahead of time by creating accounts, enabling access rights, and ensuring participants have the necessary laptop setup. Make project onboarding straightforward with easily accessible guidelines, and validate instructions by testing them with a new developer to document any specialized knowledge.

Make sure to setup a registration desk for the attendees to check in and out from the hackathon. If budget permits, provide them with unlimited supply of water and coffee. Depending upon the duration, you may have to serve three full meals and snacks in between.

Utilize collaboration platforms like GitHub for code repositories, issue tracking, and code review. Choose your company's preferred instant messaging platform for asynchronous communication, leveraging dedicated rooms for high-bandwidth discussions. Opt for your company's preferred video platform for meetings to facilitate impactful virtual face-to-face discussions. Employing familiar platforms lowers the participation barrier for employees, as they are already acquainted with these tools. Ensure virtual rooms are clearly labeled with a consistent taxonomy to easily identify team names.

Incorporate breaks, networking sessions, or social events within the hackathon schedule to facilitate interactions among participants and mentors. These intentional networking opportunities provide a valuable platform for individuals to engage with each other, share insights, and establish connections with experienced mentors. Consider creating a "hallway," either in-person or virtual hackathons, that allow attendees to engage in impromptu and casual conversations with other participants outside the formal coding rooms. This fosters serendipitous connections, encourages collaboration, and provides a more dynamic and engaging experience for attendees. Beyond coding, these breaks and social events contribute to a more enriching and holistic experience, fostering a sense of camaraderie among participants and creating a collaborative atmosphere.

Training with Workshops and Mentorship

The familiarity and skill level of hackathon participants can vary widely. Organize workshops or training sessions in advance of the hackathon to familiarize participants with essential tools, technologies, and best practices. This ensures a level playing field and equips everyone with the necessary skills.

Depending upon the participants, you may have to run introductory workshops such as an introduction to open source, version control systems, and submitting a code change by issuing a pull request. Next set of workshops may cover simple topics such as setting up a development environment, including code editors, version control tools, and setting up continuous integration. This empowers the attendees to contribute seamlessly during the hackathon. The workshops can cover intermediate topics like how to build the project, run tests, and add new documentation. Advanced topics like code review processes and providing feedback and contributing new features are also instrumental for effective participation, aligning participants with the hackathon's objectives. These preparatory workshops may span several weeks to thoroughly prepare participants for the main event.

In addition to workshops, inviting mentors with expertise in open source or the specific projects highlighted in the hackathon is crucial. Mentors play a key role in providing guidance, answering questions, and assisting participants in overcoming challenges they may encounter during the event. Their experience not only enhances the participants' understanding of the projects but also contributes to a supportive learning environment. Mentors act as valuable resources, offering insights that can significantly enhance the quality of contributions and the overall success of the hackathon. Additionally, having celebrity mentors can elevate the hackathon experience, providing participants with the opportunity to learn from diverse and seasoned experts while enjoying engaging interactions.

Create A Welcoming Environment

Foster a friendly and inclusive atmosphere so that employees feel welcome to the hackathon. Clearly communicate the hackathon's inclusivity and open participation. Emphasize that everyone, regardless of their role or expertise, is encouraged to participate. Use inclusive language in all communications to convey that diverse perspectives are valued. Highlight the diversity of participants and their contributions. Acknowledge and celebrate different perspectives, skills, and backgrounds. This recognition fosters a sense of belonging for all participants.

Develop and publicize a clear code of conduct for the hackathon. This document should outline expected behavior, respect for others, and consequences for any violations. A strong code of conduct sets the tone for a respectful and inclusive environment and signals a commitment to creating a welcoming and safe environment for everyone. If you don't know where to start, you may consider adopting the Contributor Covenant as a starting point.

A diverse group of mentors creates a more inclusive space where participants feel they can seek guidance without hesitation. Allow flexibility in team formation. Some participants may prefer to work independently, while others may want to form diverse teams. Providing options for both approaches accommodates different working styles and preferences.

Consider using GitHub's #GoodFirstIssue label for newcomer-friendly tasks, and create a dashboard displaying such issues across projects, complete with estimated hours and skill levels. This approach enhances accessibility and promotes a beginner-friendly environment for all participants.

Showcasing Results

Discuss the importance of showcasing and celebrating the outcomes of hackathons to motivate participants and the wider organization. Showcasing results in internal hackathons serves multiple purposes essential for cultivating a vibrant and innovative workplace. Firstly, public acknowledgment of participants' efforts through the display of outcomes fosters a positive and motivating environment. Recognizing their contributions not only boosts morale but also instills a sense of accomplishment, reinforcing the value of individual and team efforts.

Additionally, showcasing results contributes to knowledge sharing and cross-team collaboration. By presenting innovative solutions and successful implementations, participants have the opportunity to share insights and best practices with their colleagues. This knowledge exchange promotes a culture of continuous learning and sets the stage for future initiatives, inspiring teams to build upon each other's ideas and drive ongoing innovation within the organization. This very much fosters the open source culture and better prepares the hackathon attendees for the open source world outside the organization.

A common approach to showcase hackathon results is to create a centralized platform, such as an internal website or collaboration tool, where teams can document their projects, including project descriptions, code repositories, and relevant documentation. This ensures that the results are accessible to a broader audience, providing a comprehensive overview of the innovations developed during the hackathon. Depending upon the number of teams, you may organize a dedicated presentation or demo session where the winning teams present their projects, explaining the challenges addressed, solutions implemented, and the impact on the organization. This live demonstration allows participants to showcase their work in a dynamic and engaging manner.

A comprehensive approach to documenting hackathon outcomes involves capturing key metrics such as the number of participants, teams, and geographical locations involved in the event. Emphasizing the creation of new projects, resolution of issues, and lessons learned during the hackathon provides a more detailed and impactful representation of the results. Sharing this information with the broader community not only highlights the achievements but also communicates the overall impact and significance of the event in fostering collaboration and innovation.

Prizes and Recognition

Recognizing participants' efforts motivates them and adds an element of healthy competition to the hackathon. One effective way to recognize participants is by providing tangible incentives such as certificates and digital badges, which not only validate their contributions but also serve as a visible acknowledgment of their achievements. Often these badges can be displayed in the internal employee portal and, in some cases, on their social media profile too. Additionally, acknowledgment in company-wide communication, including newsletters and internal emails, helps shine a spotlight on participants and their impactful work. A lunch with the sponsoring executive can be very rewarding for the winning teams. Offering prizes for winning teams or outstanding contributors adds an extra layer of motivation and appreciation, ranging from gift cards to tech gadgets.

Social media can be leveraged to share success stories, using relevant hashtags to generate excitement and encourage participants to share their experiences. Featuring participants and their projects on the company internal website provides a lasting record of their accomplishments. Constructive feedback, even for non-winning projects, and avenues for improvement contribute to a culture of continuous learning and development. Consider prizes and recognition that celebrate a variety of achievements. Acknowledge not only technical prowess but also collaboration, creativity, and innovative problem-solving. This approach ensures that diverse contributions are valued.

Swag items, customized to commemorate the hackathon, add a fun and memorable element to the recognition process. Utilizing internal platforms for recognition allows colleagues to engage, comment, and share thoughts on participants' contributions, fostering a sense of community appreciation. In summary, a multifaceted recognition approach ensures a comprehensive and inclusive acknowledgment of all hackathon participants.

Recognition goes beyond tangible rewards; it's about expressing genuine appreciation for the time, effort, and creativity participants invest in the hackathon. Combining various recognition strategies ensures a comprehensive and inclusive approach to appreciating everyone involved.

Postmortem

Conducting a postmortem for internal open source hackathons is crucial for typical reasons. This reflective analysis allows the organizing team to review the event comprehensively, identifying strengths, weaknesses, and areas for improvement. By gathering feedback from participants, mentors, and other stakeholders, organizers gain valuable insights into the aspects that worked well and those that could be enhanced. By incorporating these tips, you can organize a hackathon that not only achieves its goals but also creates a positive and collaborative environment for open source contributors.

Case Studies

Let's take a look at what and how some companies did internal events to bring a cultural change in order to make open source sustainable with their business.

Blackrock

Contributed by: Mike Bowen, Technical Fellow, BlackRock

BlackRock has a rich tradition of hosting internal events aimed at promoting and fostering technical excellence and open source culture among its employees. These events serve as catalysts for learning, collaboration, and innovation, providing employees with opportunities to engage across the firm and easily lean into open source technologies, practices, and communities in meaningful and impactful ways.

The annual BlackRock Hackathon is held globally across all BlackRock offices and has been a staple of the engineering community for the last ten years. These hackathons bring together employees from diverse backgrounds, organizations, and skill sets, providing them with a platform to collaborate, ideate, and innovate around strategic initiatives, new and trending tech, and projects that typically have open source at their core. Participants work together in teams to organize, pitch ideas, and develop prototypes. Leveraging open source software provides flexibility and velocity in time-constrained hackathons. Hackathons help in fostering a culture of creativity, experimentation, and collaboration while providing an easy on-ramp to open source technologies.

In addition to hackathons, the BlackRock OSPO conducts workshops aimed at educating developers about various aspects of open source development, including licensing, community engagement, collaboration, and contribution guidelines. These workshops provide participants with practical skills, knowledge, and best practices for engaging effectively with open source projects, empowering them to make meaningful contributions and drive positive change within the organization and beyond.

Winners of hackathons are rewarded and recognized for their achievements within the organization. Moreover, open source workshop participants that attended workshops and have their pull requests (PRs) merged are given an open source contribution badge on their internal profile. The recognition serves to incentivize participation and reward execution and excellence. Ultimately, BlackRock is reinforcing the value placed on innovation and the importance of open source engagement and contribution within the organization.

These events are designed to accommodate both global participation and regional office focus in the iHubs, with virtual platforms and resources provided to facilitate collaboration among teams located in different geographic regions. This global and focused regional reach not only fosters diversity and inclusion but also enables employees from around the world to come together on the global hackathon stage and execute at the micro level within the region to share ideas and collaborate, fostering a sense of belonging and camaraderie.

The topics covered in these events vary, ranging from specific technical areas to broader discussions, many of which focus on the importance of open source in driving innovation, collaboration, and value creation. By addressing a wide range of topics and themes, these events cater to the diverse interests and needs of participants, ensuring that everyone has an opportunity to learn, grow, and contribute in meaningful ways both internally and externally.

In conclusion, internal events play a critical role in promoting and fostering technical innovation, excellence, and open source culture within BlackRock, providing employees with opportunities to learn, collaborate, and innovate around open ideas and open source technologies and initiatives. By empowering employees to engage in meaningful and impactful ways, these events drive positive change; foster a culture of openness, diversity, collaboration; and drive the organization towards greater success and impact in an increasingly interconnected and dynamic digital landscape.

Infosys

Contributed by: Naresh Duddu, AVP and Global Head of Open Source, Infosys Ltd

The Infosys Open Source Program Office (OSPO) curates a comprehensive calendar of internal and external open source events throughout the year. These events fulfill various objectives:

Employee Education and Contribution – Events provide opportunities for employees to learn about open source technologies and processes, fostering a culture of contribution. This includes

- **Technical Talks** – Industry experts from leading open source foundations and organizations deliver sessions on the latest advancements and features in the open source landscape.

- **Internal Subject Matter Expertise (SME) Participation** – Internal SMEs complement industry experts, sharing their knowledge and experience.

Open Source Awareness and Mindshare – The OSPO collaborates with Infosys-wide initiatives such as TechCohere (a comprehensive Infosys endeavor uniting architects and other technical talents), which comprises of senior members in our internal tech community, to

- **Organize Events** – Talks, quizzes, and demos raise awareness about open source and its current trends.

- **Promote Solutions** – Highlight internally developed solutions that utilize open source technologies and underscore collaborations with both internal and external stakeholders.

Event Cadence and Recognition:

- Events are held at regular intervals, providing consistent learning and contribution opportunities for employees.

- Recognition programs comprising of quizzes and awards across various categories (best article, top contributor, best speaker, best mentor) celebrates employee achievements and fosters a spirit of participation.

Global Coverage

All open source events are open to all geos and units for participation. To cover various geographies, we do reruns of the major events at different times convenient to various time zones. We have also created various chapters covering different locations to encourage local, decentralized engagement within employees.

For example, in CY2023, OSPO conducted two very successful open source events – **CodeCon** (internal contribution drive), and **HacktoberFest**.

- The events attracted participation from a large number of employees, many of whom made contributions, both code and non-code.

- The events featured multiple sessions by industry experts on open source technologies, its benefits, and collaboratively working in a team.

- Internal speakers shared insights into their personal journeys with open source – we call it "**Open Source Success Story**." This offers participants an insider's perspective on the process of engaging with open source, motivating them to embark on their own journey.

Focus on Adding New Contributors

At the beginning of CY2024, we initiated the **Zero-to-Merge** program, inspired by CNCF's **Zero-to-Merge**, to empower and inspire first-time contributors. This program comprised live sessions, activities, resources, quizzes, and mentoring. The program helped widen the contributor base and increase the contributions.

Thematic Coverage

Some of the events are generic (e.g., CodeCon) and employees are free to choose any topic of their choice for presentation or contribution. However, we do run some thematic events, e.g., OpenHack (in collaboration with our open source partners) where the focus is on Kubernetes and associated cloud native technologies. Similarly, we recently conducted "Prompt-a-thon" with a focus on creating a repository of innovative GenAI prompts as future reference.

Rewards and Recognition

These open source gatherings provide participants with a range of incentives and acknowledgments. Participants stand a chance to win appealing rewards for each accomplished open source endeavor, whether it involves code, non-code contributions, or presenting a paper. We aim to recognize both the volume and caliber of contributions, with a panel of experts singling out top contributors and exemplary submissions.

Similarly, top open source-based projects are rewarded for innovativeness and quality of adoption. In addition, these success stories are published org-wide by OSPO as part of the open source success stories mailer series.

Executive Sponsorship

All open source events are launched with a keynote from a top leader. Infosys CTO Rafee Tarafdar enthusiastically supports these events from the front by providing executive sponsorship and often delivering tech talks. These events are open to participation org-wide, including Infosys subsidiaries. Throughout these events, leaders in various technology units share their experiences and insights, inspiring participants to embrace and contribute to open source. The Infosys leadership provides extensive support for these initiatives and values the individuals who contribute to the open source community.

Reporting

We track the effectiveness of these events by measuring and tracking through multiple metrics. Some key metrices include

1. # of projects open sourced by Infosys (>200% up from CY22)

2. Improved ranking among contributor companies for Backstage (~60+ to top 10)

Intel

Contributed: Rachel Roumeliotis, Director, Open Source Strategy, Intel Corporation

Open source knowledge is an essential part of career development for software developers. With that knowledge comes that vibrant open source culture. Ongoing company-led education should be available on demand but also spotlighted in events throughout the year for alignment on how-to, inspiration from colleagues, and to clearly impart the importance of why it is part of a company's strategy.

Create an Internal Event Strategy

At Intel, our internal open source event strategy is made up of a series of events to keep open source front of mind. Each year we look at qualitative and quantitative data around: what was successful in this past year, what is currently central to open source success, and how is open source strategy being executed across the company. This input is critical to developing a plan that will educate, amplify, and empower software developers to use open source techniques and tools to enhance their work.

Our calendar this year consists of monthly meetups anchored by two cornerstone events:

- **The Open Ecosystem Summit** – A multi-track, practical event made up of sessions given by Intel employees and external partners

- **The Open Source Hackathon** – A hands-on team event where contributions are made to Intel open source projects

As you can imagine, at such a large company, open source is not the only game in town, and so we do work with other groups as well to be complementary with timing and topics. The key takeaways here are to plan ahead, keep a regular cadence going, and take opportunities to spread beyond the events you and your team generate directly.

It Takes a Village: Implementing Your Strategy

With a data-driven strategy and calendar complete, now comes the time to assemble a team. This team most likely will include not only people from your own team but also individuals like executives, engineering leaders, program managers, content creators, marketers, IT administrators, and web developers. Note that for many people on this team, involvement in internal events may be supplemental to their job focus. Take the time to present how an internal event strategy is integral to incorporating open source into the company's culture, how that leads to success for the company, and thank them for their work.

Each of these roles bring needed expertise especially for key special events:

- **Executives** – They can help shift levers to get needed resources; they can participate as keynoters emphasizing how open source technology impacts the company.

- **Engineering Leaders** – They are key to have onboard as it is their teams that will be the attendees.

- **Program Managers** – They hold everything together, a program manager will lay out the workflow, track progress, and redirect individuals as needed to reach the stated goals.

- **Content Creators** – These are your speakers, demo creators, and blog writers – content creation spans copy used to market the event to session slides.

- **Marketers** – Knowing where to go and how to get the potential audience's attention is a must; no audience, no event.

- **IT Administrators** – Company intranets, employee access, and standing up new web pages are needed; when trying to execute an event, IT needs to be present to help navigate a company's technology ecosystem.

- **Web Developers** – A web page is how the audience will be made aware of, register, and attend the event; this is the portal for the attendees.

For each of our big events, we needed multiple individuals in these areas. Be clear on roles and responsibilities; make sure someone drives each aspect of the event to ensure success. While I cannot overstate the critical nature of a strong operational team, the program must align with your overarching goals.

Craft the Right Program

The internal event strategy is based on data. It is that data that will be the basis for your program, again – what was successful in this past year, what is currently central to open source success, and how is open source strategy being executed across the company. These considerations will help to pinpoint the right tracks, sessions, and speakers. The program must provide core practical knowledge, access to new topics, techniques, and tools, and context as to why these skills are critical to personal and company success. Events will not thrive unless they yield assets for the attendees.

Intel's cornerstone events this year

- **The Open Ecosystem Summit** – This seven-track event put the importance of open source in context via keynotes from executives, how-to content on the workflows around using, maintaining, and contributing to open source, as well as insight into new technologies.

  Only in its second year, this event has seen 2000–3000 registrants from across the globe and our different business units. This major undertaking is incorporated into our core goals for the year so that there is no mistaking its importance to our overarching goals.

- **The Open Source Hackathon** – This event gives attendees hands-on experience on open source projects maintained by Intel. The mentor/mentee dynamic bolsters knowledge while offering employees guided experiences.

  Also in its second year, interest has grown year on year both in participation from open source leaders of the over 20 projects entered into the program and the 40–50 teams (250–300+ individuals) vying for the top spot each year.

Measuring Success

Software developers knowledgeable about "how to" open source, active in using and hopefully contributing to it, and who have clarity on the impact of open source choices on the company are the ultimate measure of success. But, no doubt, metrics will be wanted to gauge success. These can include registration numbers, conversion of registration to attendance percentages, number of proposals received via a call for proposals, survey results, session popularity, and feedback from the team that put on the event.

Be sure to take in the good, the bad, and the ugly in a measured way and incorporate that into the plan for next year. Remember to enjoy the journey, you are doing the important job of enabling education and inspiration – good luck!

SUSE

Contributed by: Alan Clark, Director, Emerging Standards and Open Source, SUSE LLC

Promoting an Open Source Culture: Internal Events at SUSE

At SUSE, fostering a robust open source culture is a priority, and the company organizes a variety of internal events aimed at promoting this ethos among employees. These events are designed not only to educate and engage but also to celebrate contributions to the open source community. There are several key examples outlined below that SUSE hosts to maintain, foster, and grow its open source culture, with a particular focus on hackathons, workshops, and recognition programs.

Hack Week

SUSE hosts annual Hack Weeks, a cornerstone of its internal open source culture. During these events, employees are encouraged to work on passion projects, experiment with new technologies, and collaborate across departments. Hackweek, which has been happening for 17 years, serves as a platform for innovation, allowing developers to break free from their usual tasks and explore new ideas. This initiative fosters creativity and often leads to the development of new projects, new features, or improvements to existing projects. Since its start, SUSE has dedicated a total of 120 days to Hackweek. In addition, Hackweek has generated more than 120 projects with more than 300 people participating.

Google Summer of Code and SUSE's Contribution to Open Source Culture

The openSUSE Project is sponsored by SUSE as well as other companies. Since the project's inception in 2005, it has stood as a pillar among the global open source community, consistently upholding the principles of open source and fostering active contributions to various projects. This commitment can be exemplified by openSUSE's active participation in the Google Summer of Code (GSoC), which is a worldwide program that encourages people to contribute to open source projects during their summer break.

The openSUSE Project's involvement in GSoC is driven by a desire to attract fresh perspectives and new talent to the global community. Every year, the organization highlights a diverse range of projects on 101.opensuse.org, where prospective mentees can explore detailed descriptions, connect with potential mentors, and discuss contributions. This platform not only facilitates initial engagements but also provides a structured path for mentees to propose, refine, and collaborate on projects.

openSUSE's GSoC projects range from enhancing features to developing new functionalities in AI, container management, and operating system development. Mentees learn relevant programming languages and maintain regular communication with mentors. Mentors, who are experienced contributors, guide mentees through technical challenges and help them integrate into open source communities. Many former mentees continue contributing to openSUSE and other open source projects, driven by the knowledge, skills, and passion gained during GSoC.

Supported by SUSE's sponsorship, the openSUSE Project exemplifies how corporate backing can bolster community-driven projects. This partnership ensures openSUSE has the resources to participate in GSoC and highlights the importance of collaboration between corporate entities and community projects in sustaining and growing the open source ecosystem. openSUSE offers follow-up projects and encourages mentees to attend community events, where they can present their work, receive feedback, and network.

Participation of openSUSE in the Google Summer of Code spans 15 years since GSoC began in 2006 and showcases the mentorship of more than 100 mentees. The journey of openSUSE's contributions to open source development is rich with stories of innovation, collaboration, and contribution.

Recognizing Contributions: The Annual Technology and Product Awards

In an era where innovation and collaboration are pivotal to success, recognizing the dedication and achievements for open source contributions is essential. At SUSE, this takes shape in the form of the "The Annual Technology & Product Awards." These awards are designed to celebrate the excellence, passion, and commitment demonstrated by our teams. This practice can serve as a blueprint for fostering an open source culture internally.

Nominations for the awards are open to everyone within the Technology and Product organization. Any employee can nominate colleagues who have demonstrated exceptional innovation, teamwork, and impactful contributions. A diverse and cross-functional committee then oversees the selection process to ensure transparency and inclusivity.

The awards are divided into seven categories, each highlighting specific aspects of outstanding performance. Examples include "Boldest Move on Innovation," "Top Cross Portfolio Initiative," and "Keeper of the Culture."

The awards are held annually, with the cycle starting in FY23. Winners are announced at a virtual SUSE All Hands Meeting, where the entirety of the company can celebrate in the awards.

By establishing these awards, SUSE not only recognizes outstanding contributions but also fosters a culture that values innovation, collaboration, and dedication to open source principles.

Measuring Success

The success of these internal events is measured through various metrics and feedback mechanisms. Participation rates, the number of projects initiated during Hack Weeks, and the volume of contributions to open source repositories are some quantitative measures. Additionally, qualitative feedback is gathered through surveys and informal discussions to assess the overall impact and identify areas for improvement.

SUSE continuously refines its internal events based on this feedback. SUSE's commitment to maintaining a vibrant open source culture is evident through its diverse array of internal events. From Hack Weeks and educational workshops to recognition programs and global conferences, SUSE ensures that its employees are engaged, informed, and motivated to contribute to the open source community. The active involvement of senior executives, coupled with a robust feedback mechanism, helps sustain and enhance these efforts, making SUSE a leader in promoting open source culture within the enterprise.

Summary

This chapter explained the relevance of internal events for fostering open source culture. Different types of internal events, each with a unique purpose, are explained. There was a dedicated section on hackathon with clear tips on how to organize one successfully. The chapter concludes with case studies explaining how some companies leveraged internal events to foster an open source culture.

The next chapter provides an introduction to InnerSource and its key characteristics. It provides a path from InnerSource to open source and how it serves as a valuable precursor to engaging in open source initiatives. There is an introduction to InnerSource Commons, a global community for InnerSource practitioners. Once again, there are a few case studies that explain why and how the InnerSource movement started inside an enterprise, how it was used as a stepping stone for open source, and incentive mechanisms for teams to participate in this effort.

CHAPTER 5

InnerSource

What Is InnerSource?

The term "InnerSource" was introduced by Tim O'Reilly in an article in 2000. The exact verbiage from the article is "use open source development techniques within the corporation."

InnerSource is a collaborative software development approach that applies the principles of open source development within the confines of an organization. Unlike traditional closed-source development, InnerSource encourages teams and departments to openly share and collaborate on software projects, fostering a culture of transparency, collective problem-solving, and knowledge exchange. In an InnerSource environment, developers have the freedom to access, contribute to, and improve upon codebases across different teams, promoting a more agile and innovative software development process. A deep comprehension of open source methods within organizational boundaries empowers companies to confidently and effectively contribute as productive participants within the open source community.

This approach often involves using open source-like practices, such as version control systems and a unified codebase, code review processes, test-driven development, CI/CD systems, and collaborative documentation, within the organizational boundaries. InnerSource not only accelerates development by leveraging the collective expertise of the entire organization but also aligns with open source values like meritocracy

A. Gupta, *Fostering Open Source Culture*, https://doi.org/10.1007/979-8-8688-0977-4_5

and community-driven development. It provides a framework for breaking down silos, reducing redundancy, and cultivating a collaborative culture that mirrors the dynamics of successful open source communities. Adopting InnerSource within an organization serves as a controlled and supportive environment, effectively addressing and alleviating concerns or fears that may exist. This controlled environment allows teams to gradually embrace the principles of openness and collaboration, fostering a sense of confidence in the broader open source ethos.

Key Characteristics of InnerSource

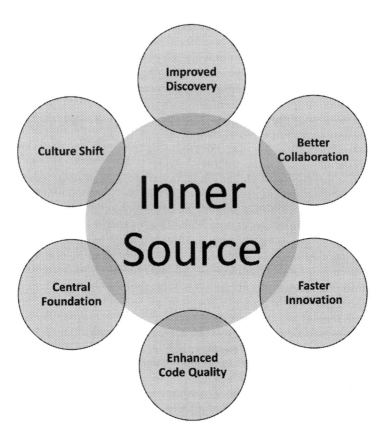

Figure 5-1. *Key Characteristics of InnerSource*

Improved Discovery

InnerSource initiatives play a crucial role in organizations by creating an environment that encourages teams to share and discover existing solutions, leading to improved discovery and reduced redundancy. In the InnerSource model, teams access centralized repositories containing codebases, documentation, and knowledge resources. This accessibility facilitates the discovery of preexisting solutions to common challenges, accelerating development cycles. Developers leverage the work of others, fostering a culture of continuous improvement based on shared experiences.

By breaking down silos and promoting shared codebases, InnerSource significantly reduces redundancy in software development efforts. Instead of independently addressing similar issues, teams collaborate on shared codebases, creating standardized solutions that can be reused across projects. This collaborative approach mitigates the duplication of efforts, streamlining development processes, and reducing overall code redundancy within the organization. InnerSource ensures teams build on a foundation of proven and reusable components.

Better Collaboration

InnerSource serves as a powerful catalyst for improving collaboration within organizations by breaking down traditional silos and fostering a culture of shared responsibility. By providing a platform for cross-team collaboration, developers from different departments can contribute to shared codebases, promoting the exchange of ideas and expertise. This cross-pollination of knowledge leads to a richer understanding of projects and challenges, enhancing overall collaboration as individuals work towards shared goals. The transparent and open nature of InnerSource, with its accessible documentation and decision-making forums, ensures teams are aligned, reducing duplication of work and promoting effective communication.

Furthermore, InnerSource encourages a shared ownership model, where multiple teams contribute to the same codebase, instilling a sense of collective responsibility. This approach fosters a collaborative mindset, leading to improvements in code quality and the development of new features. The mutual support and accountability that emerge from this shared ownership drive improved collaboration across the organization, creating an environment where individuals contribute meaningfully to projects beyond their immediate teams.

Faster Innovation

InnerSource serves as a catalyst for innovation within an organization by providing a framework that encourages experimentation, rapid prototyping, and the leveraging of collective intelligence. One of the key ways in which InnerSource fosters innovation is through its support for rapid prototyping. By allowing developers to access and contribute to shared codebases, teams can quickly prototype and test new ideas without starting from scratch. This accelerates the development process, enabling teams to experiment with different solutions, iterate on concepts, and ultimately bring innovative features or products to market more swiftly.

Furthermore, InnerSource harnesses the collective intelligence of an organization, unlocking a wealth of diverse perspectives and expertise. When developers from different teams collaborate on shared codebases, they bring their unique insights and experiences to the table. This diversity of thought fosters creativity and problem-solving, often leading to innovative solutions that draw from a broad pool of knowledge. The collaborative nature of InnerSource encourages cross-functional teams to work together, breaking down departmental silos and creating an environment where novel ideas can emerge and thrive.

Enhanced Code Quality

InnerSource elevates code quality within an organization by promoting collaborative practices and leveraging the collective intelligence of developers. Through collective code review processes, where developers from various teams review and provide feedback on each other's work, InnerSource ensures diverse perspectives and expertise contribute to more robust and well-vetted code. This scrutiny not only catches potential errors but also fosters a culture of continuous improvement, where developers learn from one another and strive for higher coding standards.

The shared ownership model of InnerSource further enhances code quality by instilling a collective responsibility for maintaining and improving shared codebases. Developers are incentivized to write clear, modular, and well-documented code, understanding its broader impact. This approach results in a more cohesive and standardized codebase, reducing inconsistencies and suboptimal practices. The transparency fostered by InnerSource, with open access to codebases and project discussions, encourages adherence to best practices and facilitates knowledge sharing, ultimately leading to higher overall code quality across the organization.

Central Foundation

InnerSource serves as a foundation for both cultural and infrastructural shifts within organizations. Culturally, it promotes open source values like transparency, meritocracy, and community-driven development. By encouraging cross-team contributions, InnerSource cultivates a culture of shared responsibility and knowledge exchange, empowering individuals to collaborate openly and align with the organization's goals.

Infrastructurally, InnerSource provides a robust framework through common version control systems and collaborative tools that support shared ownership and code collaboration. This infrastructure accelerates development cycles, standardizes software development, and enables efficient collaboration. It also enhances security by allowing centralized detection and patching of vulnerable libraries. Additionally, InnerSource facilitates continuous learning and improvement through collective code reviews and shared best practices, creating a dynamic and adaptive ecosystem that reflects open source principles.

Culture Shift

Embracing InnerSource triggers a cultural shift towards open source values, reshaping the traditional mindset of closed-source development. Transparency becomes a core tenet, as code, documentation, and decisions are open for scrutiny and contribution across the organization, fostering trust and collaboration. This openness allows team members to gain visibility into ongoing projects and the decision-making process, breaking away from proprietary practices.

Additionally, InnerSource promotes meritocracy and community-driven development. Contributions are valued based on their merit rather than hierarchy, empowering developers to participate in projects aligned with their skills. This inclusive approach encourages continuous learning and improvement, as well as a sense of ownership and pride in communal projects. As teams embrace shared responsibility for success, collaboration becomes central, accelerating innovation and creating a dynamic, engaged workplace culture that mirrors successful open source communities.

From InnerSource to Open Source

As companies embrace InnerSource, they establish a deep appreciation for the cultural and philosophical foundations of open source, including transparency, collaboration, and community-driven development. With this fundamental understanding, companies gain the confidence to actively participate in the open source community, navigating its collaborative landscape and contributing meaningfully. Such comprehension positions organizations to be productive actors, extending beyond code contributions to active engagement in discussions, providing valuable insights, and aligning their objectives with the ethos of open source collaboration.

Engaging in open source can encounter various obstacles. One prominent hurdle is the necessity for organizational approval, which involves navigating complex processes related to licensing, Contributor License Agreements (CLAs), Developer Certificate of Origin (DCO), and gauging the project's strategic significance to the business. Additionally, contributors often grapple with the fear of rejection, a common manifestation of impostor syndrome that can deter them from actively participating in open source projects. Technical barriers, such as perceived skill gaps or unfamiliarity with specific technologies that can potentially impact an organization's overall credibility, further contribute to the array of challenges.

In contrast, InnerSource provides a safe grooming ground for open source developers. It prepares individuals and teams for engagement in broader open source communities. It offers a promising solution by fostering collaboration within organizational boundaries. It provides greater flexibility for developers to participate in projects and enhance their skills without some of the external barriers associated with traditional open source contributions.

Firstly, InnerSource serves as a controlled environment within the organization, allowing team members to familiarize themselves with key principles of open source development. This includes exposure to collaborative workflows, version control systems, and transparent communication practices. By practicing these methodologies within the organizational boundaries, contributors gain the necessary skills and confidence to navigate the more expansive and diverse landscape of external open source projects.

Moreover, InnerSource provides a structured setting for individuals to understand the significance of community-driven development. This involves learning how to collaborate with peers, engage in meaningful code reviews, and contribute to shared goals. The feedback loops within InnerSource projects mimic those found in open source communities, creating an environment where individuals can refine their collaboration skills before venturing into the wider world of open source.

Additionally, InnerSource acts as a training ground for understanding the cultural nuances associated with open source participation. Contributors become attuned to concepts such as meritocracy, where contributions are valued based on their merit rather than hierarchical positions. This cultural alignment prepares individuals to seamlessly integrate into external open source projects where similar values are upheld.

InnerSource serves as a valuable precursor to engaging in open source initiatives. It functions as a practical training ground, allowing teams to assess the readiness of their repository for open source collaboration. Within the InnerSource process, developers mirror the steps involved in open source contributions by cloning the repository, following documentation to build it, conducting tests, and actively contributing code. This practice helps identify and address any internal dependencies, ensuring a clean and streamlined repository setup. Engaging in InnerSource also familiarizes developers with the typical open source workflow, involving forum participation, timely review and integration of patches, documentation writing, and assisting new contributors in their onboarding process. This internal exploration enables organizations to gauge the additional engineering effort required for maintaining such collaborative endeavors and helps in informed planning when transitioning to the open source realm. Crucially, it provides insights into the level of interest and appreciation for the contributions made within the organizational context.

If you are ready to take the next leap, Chapter 9 of Understanding the InnerSource Checklist book provides an actual checklist.

InnerSource Commons

Contributed by: Clare Dillon, Board of Directors, InnerSource Commons Foundation and Russ Rutledge, Executive Director, InnerSource Commons Foundation

Insights from InnerSource Commons: The World's Largest Community of InnerSource Practitioners

The InnerSource Commons is a global community for InnerSource practitioners. Founded in 2015 by Danese Cooper and others who wanted to share their InnerSource journeys, over 3000 individuals from at least 750 organizations have participated in the community to date. InnerSource is an evolving practice, and members of the InnerSource Commons community share their experiences through community calls, working groups, local meetups and gatherings, and an annual InnerSource Summit. The InnerSource Commons community produces outputs such as videos, articles, patterns, and research, all created to support InnerSource adoption.

InnerSource as a Stepping Stone to Open Source

InnerSource Commons members have identified various ways InnerSource paves the way for open source. Many organizations adopt InnerSource specifically to build open source skills. For example, PayPal established an InnerSource practice with this goal in mind. Comcast's Open Source Program Office reports that teams who have successfully established an

InnerSource project first are more successful when they transition to open source. The InnerSource step ensures that development teams have the necessary processes in place to allow reuse and have practiced handling external contributions in a controlled environment before going public.

InnerSource can also lead to open source in less direct ways. Some InnerSource projects become so successful internally that they naturally evolve into open source projects. For example, Spotify's Backstage started as an InnerSource initiative and was later released as open source when the team recognized its broader potential. Today, more organizations adopt InnerSource for benefits beyond open source readiness, such as improving efficiency, productivity, innovation, and developer experience. Regardless of the initial motivation, practicing InnerSource equips corporate developers to engage more effectively with open source communities.

What Are the Top Motivations for InnerSource?

The top motivation for InnerSource mirrors the reason why open source has become the foundation of today's technology industry because it enables better code reuse. The State of InnerSource 2024 report lists the top motivations for InnerSource to be removing organizational silos and bottlenecks and facilitating the creation of reusable software. These outcomes are seen to be necessary to enable innovation and increase developer productivity. Another reason for adopting InnerSource that has emerged from our research is the more general goal of knowledge sharing. Like in open source, even if they don't *reuse* source code, many developers learn by example, and seeing how others build software helps build skills and save time.

How Does InnerSource Get Started Inside Companies?

From the early days of InnerSource Commons, we have heard from passionate InnerSource practitioners who have successfully started grassroots InnerSource movements to improve software development practices from the ground up. These days, more and more organizations are putting in place formal InnerSource programs with management buy-in. The latest State of InnerSource survey reported that InnerSource originated as a bottom-up initiative in 29% of cases, 20% it came as a top-down directive, and for 36% of respondents it was a mix of top-down and bottom-up approaches.

What Metrics Do You Have to Measure the Success of the Program?

When asked about the progress on InnerSource goals, respondents to the State of InnerSource Survey 2024 reported that they had seen measurable progress in the areas of creating reusable software (46%), knowledge sharing (33%), and removing silos and bottlenecks (33%) within their organizations. The methods and metrics used to measure InnerSource's success are still evolving, and there is little consistency across the community. Some organizations use tooling provided within the source code repository to measure areas such as the number of external contributions, instances of InnerSource documentation, and code reuse. Others use surveys to measure awareness and developer experience.

Are There Certain Teams That Are Not Suitable for InnerSource?

InnerSource has the potential to improve software quality and developer efficiency in all software development teams; however, some teams can be more successful in their InnerSource efforts than others, depending on the context they operate in. The biggest blockers consistently identified by the InnerSource Commons community include organizational culture, time constraints, and a lack of management buy-in. Those teams that have leadership support, dedicated resources, and a more open mindset can be more successful in their InnerSource efforts. However, we have also seen successful grassroots community projects demonstrate that individuals can be motivated to build successful InnerSource communities of practice simply by the wish to connect with others, learn with them, and collaboratively build great software. The latest State of InnerSource survey also identified the most popular project types where InnerSource is being practiced; they include projects built with the intention of re-use (e.g., common libraries and tools), DevOps projects, and platform projects.

How Do You Incentivize Teams to Participate in This?

Over the years, we have heard many ways that InnerSource is incentivized within organizations.

From simple expressions of appreciation and stickers to badging programs, many organizations follow incentivization practices that have been proven in the open source world. Explicit leadership support for InnerSource efforts has also been reported to help motivate contributions.

Some InnerSource Commons patterns explore the idea of more formal incentivization schemes, including one advocating for dedicated resource allocation, designed to address the time constraint challenges.

Other organizations, such as Huawei, have built formal incentivization programs that extend beyond building an environment that fosters intrinsic motivations, to include monetary rewards and links to promotion pathways.

Join Us at InnerSource Commons

If you are interested in learning more about InnerSource, we would welcome you to join us at InnerSource Commons and be part of the ever-growing global community of InnerSource practitioners. Together we all work to give the gift of InnerSource to each of our organizations and to the world.

Case Studies

Let's take a look at what and how some companies have used InnerSource to bring a cultural change in order to make open source sustainable with their business.

Comcast

Contributed by: Gale McCommons, Technical Program Manager, OSPO, Comcast, Anusha Pavuluri, Technical Program Manager, OSPO, Comcast, Shilla Saebi, Head, Open Source, Comcast, Chan Voong, Technical Program Manager, OSPO, Comcast, Fei Wan, Distinguished Engineer, Comcast

InnerSource at Comcast

Comcast is a global media and technology company. Comcast is committed to open source software. We use it to build products, attract talent, and evolve the technology we use to improve the customer experience.

Comcast began their InnerSource journey in 2017 to streamline efforts and increase consistent collaboration across the company. The program was launched as the *InnerSource Pilot Program*, beginning with the onboarding of the VinylDNS project. The pilot was launched with early involvement from a PhD student at the University of Lund who was researching InnerSource at the time.

In 2020, Comcast established an InnerSource Guild that brought together experts from Security and Architecture. The guild helped cultivate an InnerSource mindset focused on transparency, collaboration, communication, and meritocracy that would accelerate software development and go-to-market products. InnerSource quickly gained traction through an educational showcase series, which led to the program's growth. Guidelines for trusted committers, governance, mentorship, and team ownership became necessary for successful InnerSource practices. In parallel, Comcast started to expand its involvement in the InnerSource Commons community by regularly participating in events, sharing best practices and insights, actively learning from other companies, and delivering a keynote address at the InnerSource Commons Summit (ISC).

In 2022, Comcast officially joined the InnerSource Commons organization (ISC) as a member and sponsor, supporting and contributing to the organization's initiatives in helping grow InnerSource practices. ISC offered common language and definitions, training resources, and a talented community that made it easier to grow an InnerSource program. With the lessons learned from practitioners, Comcast was eager to contribute back to the community. Fei Wan, Distinguished Engineer, Comcast, worked closely with ISC members to develop a Mind Map of InnerSource Patterns. The visualization categorizes patterns based on the different phases of an InnerSource program and the challenges that might appear in the respective phases.

VinylDNS: First InnerSource Project

VinylDNS is a vendor-agnostic front-end that enables self-service DNS and streamlines DNS operations. The project was initially developed at Comcast as a closed-source tool and subsequently opened internally to empower engineering teams to automate as they please while providing the safety and administrative controls demanded by DNS operators and the Comcast Security team. As adoption inside the company rapidly grew, the development team and maintainers of the project identified an opportunity for VinylDNS to fill a gap in open source DNS services available at that time. They approached the Comcast Open Source Program Office (OSPO) to partner on a plan to prepare the project for eventual open sourcing. The initial efforts involved partnering with the OSPO and VinylDNS teams to conduct a workshop with various company stakeholders. Together, we created a plan to encourage working together and cross-team collaboration through improved communication, marketing strategies, and operationalizing internal contributions to the shared codebase. Through these collaborative efforts, this endeavor began a fresh new chapter in Comcast's internal collaboration and innovation approach.

Terraform Community Modules: A Model for InnerSource

What Are Terraform Community Modules?

Terraform Community Modules are reusable, community-maintained modules designed to streamline the deployment of various common application architectures within Comcast. These modules enable application DevOps teams to provision infrastructure for their applications in minutes rather than weeks or months. By leveraging these pre-built modules, teams can quickly set up robust and consistent environments, enhancing productivity and reducing the risk of errors.

What Challenges Were There? What Lessons Were Learned?

During our cloud transformation, adopting DevOps methods revealed several challenges. The steep learning curve associated with mastering cloud technologies and DevOps practices was a significant hurdle. With expertise unevenly distributed across organizations, a few key experts emerged while many others lagged. Keeping up with constant technology updates posed a significant challenge, making it difficult to ensure that configurations and deployments remained current and compatible with the latest best practices and tools. These challenges collectively made cloud transformation a complex and time-consuming endeavor.

Terraform Community Modules accelerated cloud and DevOps adoption, reducing the time required to learn and deliver solutions while enabling faster, better innovation through collaboration. They simplified complex technologies and processes, making it easier to do things the right way.

Throughout our InnerSource journey, we learned that community building, technological simplicity, and streamlined processes for marketing, contribution, and maintenance are critical to success. Building a strong community proved crucial for both user and contributor bases; effective marketing, organizing meetups, and recognizing contributions significantly engaged and motivated team members. Simplifying the contribution and maintenance processes is essential for scalability. To achieve this, we introduced a development container and a continuous integration pipeline, facilitating easy development setup and automated test verification. These measures collectively enhanced productivity and fostered a collaborative and efficient environment.

How Does Terraform Model InnerSource for Other Projects?

Terraform Community Modules began as a collaborative initiative between a few passionate engineers. This project organically expanded across the organization, fostering a community that embraced best practices and innovation. Inspired by the success of Terraform Community Modules, this community initiated additional InnerSource projects to tackle various challenges within the company. This approach demonstrated how a collaborative, open source mindset within an organization can drive widespread adoption, continuous improvement, and effective problem-solving.

Europace

Contributed by: Isabel Drost-Fromm, Open Source Strategist, Europace AG

Europace AG runs Germany's largest transaction platform for real estate financing, building society savings and installment credits. It networks more than 700 partners such as banks, insurance companies, and other financial institutions. Thousands of users settle more than 30,000 transactions monthly with a volume of 6 billion Euros. Together with its clients, Europace develops user-centric solutions that are optimized for customer needs – financing with ease. Europace AG is a subsidiary of Hypoport SE.

With roughly 220 colleagues, Europace is responsible for the technological foundation of the platform. For a long time, teams within Europace have benefitted from high levels of autonomy, fostering innovation and allowing teams to react to customer needs quickly. Over time, though teams started to shift away from each other, even for topics where collaboration would have been beneficial. The search to counter this trend helped get executive buy-in for InnerSource as a practice.

Some teams had moved to GitHub very early on, even opening up their code repositories to others and being open to receiving pull requests. Introducing InnerSource as a practice more formally in 2017 helped structure conversations.

Hiring an Open Source expert got that process started. With time explicitly set aside to act as a dedicated community leader, we started with a two-tiered approach: as a first step, reaching out to people within the company individually – focusing on those interested in the topic but also those skeptical about the topic. These initial conversations pulled together a group of people that to this day meet regularly in a community of practice, building bridges between teams and sharing solutions to common challenges. We decided to adopt InnerSource patterns as a solution for several challenges. We decided to write up our solution for those where no fitting pattern was available and submit that as a new pattern to the InnerSource Commons. This helped in several dimensions: The resulting patterns often changed to be applicable more broadly. It helped communicate tech leadership publicly. Collecting those solutions in one – public – repository also helped track that knowledge over several years, even after people left and new people joined.

After running several experiments, more and more teams started to adopt common InnerSource practices. We used the Governance levels in conjunction with the Maturity Model to help communicate that a lot of InnerSource best practices are simply good engineering practices that help each team and differentiate the level of sharing that teams are willing to support with their projects.

Over time, it became clear that teams were in different stages concerning their understanding of InnerSource. We devised several strategies for crossing the chasm pattern to help smooth that out. We started with training for trusted committers and contributors. The contributor training was done in collaboration with the InnerSource Commons and used as an example of how sharing can lead to gaining beyond one's capabilities. Over time, it became clear that several issues that teams ran into could not be fixed at the engineering level, so we started working on a project leader-focused InnerSource training. This was again done in collaboration with the InnerSource Commons to make communication as clear as possible.

Over time, we used several surveys to understand the needs and challenges of employees with InnerSource. Our goal in increasing the understanding of InnerSource is to reduce the amount of friction that it takes for teams that depend on each other to unblock issues. As a result, we track the time it takes to ship customer features that involve InnerSource contributions. The goal with tracking this time is to spot irregularities – purely minimizing the metric obviously would be very easy to game. In addition, recently teams have started gathering metrics themselves to quickly spot bottlenecks and room for optimizations before they become huge problems.

InnerSource does come with a lot of best practices that make a lot of sense for any team – even for teams that never intend to receive code contributions from outside the team. Emphasizing the Governance levels helped us communicate to teams that there are several levels to InnerSource – and each level comes with its benefits but also with its amount of additional workload for the host team. That means that teams can make a conscious choice about which level of sharing they want to achieve. It also helped make the case for product-focused leadership for specific levels of sharing – including the additional work involved.

InnerSource helped our teams better understand open source in many ways. As many other companies, we are active users of a lot of open source projects. InnerSource helped us better understand the differences in governance between open source projects. As a result, when a new dependency comes in, teams no longer only check the license and code quality but look beyond making an informed estimate of project viability and long-term sustainability based on governance patterns that they see.

In addition, InnerSource substantially reduced the barrier to get involved with open source upstream – becoming active participants of open source projects that we rely upon daily. Not only is this part of our open source strategy for vital components that we use – those active in the InnerSource community also understand the potential for personal growth when becoming active themselves.

When it comes to teams' incentive to participate, most often collaboration between host teams and contributors happens naturally. As much as we would like teams to be autonomous, there will always be some level of dependency between teams. There will always be product features that would be easier to implement with some minor – or not so minor – changes to code that another team maintains. As a result, InnerSource contributions are often driven by product needs.

In addition, InnerSource best practices helped move several systems to a more self-service setup.

GitHub

Contributed by: Zack Koppert, Senior Manager, Software Engineering, GitHub

InnerSource has always been a part of GitHub since the beginning. When GitHub started, it was branded as a social coding platform, and so collaboration was not only how the product was built but also the goal of the product itself. As GitHub has grown over the years, so has the InnerSource practice within GitHub in terms of scale, and it still remains intact through our culture, programs, and processes.

Some at GitHub have described this as "An open source community behind our firewall." It helps us become more efficient by reducing silos and simplifying collaboration throughout the entire organization – inside and between teams and functions, as well as across teams and business lines.

GitHub has an engineering culture that welcomes code contributions and pull requests (PRs) from engineers company-wide. Many of the behaviors we see in the open source world (logging issues, submitting PRs, commenting on Architecture Decision Records (ADRs), and other discussions) are also performed in an InnerSource way inside of GitHub. Teams are highly communicative via our software tooling as well as chat systems in order to build and improve shared components.

Additionally, software languages (e.g., Ruby or Go) and other practice communities (e.g., Security and UX) organize themselves across teams to share code, best practices, and tooling. It is very common to see these self assembling activities appear as a new language or technology is introduced into GitHub.

As GitHub was founded on the ethos of open source, we didn't go through a process of obtaining executive buy-in for InnerSource as a whole. Over the years, we've outlined certain specifics to aid in our InnerSource practice such as documenting our guiding principles.

Companies often kick off their InnerSource programs by starting small. Pilot projects can help teams experiment with more open processes, democratize access to code, and document best practices before applying InnerSource more widely. Small successes can help show your internal community of developers how to make the most of their code and ship better software faster.

We use the InnerSource Commons Foundation's Maturity Model as a guide for us to self evaluate how our InnerSource practice is going. This evaluation combined with data and insights from our internal Developer Satisfaction Survey, and our internal OSPO survey, all work to paint a picture of how well we are practicing InnerSource and where we can improve.

Internal chat communities are also great ways for both sharing InnerSource knowledge as well as to see the impact this work has. It is common to see developers being connected to helpful InnerSource projects via chat and word of mouth.

We are also approached by customers who have heard about our InnerSource activities (as well as our Open Source activities) who are looking for guidance and help as they start on their own InnerSource journeys.

We evaluate InnerSource on a work project basis. There are work items that may not be appropriate to share/InnerSource, such as high-security items, but everyone should practice InnerSource. We encourage Hubbers to collaborate with whom and on what is appropriate.

Adopting InnerSource practices is like starting an open source community within your organization. As with open source, transparent collaboration mobilizes a community's collective knowledge and skills to create better software. An InnerSource community, in contrast, contains the knowledge, skills, and abilities of people and tools within a single enterprise. InnerSource helps by creating a culture of openness, a precursor to open source participation.

InnerSource is as much a cultural shift as it is a technological one – and it's important not to underestimate what a challenge this can pose to some organizations. Like their open source counterparts, InnerSource projects thrive in places where efforts naturally lean toward discoverability and reuse. It also helps to have small, cross-functional communities of the organization that share similar interests and expertise.

At GitHub, Hubbers often jump straight to open source since they are so comfortable with that way of working. We see the InnerSource to open source pipeline more common in businesses where their culture is not yet sure about operating in the open.

GitHub engineers' work on internal projects mirrors the tooling, actions, and behaviors that are used in the open source world. If an engineer is not familiar with these activities beforehand, they will quickly learn and be able to use these skills on open source projects. We are lucky to have well documented processes, training materials, videos, and experts available to train and mentor InnerSource developers on their journey to becoming open source developers.

We encourage teams to work openly across team boundaries, provide tooling that makes this type of work easier, train to make it quicker to get started, and have chat channels available to connect like-minded individuals quickly.

GitHub teams' main incentive for practicing InnerSource is the better outcomes around code quality, security, and general productivity. We hire based on engineers ability to collaborate (along with many other factors), and so this again echoes our "InnerSource is built in" engineering approach.

Intel

Contributed by: David Florey, Senior Director, Developer Solutions, Intel Corporation

Intel boasts nearly 20,000 software engineers developing firmware, drivers, open source operating systems, libraries, and more. Software teams employ a broad variety of programming languages across these stacks and execute myriad continuous integration jobs every day. This is done today through a single, common source control system and InnerSource methodology – utilizing open source best practices like pull requests, modern code review, and maintainer/contributor roles to enable cross-company collaboration and eliminate siloed development common at many large companies.

The decision to adopt InnerSource began in early 2020 with the support of executive leadership. At that time, each business unit had complete autonomy over which software tools and systems they could use to store, develop, and deliver their software. As a result, it was not only difficult to integrate software across teams but also to discover and reuse code. Each team had its own development methodology, source control paradigm, and access control to their code, making it nearly impossible to achieve the desired synergies.

With executive support, the Intel Software Group led the transformation for the company. A single source control system was chosen for the company, and countless repositories in various other source control systems across the company were migrated to the new system. It took nearly two years and continuous support from top leaders to achieve the goal. Briefly, here are some of the hurdles the transition team overcame:

1. **Need for Governance** – A system of governance was needed to ensure a consistent naming scheme, consistent use of permissions, and minimal bar of quality as repositories merged into the new system.

2. **Push Back from Teams and Managers** – Concern over deadlines and delayed releases slowed migration progress. These were resolved through timeline negotiations and some central, temporary resourcing to augment the effort.

3. **Logistics** – Rewiring existing continuous integration systems and managing growth was the final hurdle to overcome. By centralizing this effort, best practices were shared, and commonalities in the various systems were found, enabling the team to accelerate this transition.

One of the bright spots during the transition was onboarding. The transition team knew that the first hurdle (getting people onboarded) would be the most important. If that didn't go well, the pushback noted above might have become insurmountable. The team focused on creating a smooth, easy-to-integrate onboarding process.

Let's take a closer look at the anatomy of InnerSource at Intel to better understand the journey:

1. InnerSource is a single organizational structure within the unified source control system and the largest such organization. The unified source control system contains other organizations that are set up with different access control models depending on their sensitivity (i.e., sensitive IP or access restricted IP, etc.) and are therefore outside of this InnerSource effort.

2. All InnerSource repositories can be cloned (read) by all Intel developers regardless of business unit or job function.

3. Each repository has a dedicated set of maintainers.

4. Changes to a repository must go through a pull request process requiring several checks before it is approved:

   a. Modern code review (by the maintainers)

   b. Automated CI (established by the maintainers) which typically includes unit tests, code quality, and security checks.

5. Repository maintainers are encouraged to include a well-documented readme and contrib file.

Establishing this InnerSource effort, borrowing the best in classes techniques from the open source world has enabled teams to collaborate more easily. Below are some other benefits.

Feature Requests Have Become Pull Requests

InnerSource at Intel has transformed the traditional feature request process. By opening up the codebase, developers from various teams can now directly contribute to libraries or frameworks they rely on through pull requests. This organic shift towards greater transparency and collaboration has led to increased agility and speed in development, bypassing the previous black-box approach to code and feature prioritization.

Consistency Enables Continuous Improvement of Security and Quality Practices

Implementing InnerSource by centralizing code access, governance, and API support encourages continuous practices and enhances security and quality practices. InnerSource dashboards offer detailed views into the codebase and workflows, allowing InfoSec teams and Quality Champions to efficiently align repositories with company policies through pull requests.

Consistency Also Drives Easier Discovery

Tools that provide sophisticated search functionality across the codebase have enabled engineers to rapidly find projects, repositories, or experts they need for their efforts. Finding an expert in some language is as easy as searching InnerSource for the person with the most merged PRs on repos using that language.

Ease of Discovery Enables More Consistency

InnerSource makes it possible to build a consistent developer platform. In 2023, Intel began to unify continuous integration (CI) practices, tooling, and infrastructure – a feat inconceivable only five years earlier. Utilizing the InnerSource tools, the CI transition team was able to identify common CI components, interface with DevOps engineers, and rapidly transition teams to a consistent CI methodology and infrastructure.

Combined Metrics and Approaches

The more Intel engineers acclimate to open source methodologies through InnerSource, the easier it is to look at and improve practices across InnerSource and open source efforts. For example, the InnerSource team has partnered with OSPO to utilize things like OSSF Scorecards to continuously improve security practices across all codebases.

Continued Incentives

While the intrinsic incentives have driven some excellent productivity gains across the company, the InnerSource team has also developed a formal approach which includes

1. **Companywide Dashboards** – Providing team productivity and repo health statistics

2. **An InnerSource Portal** – Detailing projects across Intel to maximize collaboration

3. **InnerSource Maturity Index** – A self-assessment framework to help teams assess and improve their InnerSource efforts

The move to InnerSource was not easy, and without the tenacity of the InnerSource transition team and the consistent support from executive leadership, it might not have succeeded. Intel engineers continue to improve the system and are seeing increasing benefits from the transparency InnerSource brings.

Summary

This chapter emphasizes the pivotal role InnerSource plays in fostering an open source culture within an enterprise. It explores the alignment with open source values, collaboration across teams, and acceleration of innovation and provides real-world case studies to demonstrate successful InnerSource adoption. Additionally, it addresses potential challenges and outlines strategies for measuring and improving the impact of InnerSource initiatives.

The next chapter explains the concept of external communities and why you need to engage with them to foster open source culture. A wide range of external communities such as participating in open source projects, industry events, and open source foundations are covered. There are two set of case studies - first for open source foundations and why should enterprises join them, and second why enterprises have joined open source foundations and how it has helped them foster open source culture.

CHAPTER 6

External Communities

The globally diverse nature of open source makes engaging with external communities increasingly vital. These communities are wide-ranging covering code, industry events, and open source foundations. Typically, it starts with getting involved in an open source project either as a consumer, contributor, or maintainer. The discussion starts online through using the code, filing issues, and contributing code and docs. The desire to meet other maintainers and users of the project grows stronger as you start working with them closely. If the project belongs to an open source foundation, then you may consider joining the foundation to participate in the strategic direction of the foundation. Engaging with different channels of vibrant and active communities within these projects ensures sustainability and maximizes the impact of an organization's efforts.

Participating in Open Source Projects

Identifying suitable open source projects to contribute to begins with aligning potential projects with the organization's business objectives. This involves focusing on projects that use core technologies integral to the company's products and services, as well as those that align with strategic goals such as exploring new markets or embracing emerging technologies. By contributing to these areas, organizations can enhance their internal tools and gain valuable insights that directly support their business aims.

Each organizational need from an open source project is unique. Filing issues and waiting for the "community" to fix the bug does not work. This is where you can submit patches to the issues and work with the community to get them accepted.

The journey of engaging with open source projects often begins simply as a user of the software. This initial phase requires minimal commitment, as there's no obligation to disclose how the project is utilized within the company, the internal product roadmaps, or the project's strategic importance to the enterprise. Companies typically start by experimenting with open source software to address specific needs or enhance their existing systems. As they become more familiar with the project, they may encounter scenarios where the existing documentation or code does not fully meet their needs. At this point, the next logical step is to seek help by asking questions on the project's forums or discussion boards. This interaction not only helps resolve immediate issues but also connects the company's developers with the broader community, fostering relationships that can be valuable for future collaboration.

As the company's reliance on the project grows, so does its involvement in the community. If problems are identified, filing bugs or issues in the project's tracker becomes a common practice. In many cases, developers might also contribute patches or fixes to the codebase, which is a significant step toward active participation in the project. The importance of the project to the company can lead to an increased commitment, where contributors are encouraged to take on more substantial roles, such as becoming maintainers. Maintainers play a critical role in the project, as they have the authority to approve changes and ensure the quality and direction of the codebase. This level of involvement not only benefits the open source project by ensuring it meets the needs of a broader user base but also empowers the company to have a direct influence on the tools and technologies that are vital to its operations.

This transition across different roles in an open source project is defined by the Cloud Native Computing Foundation as Contributor Ladder.

Another key consideration is the health of the community and ecosystem surrounding the projects. Organizations should prioritize projects with an active and vibrant community, as these are more likely to be well-maintained and sustainable. There are multiple factors that define a healthy open source community.

The first factor to define a healthy open source community is around active and inclusive participation. It means the project encourages active participation from a diverse group of contributors. This includes not only developers but also designers, testers, documenters, and users. Inclusivity is critical, ensuring that all voices are heard and that there is a welcoming environment for newcomers. The community should have clear guidelines and a code of conduct to foster respectful and constructive collaboration.

An effective governance and strong leadership is the second point that indicates a healthy open source community and is essential for the sustainability of an open source project. A clear and transparent decision-making process, along with strong leadership, helps guide the project's direction, resolve conflicts, and ensure that contributions align with the community's goals. Leaders or maintainers should be accessible, responsive, and open to feedback, while also encouraging community members to take on leadership roles.

Last but not least, a healthy open source community sees regular contributions and consistent maintenance of the project. This includes timely responses to issues, regular updates, and active development of new features. A well-maintained project with good documentation, testing, and continuous integration ensures that the software remains reliable, secure, and useful to its users. It also ensures that any software vulnerabilities are addressed in a timely manner. Active maintenance also signals to the community that the project is alive and worth investing time in.

It's also important to choose projects that fit well within the broader ecosystem, including those widely used in the industry or by strategic partners. This alignment can facilitate better integration and foster opportunities for collaboration. If the project is critical for the organization, it may decide to invest in creating a healthy community around it. If the project is aligned with the broader ecosystem, then multiple companies invest in creating a healthy community around it. This makes the project less dependent upon one organization, more resilient, and less vulnerable to changes in any single contributor's priorities or resources.

Assessing the technical and cultural fit is crucial. Organizations should look for projects whose technology stack and architecture align with their own expertise and infrastructure. Additionally, choosing projects that share similar values, such as open collaboration, transparency, and inclusivity, can ensure a smoother integration of open source contributions into the organization's culture. If you want to contribute to projects where there is no internal expertise, you may consider hiring maintainers of the project or incentivize internal engineers to become maintainers of the project. This is a much more scalable approach as it allows you to tap into the collective innovation of the project, ensure your organizational needs are met on a sustained basis, and there is no technical debt by forking the project internally.

Finally, organizations must consider the potential impact of their contributions. They should seek projects where their involvement can make a significant positive difference, whether through bug fixes, feature development, or improving documentation. Projects with a strong social or ethical component may also be prioritized to align with corporate social responsibility goals. Security and licensing considerations are also essential, ensuring that the project's practices and license terms are compatible with the organization's standards and legal requirements. By taking these factors into account, organizations can identify open source projects that not only align with their strategic interests but also provide meaningful contributions to the broader community.

Open Source Events

Open source events play a vital role in the growth and sustainability of the open source ecosystem. Given the distributed nature of open source, a large majority of work happens remotely through code contributions, issue trackers, emails, and conference calls. These events provide a platform for builders and consumers of open source technologies to meet in-person, connect, collaborate, and build relationships. Face-to-face interactions foster stronger personal connections and trust among community members, which can be more challenging to achieve through online communication alone.

In-person events create opportunities for serendipitous interactions and conversations that can lead to new collaborations, ideas, and partnerships. They also allow participants to pick up on non-verbal cues during communication such as body language and facial expressions, enhancing understanding and empathy. Being physically present in a dedicated environment helps participants focus and immerse themselves fully in the event, free from everyday distractions. The energy and enthusiasm generated at in-person events can be highly motivating and inspiring, driving participants to contribute more actively to open source projects. The shared memories and experiences from in-person events contribute to a stronger and more cohesive community, with participants often reminiscing about past events and looking forward to future gatherings.

Participating in these events as a speaker, sponsor, attendee, or in any other capacity helps foster open source culture inside the company. Active participation in open source events helps to create a workplace environment where open source culture thrives, leading to more innovative, collaborative, and community-driven outcomes. It also makes the company more attractive to potential hires who value openness, transparency, and innovation. It allows employees to engage with the broader open source community which helps employees build relationships that can be valuable for both personal and professional growth. This leads to their overall job satisfaction and improved morale within the company.

By sponsoring open source events, the company visibly demonstrates its commitment to the principles of openness, collaboration, and transparency. This public commitment reinforces these values within the organization, encouraging employees to embrace and advocate for open source principles. Sponsoring events is a tangible way to give back to the open source community, acknowledging the contributions that have built the tools and technologies the company relies on. This act of giving back fosters a sense of reciprocity and respect for the community's efforts. When a company supports open source events, it encourages employees to also contribute back to the community, whether through code, documentation, or other means. This builds a culture of contribution and shared responsibility within the company. It also enhances the company's reputation by aligning with industry leaders and fostering connections that can lead to valuable partnerships and talent acquisition.

Sponsoring an open source event also allows an enterprise to visibly demonstrate its commitment to the open source community. Typically, this sponsorship comes with a visible brand presence at the event in terms of a booth. This booth can demonstrate key open source projects and initiatives from the company. Maintainers of open source projects that are employed by the company are often available at the booth to interact with the attendees. This human connection at the booth fosters deeper relationships and trust with the open source community. It provides a unique opportunity for attendees to engage directly with the project maintainers, ask questions, and gain insights into the company's contributions. This interaction not only showcases the enterprise's technical expertise but also reinforces its role as a collaborative and active participant in the open source ecosystem.

A diverse range of companies sponsoring an open source event significantly contributes to the long-term sustainability of the open source community. These sponsorships provide the financial resources necessary to organize and maintain high-quality events, ensuring that they remain accessible to a broad audience. By involving multiple companies from different industries, the event can attract a wide array of participants, fostering a richer exchange of ideas and collaboration across sectors. This diversity in sponsorship also reduces the dependency on any single organization, promoting a more resilient and balanced ecosystem. In turn, this collective support strengthens the open source community, enabling it to thrive and evolve while continuing to drive innovation and inclusivity.

Speaking at an open source event allows employees to showcase their expertise and share their insights, raising the profile of both the individual and the company within the open source community. Speakers usually share their journey of using an open source project, what worked and didn't work for them, and how they worked around the challenges. They talk about the implementation scale of the project and other surrounding technologies that had to be used to make this project work in a real-life scenario. The deployment topology of the project, such as whether the project was used on a cloud service provider or a private data center, often provides insightful details about the capabilities and limitations of the platform in a vendor-agnostic manner. This allows the event attendees to gain practical knowledge of the project and apply that information to their own environment.

Often the speaker is approached by attendees who are interested in a deep dive on certain topics presented in the talk. This leads to deeper discussion, sometimes to collaboration in the open source community and occasionally to hiring people with aligned interests. Employees who prepare and deliver presentations or talks often deepen their own understanding of the topic. They can bring this enhanced knowledge back to their colleagues, fostering a culture of continuous learning and skill development. Presenting at events exposes employees to diverse perspectives and feedback from the community, which they can bring back to the company. This cross-pollination of ideas can inspire new projects, improvements, and innovations.

By attending workshops, sessions, and talks, employees gain new skills and knowledge about the latest trends, tools, and best practices in the open source community. This continuous learning is essential for staying competitive in the tech industry. Interaction with diverse contributors and projects at open source events allows for the cross-pollination of ideas. Employees bring these ideas back to the company, enriching its internal knowledge base and sparking new initiatives. Exposure to best practices and methodologies in the open source community can lead to the adoption of similar practices within the company. This includes practices such as transparent decision-making, collaborative development, and open communication. As employees participate in and learn from open source events, they are likely to advocate for and implement open source practices in their daily work. This fosters an internal culture that values openness, sharing, and collaboration.

Open Source Foundations

Open source foundations are organizations, typically non-profit, that play a crucial role in supporting and overseeing the development of open source software projects. These foundations provide a vendor-neutral space for developers, companies, and other stakeholders to work together to create, maintain, and promote open source projects. These foundations provide a framework for governance, legal, infrastructure, and financial support that allows the project owners to focus on moving the project forward. The primary goals of open source foundations include fostering community-driven development, ensuring transparency, and promoting the widespread use of open source software.

Here are some key characteristics and functions of open source foundations.

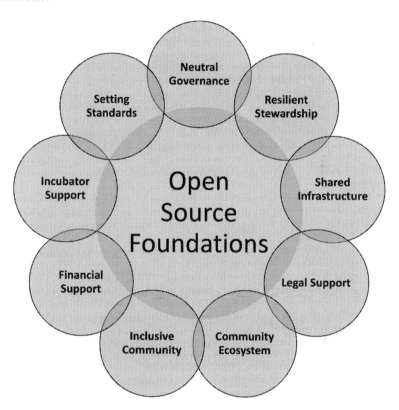

Figure 6-1. *Benefits of Open Source Foundations*

Neutral Governance

Open source foundations create governance structures that define how decisions are made, how contributors engage with projects, and how conflicts are resolved. These structures are designed to ensure transparency, fairness, and inclusivity in the development process.

Governance models may include elected boards, committees, or other organizational structures. The specific design often depends on the size and nature of the foundation and its projects.

These structures are designed to facilitate decentralized decision-making. This means that individuals and contributors at various levels have the autonomy to influence project directions. This decentralized approach ensures that diverse perspectives are considered, preventing undue concentration of decision-making power.

The governance frameworks define clear guidelines for how contributors engage with open source projects under the foundation's umbrella. These guidelines encompass processes for submitting contributions, participating in discussions, and collaborating on the development of the project. By establishing standardized practices transparently, foundations enable contributors to seamlessly integrate into the project environment, fostering a collaborative and harmonious atmosphere.

In any collaborative endeavor, conflicts are inevitable. Open source foundation governance structures incorporate mechanisms for resolving disputes and disagreements. These mechanisms may involve designated committees, mediation processes, or other established procedures to address conflicts in a fair and impartial manner. This commitment to conflict resolution ensures that issues are resolved transparently and efficiently, maintaining a positive and productive project environment.

A defining characteristic of open source foundation governance is neutrality. Foundations are committed to providing a neutral space where contributors collaborate based on the merits of their contributions rather than personal or organizational affiliations. This neutrality fosters a diverse and inclusive community where individuals from different backgrounds and affiliations can participate on equal footing. It helps prevent undue influence and promotes a meritocratic environment.

Resilient Stewardship

Foundations act as stewards for the projects under their purview, overseeing their well-being and long-term sustainability. Stewardship involves ensuring that projects adhere to open source principles, including the free and open distribution of source code and collaboration. They also provide support for project maintainers, helping them navigate challenges, foster community growth, and manage resources effectively. This stewardship role contributes to the health and vitality of the projects.

Foundations play a crucial role in safeguarding and promoting the fundamental tenets of open source development. This includes ensuring that projects under their governance adhere to principles such as the free and open distribution of source code, enabling unrestricted access, use, and modification. By upholding these principles, foundations create an environment that encourages transparency, collaboration, and the sharing of knowledge.

Project maintainers bear the responsibility of overseeing the development and maintenance of open source projects. Foundations step into a supportive role, assisting maintainers in navigating the challenges inherent in project management. This support extends to various aspects, including helping maintainers address technical issues, facilitating community engagement, and offering guidance on best practices. By providing this support, foundations empower maintainers to focus on their core responsibilities and enhance the overall effectiveness of the project.

The overall impact of foundation stewardship is reflected in the health and vitality of the projects they oversee. By upholding open source principles, supporting maintainers, fostering community growth, and managing resources effectively, foundations contribute to the sustainability and longevity of projects. This stewardship role is integral to maintaining a positive and thriving ecosystem where open source projects can evolve, innovate, and meet the needs of their users.

Shared Infrastructure

Foundations host centralized code repositories where project source code is stored, managed, and made accessible to contributors. Popular version control systems like Git are commonly used for this purpose. Centralized repositories simplify collaboration by providing a single location for developers to contribute code, track changes, and manage project versions.

Each repo is typically associated with an issue tracker, which serves as a central hub for communication among developers, making it easier to prioritize and address project-related tasks. In addition, mailing lists, forums, and other communication channels where developers and contributors can discuss project-related matters are also made available.

Continuous integration (CI) systems that automatically build, test, and validate code changes are also made available by foundations. CI systems help maintain code quality, identify and rectify issues early in the development process, and ensure that new contributions do not introduce regressions. Automated testing through CI systems enhances the reliability and stability of open source projects.

They also provide platforms for creating and hosting project documentation and collaborative tools such as wikis, project boards, and chat platforms to facilitate coordination among contributors. As projects grow, the demand for scalable infrastructure increases. Foundations ensure that the hosting infrastructure can handle the growing number of contributors, increased codebase, and expanding user base. These resources facilitate collaboration and streamline the development process.

Legal Support

Open source foundations help address legal aspects of open source software, including licensing compliance and intellectual property issues. They establish clear and standardized licensing frameworks that define the terms under which software can be used, modified, and distributed. Foundations assist projects in ensuring compliance with open source licenses. This involves verifying that contributors adhere to the licensing terms when submitting code and that the project as a whole respects the obligations imposed by its chosen license. They play a role in managing intellectual property issues related to the software developed within their ecosystem. This includes addressing concerns about patents, trademarks, and other intellectual property rights.

Foundations often provide legal guidance to project maintainers and contributors. This may involve offering resources, documentation, or access to legal experts who can help navigate complex issues. Legal guidance ensures that project teams understand the implications of their licensing choices and can address any legal concerns that may arise during the development and distribution of the software.

Foundations work to ensure that projects within their purview use licenses that are compatible with each other. Compatibility is crucial for projects that may want to incorporate code from other projects or collaborate with projects under different licenses. By promoting license compatibility, foundations contribute to a more collaborative and interoperable open source ecosystem. Multiple projects from the same foundation typically have a similar licensing framework. This simplifies the consumption of different projects from the same foundation.

In the event of legal disputes or challenges, foundations may assist in resolving issues that arise within their projects. This support can involve mediation, legal representation, or other mechanisms to address conflicts and maintain the project's integrity.

Community Ecosystem

Foundations actively work to build and nurture communities around their projects. This involves organizing events (conferences and meetups), recognizing community members, and getting feedback from the community.

Foundations organize and sponsor events and conferences, bringing together members of the open source community. Conferences often feature keynote speakers, technical sessions, and workshops, fostering a sense of community and shared purpose. These events provide a great way for developers around the world working on a project to meet in face-to-face interactions. Such engagements allow to foster deeper connections, enable more effective collaboration, and provide valuable opportunities for knowledge sharing and networking within the open source community.

Local meetups and workshops, either organized directly by the foundation or by community members, offer a more localized opportunity for engagement. These events encourage networking, collaboration, and the sharing of knowledge among participants in specific geographical areas.

Some foundations establish ambassador programs where experienced community members act as advocates and mentors. Ambassadors help newcomers navigate the community, contribute to projects, and feel integrated into the open source ecosystem.

Foundations establish feedback channels to gather input from the community. This can include surveys, townhalls, feedback forums, and mechanisms for reporting issues. The input received helps the foundation understand the needs and preferences of the community and guides decision-making.

Inclusive Community

Foundations actively work to create an environment where individuals from diverse backgrounds feel welcome and valued. Codes of conduct and community guidelines are established to ensure respectful and inclusive interactions. These guidelines articulate the values of the community, emphasizing inclusivity and diversity, and provide clear expectations for behavior. By promoting respectful interactions, addressing issues of harassment and discrimination, and creating safe spaces, the codes of conduct contribute to the development of a positive and welcoming environment. They also play a role in educating community members about the importance of these principles, ensuring accountability for violations, and encouraging the reporting of incidents. Regular reviews and updates demonstrate a commitment to adapting to evolving community needs, and the establishment of these codes underscores the foundation's dedication to fostering diversity and inclusion within the collaborative space of open source development.

Financial Support

Open source foundations rely on financial support from various sources, including member organizations, sponsors, and individual donors, to sustain their operations and initiatives. This funding is instrumental in maintaining the foundation's infrastructure, which includes hosting code repositories, maintaining communication platforms, and ensuring the availability of collaborative tools. Additionally, financial support enables foundations to organize and sponsor events such as conferences, meetups, and workshops, fostering community engagement and knowledge sharing, and conducting security audits for the projects. The funds are also allocated to other initiatives that enhance the development, visibility, and overall success of open source projects hosted within the foundation.

Incubator Support

Certain open source foundations implement incubator programs to facilitate the inception and growth of new open source projects. These programs serve as supportive environments by offering a range of resources, mentorship, and guidance to promising projects in their early stages. The objective is to help these projects evolve into sustainable and impactful initiatives within the open source community. In addition to offering infrastructure and technical resources, the foundations also offer mentorship from experienced contributors to assist project maintainers in navigating challenges and making informed decisions. Additionally, these foundations play a key role in onboarding new developers to the projects within their incubator programs. By leveraging best practices from successful projects and creating targeted training courses, they streamline the onboarding process, making it more accessible for newcomers to contribute effectively.

Regulatory Policies

The neutral and vendor-independent nature of open source foundations makes them more favorable for proposing and advocating regulatory guidelines or policies to the federal government. This is because open source foundations are perceived as impartial entities, driven by the collective interest of the community rather than the commercial objectives of specific vendors. Governments often view these foundations as stewards of shared resources, working in the public interest. As a result, recommendations or policies originating from open source foundations are more likely to be seen as unbiased, transparent, and aligned with the principles of collaboration and openness that define the open source ethos. This approach fosters trust and credibility in the regulatory and policy-setting processes, contributing to more positive and constructive engagements with the federal government.

Setting Standards

Participation in open source foundations allows organizations to have a say in the development of industry standards and best practices. This involvement allows them to share insights, contribute expertise, and influence the direction of standards and practices that govern the use of specific technologies. By actively shaping these standards, organizations can ensure that they align with the evolving needs and priorities of the broader community. This collaborative approach fosters the creation of technology solutions that are more inclusive, interoperable, and reflective of diverse perspectives. It also promotes transparency and consensus-building, reinforcing the idea that industry standards are not dictated by a single entity but are the result of collective collaboration.

In essence, open source foundations function as crucial support systems, alleviating organizations of administrative burdens and furnishing the required infrastructure. This not only establishes a necessary framework but also creates an empowering environment, enabling organizations to concentrate on their core objectives without the added complexities of managing intricate details associated with foundation setup and operation.

Umbrella Open Source Foundations

Umbrella open source foundations are foundations that oversee multiple related open source projects under a single organization. For example, the Linux Foundation is an umbrella open source foundation. The Linux Foundation serves as a home for a wide range of open source projects, providing a collaborative environment for the development, promotion, and support of various technologies. Under the Linux Foundation umbrella, numerous projects thrive in areas such as operating systems, networking, cloud computing, containers, and more. Some of the prominent projects under the Linux Foundation include the Linux operating system itself, Kubernetes (container orchestration), Hyperledger (blockchain technologies), and the Automotive Grade Linux (AGL) project, among many others. The Linux Foundation has multiple open source foundations underneath that provide a grouping of related projects. For example, the Cloud Native Computing Foundation (CNCF) has all projects related to cloud native and containers. LF AI & Data is another open source foundation in Linux Foundation that has open source projects in Artificial Intelligence (AI) and Data. Open Source Security Foundation (OpenSSF)

233

is another foundation that helps improve the security posture of open source. Other examples of umbrella foundations are the Apache Software Foundation and the Eclipse Foundation, each overseeing a diverse range of open source projects.

Such foundations offer several advantages by providing a centralized structure to oversee multiple related open source projects. These foundations streamline resource management, allowing projects to access shared technical infrastructure, legal support, and financial backing more efficiently. With a consistent governance framework, projects within the umbrella benefit from unified policies and best practices. Collaboration among projects is encouraged, leading to synergies, shared components, and a more interconnected ecosystem. The umbrella foundation also simplifies onboarding for new projects by offering an established framework for governance, legal compliance, and infrastructure. This unified approach contributes to greater visibility and branding as projects operate under a shared identity. Centralized legal support, economies of scale in cost-sharing, and common community resources further enhance the benefits of umbrella open source foundations. Strategic planning is coordinated to align the goals of multiple projects, fostering a cohesive ecosystem, while interoperability and seamless collaboration among projects are facilitated, providing users with more comprehensive solutions.

When companies heavily depend on open source projects hosted by open source foundations, it's common for them to become members of these foundations. Membership often involves financial contributions to support the foundation's operations and initiatives. The membership structure may include different levels, each offering varying degrees of involvement and benefits. Depending on their membership level, companies may gain representation on the Governing Board of the foundation.

The Governing Board is a key decision-making body within the foundation, responsible for overseeing the strategic direction and overall governance of the organization. Members of the Governing Board play a crucial role in shaping the policies and activities of the foundation.

By having a seat on the Governing Board, companies can actively participate in decision-making processes related to administrative, financial, legal, and marketing functions of the foundation. This involvement allows them to contribute to the direction of the foundation, influence key policies, and collaborate with other industry leaders and stakeholders.

Some foundations also have a technical oversight committee that provides technical leadership across all projects for that foundation. For example, CNCF has a Technical Oversight Committee that defines and maintains technical vision of CNCF, approves new projects that can be added to the foundation, and defines common practices to be implemented across all CNCF projects.

In summary, open source foundations serve as dynamic catalysts in the collaborative landscape of software development. They offer a vital infrastructure for governance, legal support, and financial backing, fostering the growth of open source projects. Through shared resources, transparent governance structures, and inclusive community-building efforts, these foundations empower diverse stakeholders to contribute meaningfully. Joining an open source foundation provides a holistic framework for integrating open source values into an organization's culture. It promotes collaboration, knowledge sharing, and innovation, ultimately contributing to the organization's growth, reputation, and long-term success in the ever-evolving landscape of technology.

Open Source Foundations Case Studies

Let's take a look at some of the most prominent open source foundations and the role they play in fostering open source culture.

Cloud Native Computing Foundation

Contributed by: Priyanka Sharma, Executive Director, Cloud Native Computing Foundation

The Cloud Native Computing Foundation (CNCF) is an open source software foundation that was created to promote the widespread adoption of cloud native computing. It was formed in 2015 when Google donated Kubernetes, a container orchestration system harnessing the demand created by Docker for containers, to create the entity within the Linux Foundation. Shortly thereafter, CNCF accepted other projects that enabled "cloud native computing." Cloud native computing enables organizations to develop and operate scalable applications in modern, dynamic environments like public, private, and hybrid clouds. The methodology has become incredibly pervasive – Gartner predicts over 95% of new digital workloads will be cloud native by next year – and success stories abound, including Spotify, IBM, Adobe, Adidas, Uber, Intuit, and Netflix, to name just a few.

The CNCF advances cloud native by supporting a community of open source, vendor-neutral projects and making projects accessible to all. It hosts and nurtures various components of cloud native software stacks, including popular projects like Kubernetes, OpenTelemetry, Argo, and Backstage. CNCF hosts the largest OSS conferences in the world, and we support cloud native learning with training and certifications.

By the Numbers

CNCF has grown to include 189 projects with over 247,000 contributors from 193 countries.

Today CNCF has

- Hosted 247,617 attendees at all events between 2015 and 2024

- Certified 154, 700 people

- 750 members

- A strong cloud native "CV" – 51% of CNCF end users have over ten years of professional cloud experience, while 37% have between 6 and 10 years

Our projects are categorized into three maturity levels (sandbox, incubating, and graduated). They are overseen by an elected body, the CNCF Technical Oversight Committee (TOC), to ensure alignment with our community's technical vision and standards.

Neutral governance is critical to creating an environment where competitors can collaborate successfully and repeatedly. The CNCF has established robust guardrails to ensure all contributors receive fair and equitable treatment through explicit rules and a transparent process.

The CNCF "sandbox" level serves as the entry point for early stage projects. Our sandbox efforts are part of our more significant, focused effort to make cloud native ubiquitous: in 2023, CNCF hosted 24 graduated projects, 36 incubating projects, and 109 sandbox projects. Incubating projects are considered stable and are capable of being used in production environments. Incubating projects are ideal for "early adopters." Graduated projects have passed through a screening and have demonstrated their sustainability to CNCF's TOC.

Importance of Open Source Foundations

Open source foundations are a critical step that allows individuals and organizations to collaborate with each other and build software in the open. Each foundation brings its own philosophy to governance and structure, and this gives donors and contributors options to choose a foundation that supports their vision. Joining an open source foundation like CNCF is crucial for enterprises looking to foster an open source culture for several key reasons:

1. **Neutral Collaboration Space** – Foundations provide a vendor-neutral home for open source projects, allowing organizations to collaborate on equal footing without any organization taking precedence. And CNCF was unique in that it brought big tech players together around a shared vision – Kubernetes – really for the first time.

2. **Established Governance** – Projects within foundations operate under well-defined governance models, which provide clarity and confidence to enterprises looking to adopt the technology.

3. **Improved Sustainability** – Foundations help projects become more sustainable by providing diverse financial, legal, marketing, and other support beyond what any single company could offer. And that level of support continues even when projects have "graduated."

4. **Credibility and Trust** – Having projects within the fold of respected foundations like CNCF lends credibility, which can accelerate enterprise adoption.

5. **Employee Opportunities and Job Satisfaction**
   – No organization can give employees *everything* necessary to grow into future roles, but time spent as a contributor or maintainer at CNCF can provide networking, mentoring, hands-on technical training, cultural exchange, experience with governance, and industry insights. The employer and the employee benefit, as does the open source community.

Here's how one organization has leveraged CNCF to change its culture: Adobe demonstrates the impact of contributing to CNCF and how it can drive change within a company. The company has contributed to 46 different CNCF projects and regularly engaged in constructive feedback exchanges with maintainers, end users, and contributors. This has led to product enhancements that benefit Adobe and the wider community. Despite a successful development process, the company boldly shifted to an advanced internal developer platform powered by open source initiatives like Argo. This move has positioned Adobe as a leader in this increasingly important sector. Adobe's collaboration with CNCF has enabled it to stand out in a competitive landscape, allowing it to influence the future of cloud native.

Impact on Open Source Culture

CNCF has helped nurture a vibrant cloud native open source ecosystem and culture in a few key ways:

1. **Cultivating Communities** – CNCF helps cloud native open source communities flourish through events like KubeCon + CloudNativeCon, webinars, and extensive marketing support. Diversity, equity, inclusion, and accessibility are built into everything we do.

2. **End User Community** – Our End User Community includes over 150 top companies and innovators who meet regularly to share adoption best practices and directly influence project roadmaps, which leads to value for enterprises looking to learn from peers. We enjoy the largest known ecosystem of end users in a foundation, and this benefits our projects and contributors in every aspect of development and maintenance.

3. **Training and Certification** – CNCF provides training and certifications for crucial projects like Kubernetes and Prometheus, which help build critical talent within organizations.

4. **Conformance Programs** – The conformance program ensures interoperability for projects like Kubernetes, giving enterprises the confidence to adopt and build upon open source technology. This program is one of the reasons for the ubiquity of Kubernetes.

5. **Information Exchange** – Nothing is more meaningful than learning from others in the same situation. Last year, Kubernetes Community Days gathered over 10,000 people across 24 countries in 32 virtual, in-person, or hybrid meetups to exchange best practices and experiences and help grow the cloud native community. The power of the grassroots network cannot be overestimated.

Eclipse Foundation

Contributed by: Mike Milinkovich, Executive Director, Eclipse Foundation AISBL

Headquartered in Brussels, Belgium, the Eclipse Foundation exemplifies how an open source foundation can drive technological innovation and foster global collaboration. With over 400 projects, the Foundation fuels innovation across enterprise, cloud, automotive, embedded systems, IoT, mobility, and other domains. Supported by a dedicated community of over 2,000 committers from more than 50 countries and over 350 member organizations, the Foundation oversees a codebase representing a collaborative technology investment exceeding 25 billion euros as of 2024.

Established in 2004, the Eclipse Foundation began as a vendor-neutral hub for the Eclipse IDE project. The Eclipse Platform and ecosystem is globally trusted by developers and businesses in various industry sectors. With millions of users and tens of millions of annual downloads, the Eclipse IDE remains one of the world's most popular desktop development environments. However, the Foundation's influence now spans well beyond the IDE.

Today, the Foundation supports over 20 Working Groups, each tailored to specific community goals. Operating under a 'foundation-as-a-service' model, these collaborations allow industry stakeholders to work together without the overhead of establishing new legal entities while offering customized governance models to fit diverse technology needs.

Working Groups like Software Defined Vehicle (SDV), Adoptium, Jakarta EE, Eclipse Dataspace, Cloud DevTools, and Eclipse IoT play a crucial role in advancing and supporting open source technologies vital to their industries. Valued in the billions of euros, these initiatives highlight the economic impact of collaboration.

The Eclipse Foundation has a proven track record of hosting emerging technologies and uniting industry stakeholders to drive innovation and create vibrant new ecosystems. Its professional staff provides core services to Eclipse project committers, contributors, users, and adopters, including governance, community and ecosystem development, marketing, infrastructure, and more. The Foundation is also committed to open source supply chain security – employing a professional security team, conducting third-party audits, and serving as a CVE Numbering Authority to manage vulnerabilities.

Joining an open source foundation like the Eclipse Foundation can transform how a company leverages open source, fostering a robust culture within the enterprise. Open source is a strategic asset that drives digital disruption and innovation, empowering businesses to harness collective intelligence, agility, and innovation.

Participation in an open source foundation allows enterprises to access a vast network of collaborative development opportunities, accelerating product development cycles. Engaging with the Eclipse Foundation allows companies to shape technology to meet strategic and operational needs, ensuring it evolves to address real-world challenges.

The Eclipse Foundation's Working Group model promotes transparency and inclusiveness, fostering an open culture that facilitates collaboration and innovation. This approach reduces costs, accelerates technological advancements, and enhances software quality and security. The Eclipse governance model emphasizes collaboration and innovation, providing a structured environment where businesses can confidently contribute to and benefit from shared technological progress.

The Eclipse Foundation empowers people and organizations to collaboratively address a range of challenges, from funding critical projects to developing specifications. With a commitment to good governance, community development, and a vendor-neutral approach, the Foundation is a catalyst for industry collaboration that drives innovation.

Consider the Adoptium Working Group as an example. Adoptium is pioneering open source software supply chain security with Eclipse Temurin, a widely adopted OpenJDK runtime. As of 2024, Temurin holds approximately 18% of the Java market share, making it the industry's second most popular JDK distribution[1]. Its frequent community-driven updates contributed to a 50% year-over-year increase in enterprise adoption from 2023 to 2024. These efforts, facilitated by the Eclipse Foundation, drive innovation while ensuring high standards of security and reliability, lowering barriers to adoption, and setting a benchmark in the open source ecosystem.

Emphasizing software security, the Eclipse Foundation has implemented rigorous practices and infrastructure enhancements to address vulnerabilities and supply chain attacks in today's complex software development landscape. Temurin plays a pivotal role in this strategy, enjoying broad community support and integration across diverse applications, from IoT to cloud platforms. This underscores the Foundation's commitment to delivering secure, high-quality runtimes, reinforced by the establishment of the Eclipse Foundation Security Team in 2022.

Notable milestones through Eclipse Foundation collaborations include Jakarta EE's substantial growth since its 2018 launch. Leading Java innovators like Fujitsu, IBM, Microsoft, Oracle, Payara Services, Red Hat, SAP, Tomitribe, and others collaborate to advance enterprise Java technologies, facilitating the migration of mission-critical applications to the cloud. Jakarta EE has revitalized the enterprise Java ecosystem, inspiring the development of new Jakarta EE-compatible products and demonstrating successful vendor-neutral collaboration.

The case of Payara Services illustrates how joining the Eclipse Foundation enables companies to leverage open source for a competitive edge. Since joining in 2017, Payara has found an unexpected level of equality and collaboration within the community, providing both brand visibility and significant influence on projects like Jakarta EE. By engaging in the Jakarta EE Working Group, Payara could advance technological innovations crucial to their business model while ensuring compatibility with industry standards. Moreover, the Foundation's inclusive and affordable membership structure supported Payara's strategic goals, fostering a culture of open innovation essential for staying competitive in the tech industry.

Obeo's experience highlights the strategic benefits of integrating open source into corporate strategy through active participation in the Eclipse Foundation. Founded in 2005, Obeo operates in France and Canada, developing software technologies for visual and collaborative modeling solutions used in aerospace, defense, energy, and transportation. By leveraging open source, Obeo has gained brand exposure and credibility through contributions to and use of the Eclipse community resources. Deep engagement with Foundation projects and governance has enhanced Obeo's product offerings and influenced new standards and technologies critical to its business, such as Eclipse Sirius and EMF Compare.

Aligning with the Eclipse Foundation has facilitated Obeo's growth, enabling it to expand its reach globally and collaborate with industry leaders. The Foundation's vendor-neutral and collaborative environment has also allowed Obeo to participate in shaping industry-wide innovations while internally fostering an open source culture. This approach has driven Obeo's business growth and positioned it as a leader in its field.

Open Source Initiative

Contributed by: Stefano Maffulli, Executive Director, Open Source Initiative

The Open Source Initiative (OSI) is a non-profit corporation founded in 1998 with a global mission to educate about and advocate for the benefits of open source and to build bridges among different constituencies in the open source community.

As the leading voice on the policies and principles of open source, the OSI helps build a world where the freedoms and opportunities of open source software can be enjoyed by all.

License and Legal

As a standards body, the OSI maintains the Open Source Definition (OSD) for the good of the community. The Open Source Initiative Approved License trademark and program creates a nexus of trust around which developers, users, corporations, and governments can organize open source cooperation. Many governments, international non-profit organizations, multinational corporations, and global open source communities rely on the OSI, the OSD, and OSI Approved Open Source Licenses for identifying open source software, development communities, and distribution models.

Policy and Standards

In addition to serving as an anchor for open community consensus on what constitutes open source, the OSI plays an important role in monitoring policy and standards-setting organizations. The OSI policy and standards program, established in 2020, provides support for legislators and policy makers, educating them about the open source ecosystem, its role in innovation, and its value for an open future. For example, OSI formed the Open Policy Alliance, uniting non-profit organizations to participate in responding to public requests for comments and other policy-related activities related to open source software, and open-adjacent interests such as content, research, and education.

ClearlyDefined Project

OSI also serves as the host for ClearlyDefined , an open source effort created in 2017 to curate a centralized data store for open source software licenses. With the move towards SBOMs (Software Bill of Materials) everywhere, organizations will face great challenges to generate these at scale for each stage on the supply chain, for every build or release. This is where ClearlyDefined comes in, by serving a cached copy of licensing metadata for each component through a simple API. Users will also be able to contribute back with any missing or wrongly identified licensing metadata, helping to create a database that is accurate for the benefit of all.

Advocacy and Outreach

OSI convenes global conversations with stakeholders, non-profits, corporations and individuals through its advocacy and outreach programs. Aware that software technologies change, OSI investigates the impacts of those changes with its wide network of affiliate organizations, providing a well-informed voice to ongoing debates around open source, such as the current debate around Open Source AI.

Defining Open Source AI

The traditional concept of software is not sufficient to describe the new artifacts necessary to create and deploy artificial intelligence (AI) systems. These systems depend on data and create new artifacts that don't fit squarely in the concepts of source code. Ensuring AI systems are free to use, study, share, and modify is an effort that will benefit everyone, yet what it means for an AI system to be open source is a question we've yet to answer. In 2022, the OSI started coordinating "Deep Dive: AI," a global process to sharpen collective knowledge and identify the principles that lead to a widely adopted Open Source AI Definition. Just as the Open Source Definition serves as the globally accepted standard for open source software, so will the Open Source AI Definition act as a standard for openness in AI systems and their components.

At the time of this book's publication, the "Deep Dive: AI" open process has resulted in a massive body of work, including podcasts, panel discussions, webinars, published reports, and a plethora of town halls, workshops, and conference sessions around the world. After months of bimonthly town hall meetings, draft releases, and reviews, the OSI is nearing a stable version of the Open Source AI Definition. The OSI is embarking on a roadshow of workshops to be held on five continents to solicit input from diverse stakeholders on the draft definition. The goal is to present a stable version of the definition in October 2024 at the All Things Open event in Raleigh, North Carolina.

The Deep Dive: Defining Open Source AI co-design process is made possible thanks to grant 2024-22486 from the Alfred P. Sloan Foundation, donations from Google Open Source, Cisco, Amazon, and others, and donations by individuals. The media partner is OpenSource.net.

The Power of the Open Source Definition

The Open Source Definition plays a central role in facilitating global innovation, research, and economic growth. According to a recent Harvard Business School paper, the estimated value of widely used open source software is $4.15 billion, but the demand-side value is much larger at $8.8 trillion.

The Open Source Definition offers a clear understanding of the rights of the stakeholders, and this clear understanding enables everyone to take advantage of the immense value provided by open source software, allowing permissionless innovation and frictionless collaboration across companies. It's estimated that companies would need to spend 3.5 times more on software than they currently do if open source software did not exist.

The OSI and its License Review Working Group maintain a database of approved licenses, offering a comprehensive and authoritative listing of all licenses so organizations know that the license they choose for their project allows their software to be freely used, modified, shared, and monetized in compliance with the Open Source Definition. This database of approved licenses simplifies procurement and compliance because organizations can rely on the rigorous license review process from the OSI. Additionally, the approved licenses database serves as a valuable tool to simplify M&A and other legal due diligence.

Besides maintaining an always up-to-date license database, the OSI also monitors policy and standards-setting organizations that develop regulations that may impact open source software. These regulations include, for example, the Cyber Resilience Act (CRA) in Europe and Securing Open Source Software Act in the US. More recently, the OSI is also monitoring AI policies that may impact the development and commercialization of Open Source AI, including the European AI Act and the White House's AI Executive Order. The OSI participates in educating and informing public policy decisions so that organizations that use and commercialize open source software can innovate and thrive.

By supporting OSI, organizations and individuals secure a level playing field by funding a truly independent organization that defends the principles of the global open source ecosystem, from economic actors to volunteers and amateur developers to academia to non-profit organizations. This support helps foster an open source culture that ensures that software development collaboration and innovation remain accessible to all, breaking down barriers to entry and empowering a diverse community of contributors to drive technological advancements for the benefit of society as a whole.

Open Source Security Foundation

Contributed by: Omkhar Arasaratnam, General Manager, Open Source Security Foundation

Introduction to OpenSSF

Open Source Security Foundation (OpenSSF) is a global initiative to strengthen open source software security. Established in 2020 as part of the Linux Foundation, OpenSSF seeks to bring together stakeholders from the private sector, the public sector, and the community to improve the security of open source software for everyone.

Security Within Open Source

The distributed nature of open source development means it is difficult to determine whether the code produced by an open source project meets appropriate security invariants – security-related requirements that must be present at all times.

Writing secure code is challenging in software development. Over 90% of commercial software is estimated to contain open source components. Incorporating open source software in any project involves several considerations. These considerations can be non-technical, such as the license, or technically specific, such as the language the project is written in or its performance characteristics.

Historic Security Issues in Open Source Software

Open source security came into the spotlight in 2014 when a security defect in the popular cryptographic library OpenSSL was discovered. This vulnerability, called Heartbleed, became notorious due to the broad use of OpenSSL on internet-facing servers, resulting in many systems under potential attack.

In 2021, a vulnerability called Log4Shell was disclosed in the broadly used Java library Log4j. Log4Shell's disclosure occurred at the end of 2021, typically a holiday season in North America and Europe. Log4Shell resulted in staff being called back into the office from their holidays and significant overtime to remediate the vulnerability.

Most recently, in 2024, the popular compression package xz-utils had a backdoor inserted into its codebase through social engineering. While most security vulnerabilities are attributed to human error, the xz-utils backdoor appeared to result from a social engineering attack. After discovery, several public and private disclosures of similar attempts against other prevalent open source packages were made, thus bringing an additional potential malicious threat vector into scope.

Projects, Governance, and Scope

As of 2024, OpenSSF oversees about 20 projects and ten Special Interest Groups (SIGs) across ten different workgroups, each focusing on a different aspect of open source security. These projects range from software repository security best practices and secure software development practices to community engagement initiatives. These are referred to collectively as the Technical Initiatives (TI) of OpenSSF.

Organizations can join OpenSSF as a Premier, General, or Associate Member.

Each Premier member has a seat on the Governing Board. General and Associate members elect representatives from their membership to represent their interests as a class. The board also has a Security Community Individual Representative (SCIR), elected by the community to represent their interests.

OpenSSF Technical Advisory Council (TAC) oversees the various TIs of OpenSSF.

OpenSSF's scope is global, with members and contributors spanning North America, Europe, Asia, and beyond. This international focus is critical because the open source ecosystem is inherently global, with software projects and developers from diverse backgrounds and regions.

Fostering Open Source Culture Within Enterprise

Foundations like OpenSSF provide a community through which many facets of the community, including organizations that may be commercial competitors, can collaborate on topics for the common good. Improving the security of open source software isn't a commercial competitive advantage for any organization; it's a common good from which we can all benefit. While enterprises have often used open source software as part of their software development, there hasn't always been a reciprocal contribution to the community. The OpenSSF provides a neutral, trusted nexus for organizations and the community to collaborate on projects to improve open source security. Foundations also provide neutral governance through which open source projects can thrive beyond the interest of any single organization or maintainer.

OpenSSF Scorecard for Open Source Software

OpenSSF Scorecard was created as a way for open source developers to

- Understand the security properties of open source projects that they're consuming

- Inform their consumers of the security properties of the project they've produced

Like any incentive structure, the goal of the OpenSSF Scorecard is to provide positive reinforcement to encourage open source projects to embrace security best practices. Each test has a risk level corresponding to the significance of the security control.

There are numerous critical, high-medium, and low-risk checks available, with new checks under active development. While no evaluation scheme is perfect, the OpenSSF Scorecard provides robust insight into a project's compliance with well-regarded security invariants.

Today, OpenSSF Scorecard regularly scans over 1.3 million open source repositories a week, bringing insight into a variety of major projects across the ecosystem. Users are also able to run OpenSSF Scorecard against their internal or private repositories if there are reasons they cannot use the public good instance. For those that elect to use the public good OpenSSF Scorecard service, onboarding can be done quickly and simply.

Case Study: US Office of the National Cyber Director (ONCD)

The Office of the National Cyber Director is an agency in the United States Government statutorily responsible for advising the President of the United States on matters related to cybersecurity. In 2024, ONCD released a paper titled "Back to the Building Blocks." This paper focused on a number of areas that industry should focus on to ensure that software is more resilient to cybersecurity threats.

ONCD emphasizes the importance of metrics and measurements to empower software producers to inform consumers with the information needed to make informed decisions about the security of their software. These metrics can also help drive positive outcomes in the development process by providing an incentive for the adoption of security best practices. Tools like OpenSSF Scorecard can provide a consistent, well-understood method of evaluating these security invariants and ensuring that open source contributors and maintainers are focusing on improving their products by using best practices.

Conclusion

Open source software is a critical part of modern society. The distributed heterogeneous nature of open source software development has led to countless innovations we enjoy today. OpenSSF has rapidly established itself as a leading voice in the open source security landscape. OpenSSF provides a home for numerous projects that help improve the security of the open source ecosystem. Regardless of the project, purpose, or origin, establishing a uniform baseline for security ensures that the digital public good of open source software is secure. OpenSSF Scorecard is a tool that the community and enterprises have embraced to improve the consistency, consumption, and production of open source software. Join us in making open source software secure for everyone.

OpenUK

Contributed by: Amanda Brock, Chief Executive Officer, OpenUK

OpenUK is a unique organization founded in 2020 with the purpose of UK leadership and global collaboration in "Open Technology." As one of the youngest organizations of significance across open source, it operates on three pillars: community, legal and policy, and learning. It has generated probably the biggest communities built around open source which does not have a code or data deliverable at its heart and is one of only two organizations in the world founded to undertake open source policy work – notably, individuals in the UK set both up.

From its instigation, OpenUK has focused on "Open Technology." This started out referring to the three opens which it believed captured all opens: open source software, open hardware, and open data. Its approach is in the tradition of open source projects where participants do not "pay to play" and anyone can participate without payment. Its leadership and participants are mainly volunteers with a small staff.

Of the characteristics that make it unique, despite it focusing on business and effectively creating the UK's geographic industry organization, it focuses not on businesses but people for its participants. This is important for any organization outside of the United States, as the bulk of companies based on open source are located in the United States, and many people are employed by those US corporations despite living in different geographies. Its focus on people has been enhanced by the understanding that if OpenUK was to instead focus on local companies, not people in the business of open tech, the vast majority of its participants would be excluded. This has become referred to as the "submarine under the digital economy," where the UK's open source communities are employed or employ people globally. They contribute a huge amount to the UK economy but are largely unseen locally as a home-working community employed across the planet.

By focusing on the people in the geographic area, Open UK fulfills a role as a convener of the business community, and the organization has been able to give that community a cohesive voice. That voice is exercised in law and policy through a group of highly skilled legal experts with deep experience in open tech who have responded to various legislation in the UK, US, and EU.

To recognize the people in the open tech communities in the UK, OpenUK has built a recognition program with an award and an annual New Year's Honours List. In their fifth year, the Awards culminate in the presentation of 12 categories of awards at a black-tie event at the House of Lords, which has truly become the Oscars of Open Source. The Honours List is a very British tradition, and the list is traditionally shared each year by the UK Monarch at New Year to recognize individuals of achievement, who are each presented with a medal. Initially, a piece of fun, the Honours List – shared each year at midnight on New Year's morning – has become a highly anticipated opportunity for OpenUK to recognize the achievements of up to 100 individuals. The cache attached to these awards and the associated Honours List has enabled OpenUK to promote the achievements of UK-based individuals.

On the policy front, being young has allowed OpenUK to be innovative. OpenUK has convened the conversations on key issues like sustainability. It was the first open source organization to share a Sustainability Policy and to appoint a Chief Sustainability Officer, in the run-up to the major

event it held at COP26 in Scotland, where it delivered the first version
of its Data Centre Blueprint. It has since also delivered an EV Charging
Blueprint, and the Data Centre Blueprint was used to build challenges for
the KubeCon Europe hackathon in Paris in 2024.

Although the UK had recently exited from the EU through Brexit,
OpenUK engaged in the EU Gaia-X project as a day one member and is the
UK's Hub Coordinator for Gaia-X, engaging with the EU, around both its
cloud project and the build of data spaces.

OpenUK has undertaken reporting since 2021, and its work on the
value of open source software, based on data gathered from its annual
survey, is now in its fourth year. As a small and agile organization working
with an academic research partner, OpenUK has pushed the envelope in
reporting in open source software and has calculated the local "value" of
open source software to the UK for four years. It was the first organization
in the world to take a value instead of a replacement cost basis for its
calculation. Its case studies, thought leadership and reporting are now
driving OpenUK's research arm forward to instigating an academic Fellows
Network. The Fellows will work collaboratively with the OpenUK Advisory
Boards, spanning topics including AI, healthcare, security, sustainability,
space, quantum, and finance to build rigorous research and ongoing
thinking in these spaces.

OpenUK's skills work began with two kids camps, the second being
runner-up in the GNOME Community Challenge. These introduced young
people to open source, and 8,500 digital gloves were shared with teenagers
to encourage them to learn open source coding languages and skills while
teaching them the meaning of open source software and the Open Source
Definition. It is currently working on a program to encourage first-time
contributors to open source projects where they gain greater skills and
learn about key projects and packages relevant to their future employers.

All of OpenUK's work will lead to the building of the next generation
of open technologists in the UK, encouraging an environment where open
source software, hardware, data, standards, and AI are better understood

and regulated, but also building out on its being a center of excellence. The goal is to encourage more new contributors into open source software over the next few years to see an increase in the contributions from the UK and for that to support businesses in the UK and across the globe with a strong UK-based employee and founder base.

Now that you've learned about some of the open source foundations, let's learn about why some organizations participate in them and what they get out of it. Each case study highlights some of the foundations that they sponsor and are part of it. The case studies highlight the incentive mechanisms in the organization for employees to take leadership roles that may not be directly contributing to the bottom line. Finally, there are specific examples of how joining a particular foundation has helped build an open source culture in the enterprise.

The Apache Software Foundation

Contributed by: Brian Proffitt, VP, Marketing and Publicity, The Apache Software Foundation

Since its founding in 1999, The Apache Software Foundation (ASF) has served as the global home for open source software the world relies on. It exists to provide software for the public good by sustaining open source projects in perpetuity. As the world's first and prominently known open source software foundation, its members believe in the power of community over code known as The Apache Way. Thousands of people around the world contribute to over 320 ASF open source projects every day.

The foundation differs from other software foundations in the open source sector, as it was originally incorporated as a U.S. 501(c)(3) not-for-profit organization. This classification means that the ASF is a charity for the public good. This distinction aligns with the ASF's mission of creating software for the public good is something its leadership and members take very seriously. The software produced under the ASF's umbrella comprises much of the core infrastructure of today's Internet, cloud computing, and big data technologies.

That the foundation is operated almost exclusively by volunteers makes that achievement all the more outstanding. Our leadership is elected by the ASF members, who are nominated and elected into the ASF themselves. Our leadership is composed entirely of volunteers who are committed to advancing ASF's mission of providing software for the public good. Billions of users benefit from the ASF's freely available open source software, and countless non-ASF-developed software applications have been distributed under the terms of the popular Apache Public License.

As a charitable organization, the ASF runs a very lean operation, spending 10% or less on overhead. Donations to the ASF also help offset day-to-day operating expenses such as legal and accounting services, brand management, public relations, and general office expenditures. Because of this, the ASF is an ideal home for open source projects seeking an even playing field for individuals to collaborate equitably.

Community over Code

"Community over code" is not just the name of the ASF's conference; it is also the ASF's way of saying the foundation values sustainable projects' communities above the value of the code itself. Fixing broken code is much easier to do than repairing a broken community, so keeping a community engaged and thriving is a critical piece to open source sustainability.

This doesn't mean code isn't important, too: building something together is the focal point of the strongest communities. But while great code may become a tool that everyone uses, a great community around will create and maintain a project that has a far greater long-term impact. Diversity is also a cornerstone of a thriving community. ASF Diversity and Inclusion is a project dedicated to understanding and promoting the diversity and inclusion within ASF projects.

The philosophy also emphasizes the importance of non-code contributions. Open source is more than just developers building software with code; it's about writers creating documentation, organizers running events, artists designing logos – all talented people creating something that lasts longer than what they are building: a true community.

The Apache Way

The ASF's collaborative, meritocratic community development process, known as "The Apache Way," is highly emulated by other open source foundations and the subject of numerous industry case studies. When projects come into the ASF, they undergo an Incubator phase that not only ensures the project's development is well-managed but also that the project's community is well-governed and sustainable. After a project is accepted into the ASF, it is overseen by a Project Management Committee (PMC), a self-selected team of contributors that guides the project's day-to-day operations, including development and product releases.

ASF projects and their communities are diverse and focused on the activities needed at a particular stage of the project's lifetime, including nurturing communities, developing code, and building awareness. They all embrace

- **Earned Authority** – All individuals are given the opportunity to participate, but their influence is based on publicly earned merit – what they contribute to the community. Merit stays with the individual, does not expire, is not influenced by employment status or employer, and is non-transferable to other projects.

- **Community of Peers** – individuals participate at the ASF, not organizations. The ASF's flat structure dictates that roles are equal irrespective of title, votes hold equal weight, and contributions are made on a volunteer basis (even if paid to work on ASF code). The ASF community is expected to treat each other with respect, in adherence to our Code of Conduct.

- **Open Communications** – as a virtual organization, the ASF requires all communications related to code and decision-making to be publicly accessible to ensure asynchronous collaboration, as necessitated by a globally distributed community.

- **Consensus Decision-Making** – ASF projects are overseen by a self-selected team of active volunteers who are contributing to their respective projects. Projects are auto-governing, with a heavy slant towards driving consensus to maintain momentum and productivity.

- **Responsible Oversight** – The ASF governance model is based on trust and delegated oversight. Rather than detailed rules and hierarchical structures, ASF governance is principles-based, with self-governing projects providing reports directly to the Board. ASF committers help by making peer-reviewed commits, employing mandatory security measures, ensuring license compliance, and protecting the ASF brand and community at-large from abuse.

The Apache Way is a living, breathing interpretation of one's experience with the ASF's community-led development process. While the Apache Way may seem like common sense to anyone familiar with open source, when it was first created 25 years ago, there were few guidelines on how to create sustainable open source projects. Through these guidelines, the ASF and the Apache Way set the tone for open source best practices in the very early days of open source.

Moving Forward

For 25 years, ASF has led innovation in open source, pioneering industry standards including licensing and security to deliver software you can rely on – all powered by communities steeped in the Apache Way.

As we move onwards into the next 25 years, the ASF is committed to preserving open source ideals through education, community, and public policy – with independence as a core value.

The Linux Foundation

Contributed by: Chris Aniszczyk, Chief Technology Officer, Linux Foundation

In the last couple of decades, The Linux Foundation (LF) has grown from being out of simply a neutral home for the Linux kernel to a full-fledged open source "foundation as a service" to a wide umbrella of open technologies from Argo to Zephyr. Today, the LF is one of the largest global open source foundations in the world, with over 1800 members worldwide sustaining over 1.7 billion lines of code contributed across 1000 projects.

The LF hosts many sub-foundations, such as the Cloud Native Computing Foundation (CNCF) or OpenJS Foundation and/or even the PyTorch Foundation, covering many technology areas and industry verticals such as finance and automotive. These projects and sub-foundations are not purely software-based only, the LF hosts open data projects such as the Overture Maps Foundation to even open hardware designs via the RISC-V foundation. Recently, the LF communities have also even started to build industry specifications and standards. The Joint Development Foundation (JDF) is the home to many of these specifications covering technologies such as GraphQL, video codecs, decentralized identity, content provenance, and more. JDF is now also approved as an ISO JTC1 PAS submitter, meaning that LF projects can now follow a path to becoming an international standard.

The LF is truly a unique global organization that hosts foundations such as RISC-V, which is based out of Switzerland, and/or even LF Europe, which is based out of Belgium, to support the needs of the growing European open source ecosystem. Furthermore, the LF has

In 2023 alone, cumulative trainee and certification enrollments exceeded 3 million, with over 1,000 people taking an LF Training exam each week on average. The LF helped organize 256 events with 3,581 talks delivered by 4,576 speakers, gathering 120,000 attendees from 17,764 organizations in 160 countries. For example, the LF handed out $1.64 million in community travel funding and registration scholarships in 2023 to attend career-changing events; this included 548 diversity travel scholarships and 362 needs-based scholarships. Also since its inception, the LF has paid over $1.5 million to nearly 500 mentees participating in the LFX Mentorship program to contribute directly to open source projects.

Part of the greatest value that open source foundations bring is the creation of a neutral collaboration hub for everyone participating in, and taking a dependency on, a project. The LF offers their communities

- Distributed ownership
- Level playing field
- De-risking open source
- Open community governance

Joining an open source foundation is critical to fostering open source culture in the enterprise because there's no better way to learn how to do open source than by doing it in a neutral and professional setting. In open source foundations, you get to collaborate with your industry peers and community members to evolve open technology to meet your business needs. Some examples of how this can work in practice are looking at TODO Group case studies like Porsche [https://todogroup. org/resources/case-studies/porsche/] which went through a digital transformation exercise of moving software development in-house leveraging lessons from open source communities. Other examples can be cleaned from CNCF End User Journey reports like from Spotify: `https://www.cncf.io/reports/spotify-end-user-journey-report/`

> *...who built its own container orchestration system. After starting their migration to the public cloud in late 2016, the team realized it would be better to adopt an open source orchestration tool that was widely adopted and had a growing ecosystem of users and compatible tools. Having a team dedicated to the internal tools upkeep and functionality would be more time consuming than adopting a solution that was supported by a larger open source community, and that would quickly outpace what a small team could do when it came to features. So Spotify turned to Kubernetes and the burgeoning CNCF community, which had more than 50,000 contributors at the time.*

Another example is Adobe who has improved its internal practices and products from learning from open source communities according to an engineering leader: `https://www.cncf.io/reports/adobe-end-user-journey-report/`

> *Because it's open source, this is a way that we could pay this forward for other end users but then I also get the net benefits of meeting a lot of people in the community. The dialogue really helps us to improve the products that we then bring back to our company.*

These are just a few examples where organizations have benefited from joining open source foundations that can improve engineering and internal product practices.

In conclusion, the LF is one of the largest open source global organizations in the world dedicated to creating the largest shared technology investment in the world. This would not have been possible without first building a governance model that organizations could trust to work for them, then building value-added support programs to support scale. The design goal has been to build the best upstream community model for downstream commercial solution providers and users.

Finally, the LF organization's values are helpful, hopeful, and humble. Those values extend themselves through how the organization sustains open source communities. The LF truly takes care of all the boring but important stuff necessary to support projects so that developers can focus on development. This includes events, marketing, infrastructure, finances for projects, training and education, legal assistance, standards, facilitation, and more. These are all critical for organizations looking to foster open source culture in the enterprise and depend on open source software critical to their business.

Case Studies

Let's take a look at why some organizations have joined open source foundations and that helps bring a cultural change in order to make open source sustainable with their business.

Bloomberg

Contributed by: Alyssa Wright, Open Source Program Office, Office of the CTO, Bloomberg

Bloomberg + Foundations = Stewards of Sustainable Open Source

Bloomberg's Open Source Program Office (OSPO) and Corporate Philanthropy team work together to facilitate the engagement of the company's engineers with open source foundations in order to support their ecosystem work, as well as cultivate a vibrant open source culture within its walls. By actively engaging with foundations, the firm's engineers are empowered to become leaders in a variety of open source communities, promoting innovation, and reaping significant business and professional benefits.

The Power of Open Source Foundations for Bloomberg's Business

Open source foundations play a pivotal role in fostering a secure and thriving open source software landscape. These non-profit organizations provide essential elements for project sustainability and growth, fostering a collaborative environment that benefits project maintainers and users. Some of the crucial things that open source foundations contribute include

- **Governance and Structure**: Foundations establish frameworks for project management, code review, quality control, and legal governance. This transparency builds trust in open source software's integrity and security.

- **Community and Support** – Foundations cultivate developer communities around specific projects. These communities provide a platform for knowledge sharing, collaboration, and mutual support, enabling developers to seek help, troubleshoot issues, and contribute their expertise.

- **Financial Backing** – Many foundations provide financial resources to support project development and maintenance, as well as community events. This backing allows projects to attract and retain talented contributors, ensuring the projects' continued growth and evolution.

- **Security Guardrails** – Collaborative and transparent governance structures create shared accountability for projects' security and direction. This contrasts with single-vendor "open-core" models, in which security practices and roadmaps may be less transparent and accountable to the end-user community.

Taken together, open source foundations ensure the long-term stability and sustainability of open source projects, giving Bloomberg confidence in a project's reliability, security, and longevity.

Beyond Business Value: Cultivating a Collaborative Culture

While the business case for open source engagement is clear – access to innovative technologies, reduced development costs, and exposure to a wider talent pool – Bloomberg's OSPO recognizes the additional value that supporting open source foundations brings to the company. Bloomberg actively participates in more than twenty different open source foundations, fostering an environment of collaboration that extends beyond code and emphasizes teamwork, knowledge sharing, and problem-solving. Engineers who contribute to open source projects alongside diverse teams in the "foundation context" bring back a spirit of open communication and a commitment to shared goals within our "internal context." This fosters a more innovative and efficient in-house environment where teams can work together more effectively to tackle complex challenges.

Incentivizing Collaboration: Fueling Open Source Foundation Engagement

Bloomberg recognizes the intrinsic value of open source contribution – the opportunity to learn, grow, and make a real global impact. The company's OSPO also understands the importance of providing additional incentives to encourage employee participation at the foundation level, addressing both professional development and the desire to give back:

- **Professional Growth** – Taking leadership roles in open source foundations offers valuable opportunities to hone leadership and communication skills. Bloomberg engineers gain experience working in collaborative environments, navigating diverse perspectives, and influencing the direction of open source projects. Building relationships with other open source developers expands their professional networks and opens doors to future opportunities.

- **Industry Recognition** – Active participation in open source foundations can significantly enhance an engineer's reputation within the tech industry. Holding leadership positions, contributing code or documentation, and presenting at foundation events and technical conferences demonstrates both expertise and thought leadership. This recognition strengthens professional networks and fuels future career growth.

- **Shaping the Future of Technology** – Open source foundations are at the forefront of innovation, defining the direction of critical technologies that Bloomberg relies on. By actively participating in these organizations, Bloomberg engineers have a direct say in shaping the roadmap and technical specifications of these technologies, ensuring they remain aligned with Bloomberg's strategic needs.

Leading by Example: Bloomberg's Impact on Open Source

Bloomberg's commitment to open source foundations extends beyond simple participation. We boast a strong record of leadership and technical expertise within these communities, as evidenced by these examples:

- **Apache Software Foundation (ASF)** – Multiple Bloomberg engineers have served on the Project Management Committee (PMC) for Apache Solr, a search platform for large data volumes.

- **Python Software Foundation (PSF)** – Several Bloomberg engineers are core developers for CPython, the reference implementation of the Python programming language. The company also employs PSF Fellows, the maintainer of essential Python ecosystem tools like pip, virtualenv, and auditwheel, and has funded key roles within the CPython core dev team and the Python Packaging (PyPA) ecosystem.

- **Cloud Native Computing Foundation (CNCF)** – Bloomberg engineers make key contributions and serve in the leadership ranks of Cloud Native Buildpacks and KServe, a highly scalable ML model inference platform that runs atop Kubernetes.

- **NumFOCUS** – Bloomberg engineers helped develop and continue to actively contribute to various projects within the Project Jupyter ecosystem (e.g., bqplot, ipydatagrid, and ipywidget) that further enhance its capabilities for data science and interactive computing.

- **Ceph Foundation** – A Bloomberg engineer sits on the Ceph board, representing the viewpoints of enterprise users. Our engineers have also contributed projects related to enterprise use cases (e.g., Ceph telemetry systems, real-time distributed Layer 7 QoS stack, and S3 notifications and IAM features).

These are just some examples of how Bloomberg engineers are leading the way in open source communities. Their active participation brings not only technical expertise to these projects but has also fosters an internal culture of collaboration.

Foundations: The Place to Learn Open Source Culture

By actively engaging with open source foundations, Bloomberg's OSPO has nurtured a culture of open source contribution and collaboration within the company. This has fostered innovation, strengthened Bloomberg's technical capabilities, and has positioned the company as a leader within the open source community. The impact goes beyond just code; it has generated a spirit of teamwork and knowledge sharing that has broadly benefited both Bloomberg and the global tech sector.

Dell

Contributed by: Barton George, Developer Community Manager, Dell Technologies

Leveraging Open Source Foundations to Move Faster, Drive Standards, and Shape Technologies

Dell Technologies' participation in open source foundations began in 2008 when it became a sponsor of the Linux foundation. Dell's open source culture has evolved over time to allow individual groups and teams the freedom to join foundations or initiatives aligned to their goals.

By participating in open source communities, Dell moves faster with less costs, helps drive standards, and advances the industry. Over the past 15 to 20 years, Dell sponsored or participated in more than a dozen open source foundations, projects, and initiatives, including the Open Stack Foundation, the Cloud Foundry Foundation, the Open Source Security Foundation, the Cloud Native Compute Foundation, the Eclipse Foundation, the Open Container Initiative, the Core Infrastructure Initiative, the Open HPC Project, the Open Programmable Infrastructure Project, Software for Open Networking in the Cloud, and the Yocto, Anuket, and Nephio projects.

The Benefit of Collective Innovation

Open source foundations or projects, like those above, are collaborative communities. Within these communities, companies and individuals come together to build, maintain, and innovate around specific technology or groups of technologies. This collaboration allows organizations to decrease costs, increase speed, and potentially shape technology or even the industry. These communities see very large companies that historically don't work together collaborating on the development of technology. Each company contributes its best technical people and ideas to projects, resulting in a collective output that surpasses what individual organizations could achieve alone. In these situations, the investment of any individual company is small, but the return of the collective investment is a powerful way to efficiently deliver an outcome.

Communities Facilitate Standardization Within the Industry

As Dell became more involved in open source communities, it recognized that these groups were often more effective at achieving consensus and driving traditional standards for the betterment of the industry. This realization helped evolve Dell's open source culture. Technologies like

Kubernetes, the Open Container Initiative, and even the Cloud Foundry Foundation were standardized and achieved compatibility through open source community efforts. Dell realized that open source doesn't eliminate differentiation; instead, shifts it. In the proprietary world, differentiation comes from unique ideas, even poorly executed ones. With an overarching commitment to "community-defined," open source differentiation comes from system integration, speed, and quality of execution.

Here are a few examples illustrating the power and efficiencies driven by communities:

- **EdgeX Foundry Foundation** – Dell created, led, and donated the code for The EdgeX Foundry Foundation. At the time, Dell wanted to extend its Internet of Things (IoT) offerings. Given the fragmentation of the landscape, Dell recognized a common framework for IOT Edge was needed – so it started building one. After investing two years in the effort, Dell acknowledged more resources and broader support were necessary to create an industry standard framework. It needed a community. Creating an open source foundation was unfamiliar territory for Dell and required a significant cultural shift. With the guidance of the Linux Foundation, Dell's IoT division embraced the idea of contributing its code to start the foundation. In 2017, the Dell-led EdgeX Foundry Foundation launched with more than 50 members. Today, the foundation includes multiple projects, such as Alvarium and Akraino. Dell maintains a representative on the foundation's board, who also serves as the lead architect for project Alvarium.

- **Cloud Foundry Foundation** – Dell was one of seven platinum members of Cloud Foundry Foundation. Dell's CTO was elected as the Foundation's board chair, responsible for strategic and operational leadership of the Foundation. In its time, Cloud Foundry was a significant step in the IT infrastructure stack, delivering an open, standardized architecture for cloud native applications.

- **Cloud Native Computing Foundation (CNCF)** – The same year Dell launched the EdgeX Foundry, it joined the Linux Foundation's CNCF. The CNCF's mission was to support the adoption of cloud native computing. Dell actively participated in two CNCF projects: the creation of a Container Storage Interface (CSI) and the development of a common container standard.

  - **Container Storage Interface** – Originally, Kubernetes was unable to integrate with traditional enterprise storage. Dell collaborated with other members of the community to create the Container Storage Interface, allowing the traditional storage world to communicate with the cloud native world.

  - **Open Container Initiative** – The Open Container Initiative (OCI) defined a standard container format, enabling interoperability among container tools. This standardization led to wider adoption of modern container architectures and, more broadly, cloud native applications.

- **OpenSSF** – Similar to the early days of container technology, today's open source security software landscape is characterized by disparate and incompatible solutions. The Open Secure Software Foundation (OpenSSF) is taking the same approach as the OCI to unify security solutions through common standards and formats. By participating in OpenSSF, Dell collaborates with other industry leaders to address and mitigate security risks in the open source ecosystem. This involvement aligns with Dell's broader strategy to contribute to and support initiatives that improve software security across the industry.

The examples above demonstrate Dell's deepening involvement in open source communities, which serves as a significant driver of its open source culture. Dell actively creates and participates in foundations and projects, influencing the direction of key technologies. Additionally, it has established a robust open source culture that values contribution, innovation, and community-driven development. Through senior-executive supported engagement, Dell Technologies continues to drive forward the principles of open source within the organization and the broader IT industry.

Infosys

Contributed by: Naresh Duddu, AVP and Global Head of Open Source, Infosys Ltd

Modern architecture is powered by open source, but before adopting open source software, clients often have several questions. Security is paramount, with concerns about vulnerabilities and the timely application of patches. Support and maintenance are crucial, as clients need reliable assistance and assurance of the software's longevity. Legal issues, such as compliance with open source licenses and avoiding intellectual property risks, also weigh heavily. Clients scrutinize the software's quality and reliability, evaluating its maturity, performance, and scalability. The strength and activity of the community and ecosystem supporting the software largely influence the decision, alongside concerns about potential vendor lock-in despite the open source nature.

Open source foundations act as linchpins, convening contributors, sponsors, and users to foster innovation. By promoting a culture of standardization and interoperability, they ensure the legal, secure, and sustainable growth of open source projects and communities. This neutral governance model, championed by organizations like the Cloud Native Computing Foundation (CNCF), encourages wider enterprise adoption by fostering trust and long-term project sustainability.

Legacy systems within a majority of Fortune 500 companies pose a significant challenge to their agility compared to modern, digitally native organizations. To expedite their modernization efforts, many of these companies are embracing platform-centric approaches and leveraging cutting-edge open source projects such as ORA2PG and Konveyor to facilitate a more rapid transition. Infosys has also developed industry-leading platforms like Infosys Live Enterprise Application Development Platform, built on technologies and projects that are governed by open source foundations.

Infosys, committed to staying at the forefront of technology, leverages partnerships with open source foundations. Infosys holds membership in various other foundations such as the Cloud Native Computing Foundation (CNCF), Linux Foundation Networking (LFN), Linux Foundation, and Hyperledger Foundation. We also actively participate in industry-focused foundations like Open Banking, BIAN, TMForum, and OpenManufacturing.

Through partnerships with open source foundations, Infosys gains early insights into technology and industry trends, fostering faster innovation. This empowers us to deliver superior client support and champion their interests by influencing the technical direction and governance of open source projects. We share our feedback and insights, as exemplified by our proposed Northbound Integration (NBI) Adapter component in Nephio leveraging TMForum 664 Open APIs and the proposed alternative frameworks of Quarkus/Native for rewriting Springboot-based microservices in ONAP to improve performance.

There are instances where clients have collaborated with us on specific open source initiatives. For example – A European energy giant is coinvesting with us to build open source extensions and enhancements to the Geonode project.

Incentivizing Open Source Leadership

In alignment with the Infosys ESG Vision 2030 to enable digital skilling at scale, Infosys aims to empower over 10 million people with digital and life skills by 2025 through its digital literacy initiative launched in 2021 – Infosys Springboard. Springboard has several million registered learners, 30% being female learners. The platform currently includes about 17,000+ courses and 162,000+ learning resources across digital technologies, computer science, engineering, and life skills. This platform has content in 20+ regional languages to promote inclusivity and access. The platform, powered by Infosys Wingspan, is accessible free of cost to any curious learner from Class 6 to lifelong learners. Educational institutions can use the platform to bring industry relevance to the academic curriculum and monitor the learning progress of their students on the platform.

There are 8 million people with complete blindness in India. Infosys and LV Prasad Eye Institute (LVPEI) came together, bringing innovation and technology into SightConnect, an AI-powered mobile app that helps in early detection of eye illnesses, with a goal to make eye care accessible to all. The digital services built based on open architecture are aligned to the Ayushman Bharat Digital Mission (ABDM).

Infosys has empowered over 114 million lives through "technology for good" initiatives across e-governance, healthcare, and education, as of FY2023.

We began collaborating with Modular Open Source Identity Platform (MOSIP) in early 2023. Through this collaboration, Infosys demonstrates its commitment to using technology for social good and empowering individuals with secure and reliable digital identities.

We provide multiple opportunities to employees to work on their passion outside of regular work. All our development centers are operated by executive councils made up of volunteers. Employees also take leadership roles for various other initiatives, e.g., open source adoption, various "tribes" or guilds related to pursuits other than their regular work.

While these endeavors may not have a direct impact on the bottom line, the organization encourages and incentivizes such initiatives through a range of awards, rewards, and recognition programs. Contributions to open source projects are formally acknowledged and rewarded by being included in the goal sheets of our key technical talents. Infosys also takes such leadership effort into consideration while assigning future roles and promotions. There is a system of "skill tags" within Infosys where employees get recognition for their technical and professional development.

Example – How Joining CNCF Has Helped Us Build Open Source Culture

Our engagement with foundations is twofold: we actively promote contributions to open source projects supported by the foundations while also staying abreast of emerging trends and innovations to integrate them into our client projects.

Prior to attaining platinum membership, our engagement with CNCF primarily revolved around contributing to Kubernetes documentation. In addition, Infosys hosted the KubeDay event in 2019 at our Bangalore campus.

In Jan 2023, Infosys became a platinum member of CNCF. Subsequently, our involvement has significantly broadened. We established a Cloud native Interest Technology Group, dedicated to exploring and advancing new technologies and trends. Additionally, we empowered a team of architects specializing in cloud native technologies, actively advocating for open source solutions within client projects. We regularly invite open source tech leaders to speak at our events.

To train and inspire new contributors, we have introduced our internal "Zero-to-Merge" program, modeled after the CNCF Zero-to-Merge initiative. This program assists participants in progressing from a fundamental understanding of open source to submitting their first pull request. This program saw thousands of participants who benefitted from mentoring and talks by open source enthusiasts.

Similar to CNCF, our platinum membership with LF Networking foundation has helped us establish executive connects. We participated in multiple events like MWC Barcelona, LFN Dev, and Testing Forum and won 2 awards at DTW Copenhagen (Outstanding Catalyst – Business Growth, and Best Innovation).

Intel

Contributed by: Shirley Bailes, Director, Open Source Community and Evangelism, Intel Corporation

Open source software (OSS) has fundamentally transformed the technology sector, promoting collaboration, transparency, and community-driven innovation, resulting in world-changing software used by 90% of companies around the globe. Central to the success of open source projects are the foundations and non-profit organizations that nurture and sustain them. These foundations provide governance, resources, and advocacy, creating an environment where open source culture can thrive. We'll explore the roles of these foundations, Intel's motivations for joining them, and the ways in which the company's involvement and internal incentive mechanisms have strengthened open source culture.

The Role of Foundations in Fostering Open Source Culture

Foundations offer a formal governance structure for managing open source projects, ensuring adherence to best practices and community standards. The Linux Foundation (LF), for example, oversees critical projects like the Linux kernel, establishing advisory boards and technical committees to guide development. Similarly, the Apache Software Foundation (ASF) uses a meritocratic model where project decisions are made collectively by contributors, fostering a collaborative yet structured environment.

Foundations often provide essential resources such as funding, infrastructure, and tools necessary for project development and collaboration with the goal of alleviating financial and logistical roadblocks that stifle innovation and growth. The Linux Foundation offers funding through sponsorships and provides essential infrastructure like servers and development tools. Similarly, organizations like the Software Freedom Conservancy and the ASF assist projects, such as Outreachy and Apache Spark, with legal support, project management tools, and collaborative platforms – vital resources for ensuring that open source projects can thrive and evolve.

Beyond governance and resources, foundations promote open source principles and foster community engagement, which are critical to the long-term health of a project. Events such as the Open Source Summit and KubeCon + CloudNativeCon bring together developers and industry leaders to share knowledge and discuss technological advancements. Community-driven events like Community Over Code and FOSDEM aim to support interaction and education within open source communities, which are comprised mainly of volunteers. These efforts enable developers to connect and raise awareness about open source technologies that move the entire industry forward, as well as encourage new contributors to get involved.

Intel's Engagement with Open Source Foundations

Intel's commitment to open source reflects its core belief that open ecosystems are more powerful than closed ones and that commitment to openness extends to silicon. Since the early days of Linux and the founding of the Linux Foundation, Intel has collaborated with open source organizations to help align its technology initiatives with the latest industry standards. One of the top contributors to the Linux kernel and a top contributor to Kubernetes, Intel belongs to over 700 open source foundations and standards bodies and actively maintains, or contributes to, over 450 community-managed projects. Intel's participation is a win-win for both the company and the community for several reasons.

Collaboration – Intel actively participates in various communities to foster collaboration among developers, researchers, and industry experts. This collaborative environment encourages the sharing of ideas, promotes the development of new features and optimizations, and drives innovation forward. For example, in 2024, Intel launched the Open Platform for Enterprise AI (OPEA) with the goal of streamlining the implementation of enterprise-grade generative AI by creating standards and frameworks that all organizations could use to start realizing benefits from their AI investments faster.

Accessibility and Adoption – By working with key foundations and projects, such as the Linux Foundation, the PyTorch Foundation, the Open Source Security Foundation (OpenSSF), the Unified Acceleration Foundation (UXL), and many others, Intel helps increase the accessibility and adoption of new frameworks and tools. Intel's contributions, including developer tools and educational resources, empower developers to effectively use its technology, promoting a diverse and inclusive ecosystem.

Sustainability – Intel's support for open source projects and open standards creates a level playing field for multiple vendors and contributors to thrive, fostering innovation and preventing vendor lock-in.

This benefits developers, users, and the global tech industry. As a member of the Open Compute Project since 2011, we're leveraging our leadership role in the Open Compute Project (OCP) Sustainability Initiative to develop standards for power usage effectiveness (PUE) and IT energy efficiency.

Corporate Responsibility – Foundation membership in its various forms across the ecosystem provides several opportunities. Leadership in the form of governing board seats, technical advisory boards, and marketing committee roles provides a platform to influence the direction and development of key projects, ensuring representation.

Community Building – Foundations connect organizations, facilitating the exchange of knowledge and resources and fostering valuable relationships and collaboration opportunities. For instance, Intel's contributions to the Zephyr Project help enhance its real-time operating system capabilities, while its involvement with the Open Source Initiative supports broader open source principles and practices. Similarly, Intel's engagement with the eBPF Foundation advances the development of eBPF technologies, supporting innovation and performance improvements in networking and security. Through these key partnerships, Intel not only supports individual projects but also contributes to a broader ecosystem of collaboration and knowledge sharing within communities.

Internal Culture – Intel's active participation in foundations and projects helps build a strong ecosystem that benefits developers and end-users alike. Through our open source program office (OSPO), Intel employees can contribute to open source projects they care about to optimize their products, test out new ideas, or simply take an active role in efforts that matter to them. As a result, Intel is responsible for making the third-most commits to Linux Foundation projects of all time.

Community Best Practices – Intel has a long history of contributing to and supporting open source communities. The company supports the Contributor Covenant, adheres to the Open Source Initiative (OSI) approved licenses for its open source projects, and leverages the tools and best practices for security dashboarding developed through the OpenSFF to identify and mitigate vulnerabilities in their projects.

A Commitment to Future Innovation

"Innovation thrives most when people can come together and collaborate in a transparent environment. That kind of open ecosystem is the foundation of our approach at Intel – and why we launched the first global sustainability summit for the semiconductor industry," said Intel CEO Pat Gelsinger; "It's how we continue to democratize computing, achieve new breakthroughs, and improve productivity for our partners, developers, and customers."

Summary

This chapter explained the relevance of engaging with external communities to foster open source culture. These communities range from participating in open source projects, industry events, and open source foundations. A transition between different roles in an open source project and key criteria of a healthy open source community are discussed in detail. Participation in open source events as a speaker, sponsor, or attendee and how these benefit in fostering open source culture are explained in detail. Key characteristics and functions of open source foundations are explained next. Like other chapters, this chapter has case studies from several open source foundations and how they help foster open source culture. There are also case studies from different enterprises on why they join open source foundations, incentive mechanisms in their company for employees to take leadership roles that may not be directly contributing to the bottom line, and how overall it helps foster the open source culture.

The next chapter explains how employees at different levels of the companies need to be enabled to foster an open source culture. It explains training programs that can educate employees at the worker level as well as within the management. The relevance of a consistent language and creating an internal and external website are explained next. Finally, incorporating the company's open source philosophy into employee onboarding, how to cultivate enthusiasm, and creating incentive mechanisms to reinforce the culture are explained.

CHAPTER 7

Employee Enablement

Enabling employees at different levels of the company is critically important to ensure open source culture is flourishing within an enterprise. This inclusivity spans across different echelons, encompassing worker bees, line managers, middle management, and executives. The different layers, of course, depend upon the size of an organization. Each stratum plays a unique and complementary role in nurturing an environment where open source principles thrive.

At the foundational level, worker bees, often comprising developers, engineers, and contributors, are the lifeblood of open source initiatives. Enabling them involves providing the necessary training, resources, and collaborative platforms to actively engage with open source projects. Their direct involvement in coding, testing, and documentation contributes significantly to the hands-on execution of open source practices and moves the project forward.

Moving up the hierarchy, line managers play a pivotal role in facilitating the integration of open source methodologies within their teams. Their role involves aligning team goals with the broader organizational strategy, ensuring that open source contributions align with business objectives. Acting as intermediaries between upper management and their teams, line managers play a vital role in ensuring that their teams feel adequately supported and empowered to engage in open source work, while also communicating progress and outcomes upward through the organizational chain.

For middle management, the focus shifts to strategic alignment and resource allocation. Enabling this tier involves equipping managers with the knowledge to make informed decisions about incorporating open source practices into broader organizational initiatives. Middle managers act as advocates, driving the adoption of open source methodologies across multiple teams and projects.

At the executive level, fostering an open source culture requires a top-down approach. Executives need to champion the cause, articulating a clear vision for how open source principles align with the company's mission and values. Their enablement involves understanding the strategic implications of open source contributions, allocating resources, and advocating for a culture that promotes collaboration, innovation, and community engagement.

Let's dig further into specific initiatives that can be done for employee enablement.

Training Programs

Run regular workshops to provide employees with an opportunity to acquire and enhance specific skills relevant to open source contributions. It's equally important to educate employees at the foundation level as well within the management.

Clyde Seepersad, Sr. Vice President and General Manager, Education at Linux Foundation, says, "The ongoing shift towards collaboratively developed software for the 'bones' of most modern systems has changed the game when it comes to technical training. Proprietary product training made available with purchase is out and vendor neutral courses for the baseline technologies are in. This approach positions employees to be savvier about the product implementations they choose."

By focusing on these foundational technologies, employees are not just learning how to use a single product; they're gaining a deeper understanding of the principles and systems that underlie a wide range of software implementations. This knowledge makes them more adaptable and versatile, better equipped to evaluate, integrate, and optimize various tools and solutions, regardless of the vendor.

Some of the most common workshops for worker bees are suggested below and help them get ready to embrace the open source philosophy. The Linux Foundation offers plenty of online resources at `https://training.linuxfoundation.org/` that range from getting started with an open source project to the latest bleeding-edge technologies. A lot of the introductory courses are free and thus allows you to start immediately. New courses are added all the time so consider saving this website and revisit whenever there is a need.

- **Introduction to Open Source** – The objective of this workshop is to familiarize participants with the principles and benefits of open source. The contents can include basics of open source, history, licenses, and the widespread impact on technology. The Linux Foundation's Open Source Best Practices track is a great collection of courses to start with.

- **Tools and Infrastructure** – A wide variety of tools are used to ensure the collaborative and dynamic nature of open source projects. These tools range from version control, continuous integration, automated testing, containerization, infrastructure-as-a-code, monitoring, and observability. These workshops will introduce participants to tools commonly used in open source development. For example, Git is the most popular version control system used for open source projects. A workshop to equip participants with essential version control skills using Git would help them to contribute to a large range of projects. The content may contain

Git basics, branching strategies, collaborating on repositories, and resolving conflicts. For example, Learn Git & GitHub at Codecademy helps you get started with Git.

- **Code Review and Collaboration** – Code reviews help ensure that potential issues, bugs, or code smells that might have been missed by the author can be identified and addressed before merging. This workshop will teach participants the art of code review and collaborative coding. An important element of code review is providing constructive feedback and is included in the workshop.

- **Contributing to Open Source Projects** – This workshop will provide hands-on experience on contributing to existing open source projects. This can involve how to find projects matching your skill sets, creating issues, submitting pull requests, and collaborating on GitHub or similar platforms. Refer to Appendix B for ten non-code ways to contribute to open source.

- **Documentation Best Practices** – Documentation is typically the entry point for any project. This workshop will emphasize the importance of documentation in open source projects. Specifically, it will teach writing README files, project documentation, and creating effective user guides.

- **Licensing and Compliance** – A basic understanding of different licenses would be very helpful to participants. This workshop will educate participants on various open source licenses and compliance. It will provide an overview of popular licenses, legal considerations, and ensuring compliance. You may like to consult closely with your organization's legal team for legal advice anyway.

- **Project Management** – Project management is crucial for the success of open source projects, playing a pivotal role in maintaining order, maximizing efficiency, ensuring quality, and fostering collaboration among diverse contributors. This workshop will explore effective project management strategies for open source projects. It will involve setting up projects, issue triage and tracking, timeline and release management, and effective communication with the community.

- **Culture and Community Building** – Open source community is very particular about transparency, collaboration, and inclusion. Instill the values of open source culture and community engagement with different workshops. The workshop content would show how to build inclusive communities, effective communication, and resolving conflicts. Helping understand the purpose of code of conduct would be an essential part of this workshop.

- **Hackathons** – Organize hackathons that allow employees to come together and practice the skills mentioned above in a guarded environment. Employees can practice how to pick a project to contribute to, sending their first pull request, providing and accepting feedback on code reviews, updating documentation, and much more.

Workshops for management and senior executives aimed at conveying the value of open source culture can be designed to provide a comprehensive understanding of the benefits, strategies, and best practices associated with open source. Here are several workshop ideas:

- **Introduction to Open Source** – It's important to familiarize executives with the core concepts of open source, including its history, principles, and the collaborative nature of the community. The content may be an overview of open source philosophy, key terminology and principles, and successful case studies of open source projects.

- **Business Impact of Open Source** – Demonstrate how adopting open source practices aligns with business goals and can accelerate innovation, reduce costs, and enhance competitiveness. The workshop content would typically include how cost savings and efficiency gains can be achieved. It will provide concrete examples of how innovation and development can be accelerated by leveraging open source. The competitive advantages of adopting open source need to be clearly explained.

- **Open Source in Digital Transformation** – Showcase how open source technologies play a pivotal role in digital transformation and modern software development. The majority of bleeding-edge development in cloud-native technologies, continuous integration, and microservices architecture is happening in open source. Sharing examples of how other organizations that have similar businesses to yours have embraced open source and been able to accelerate digital innovation would be very helpful.

- **Risk Management and Compliance** – There is an irrational fear and concern that open source is less secure and has more licensing and legal issues. This is primarily because of a lack of knowledge. It needs to be directly addressed by sharing open source licensing models, how open source improves security dramatically, and legal considerations and compliance.

- **Corporate Social Responsibility** – Emphasize the community-centric nature of open source and its alignment with corporate social responsibility (CSR). The workshop can talk about how open source contributes to social impact projects and allows to build and engage with communities.

Consistent Language

It is critical for an enterprise to set up up a consistent language about understanding the term "open source" across the organization. Teams or organizations would put their source code outside the firewall and call it "open source." That is "source available," as the teams may not take any external contributions, have limitations on commercial use, the sharing of modifications, or the ability to distribute modified versions of the software. There may be a business need for projects to exist in that state, and they fall within a spectrum between proprietary, closed source, and fully open source, offering a middle ground where users can access the source code but with certain restrictions. But this should not be confused with open source. Educating teams to be consistent and deliberate about this terminology will bring clarity to everybody within the organization. If the teams want to go this route, then they should clearly label the project so. It is about setting expectations.

"Open source washing" refers to the practice of falsely labeling or marketing a product, project, or initiative as open source when it does not truly adhere to the principles of open source software development. This term draws parallels to "greenwashing," where companies misrepresent their environmental practices to appear more environmentally friendly than they actually are. This "open source washing" may mislead consumers, developers, or organizations into thinking they are supporting or adopting open source solutions, when, in reality, the commitment to openness may be limited. This can lead to broken trust at multiple levels:

1. **Consumer Trust** – Consumers, whether they are individual users or other organizations, often rely on the transparency and collaborative nature associated with true open source projects. If an organization falsely labels their project as open source without adhering to the principles of open collaboration and transparency, consumers may feel misled or deceived. This can damage the reputation of the organization and erode trust with their user base.

2. **Developer Trust** – Developers are often passionate about open source principles and may choose to contribute to projects based on their belief in the ethos of collaboration and openness. If a project falsely claims to be open source but doesn't accept external contributions or share modifications, it can disillusion developers who may have been interested in contributing. This can lead to frustration and a loss of trust in the organization behind the project.

3. **Organizational Trust** – Within the organization itself, misusing the term "open source" can create confusion and undermine trust among teams. If different teams within the organization have varying understandings of what constitutes open source, it can lead to miscommunication, inefficiencies, and ultimately a breakdown in trust between teams and leadership.

4. **Industry Trust** – Open source has become a cornerstone of modern software development, with many organizations and industries relying on open source solutions. When organizations engage in "open source washing" by falsely labeling their projects as open source, it can undermine trust within the industry as a whole. This can have ripple effects, affecting partnerships, collaborations, and the overall reputation of the industry.

To mitigate the risk of broken trust, organizations must prioritize clear and consistent communication about the nature of their projects and adhere to the principles associated with open source. Educating teams about the importance of accurately representing the openness of their projects and fostering a culture of transparency and collaboration can help build and maintain trust both within the organization and with external stakeholders.

Central Website

There is a need for a central website targeted at employees and another one for the open source community outside the organization. They both serve unique purpose and are critically essential to foster open source culture inside the enterprise. It is interesting to note that sometimes publishing content on an external repository helps more with fostering an open source culture inside the company. We will talk more about this point a bit later, but first let's understand what the purpose of these repositories is and what typically goes on them.

Internal Website

An internal website is only accessible to employees within the organization. This website serves as a centralized hub for employees, offering clear visibility into the company's open source policies, initiatives, and opportunities. This central website becomes a one-stop shop for everything open source at the company. This website provides a single source of truth for documentation, guidelines, and resources related to open source projects. It includes guides, manuals, and best practices to help team members understand and use open source tools effectively. The internal wikis, FAQs, and troubleshooting guides for open source projects are listed as well.

The website offers valuable insights into engaging with and contributing to open source projects within the company. It contains information about the internal code repositories and documentation about how to check out the source code and how to contribute code. It also features tools facilitating the open source contribution approval process and compiles playbooks with step-by-step instructions for managing various aspects of open source projects. Such a website helps streamline processes, enhance collaboration, ensure compliance, and foster a culture of innovation and continuous improvement within the organization.

The website acts as a prime advertising space for internal workshops, training sessions, hackathons, and summits, ensuring maximum visibility for these initiatives. By consolidating all pertinent information in one location, the central website simplifies navigation and facilitates easy access to details related to the company's open source endeavors, eliminating the need to sift through multiple channels.

External Website

While an internal-facing website is targeted at employees within the company, an external-facing website that raises awareness about the enterprise's open source engagement is equally relevant. This website shares the open source projects created by the organization highlighting their benefits and features to attract users, contributors, and collaborators. This comprehensive information is designed to attract a diverse audience, including potential users who can benefit from the software, skilled contributors eager to improve and expand the projects, and collaborators who see the value in partnering for mutual growth.

The website also highlights the open source projects that are created by others and where developers of the organization contribute. This allows the organization to demonstrate its wide range of developers' expertise and engagement in the broader open source community. This can enhance the organization's reputation as a leader in open source development and innovation. Highlighting project maintainers and key employees in leadership roles provides a human touch to the company's involvement. Developers who contribute to well-known projects may receive individual recognition for their work, further boosting their professional profiles and credibility. Demonstrating active participation in open source projects reinforces the organization's commitment to supporting the broader developer community. This engagement can foster goodwill and support from the community, potentially leading to increased contributions, feedback, and adoption of the organization's own open source initiatives.

The website is an ideal candidate for deeply technical content to demonstrate the depth of the company's open source engineering expertise. By publishing in-depth technical blogs, the organization can demonstrate its knowledge and skills in specific areas of open source development. This not only positions the company as a thought leader but also instills confidence in users and contributors about the quality and reliability of its projects. By offering a variety of content formats – such as written blogs, video tutorials, and podcasts – the website can cater to diverse learning preferences within the community. This inclusivity encourages broader engagement and participation. Regularly posting news and updates about the organization's projects keeps the community informed about the latest developments, upcoming releases, and significant milestones. This transparency fosters trust and engagement among users and contributors.

Any participation in an open source event should be highlighted on this website. This would typically involve creating a page dedicated to an event. A dedicated event page provides detailed information about the organization's presence, including booth location, schedule, and activities. This ensures that attendees can easily find and engage with the company during the event. Highlighting specific demos and code samples that will be showcased at the booth allows potential attendees to understand what they can expect and encourages them to visit. This can create excitement and anticipation around the organization's offerings. Listing talks given by the organization's developers emphasizes the expertise and thought leadership within the company. A dedicated event page serves as a valuable resource for post-event follow-up activities. It can be used to share highlights, key takeaways, and outcomes from the event, helping to maintain momentum and engagement with the community.

It is important to make sure that this external website is a top-level domain, such as open.intel.com, and is not hiding under some other domain. This is a clear signal to users that the organization is serious about its open source initiatives. It helps build trust among developers, contributors, and users who are more likely to engage with a reputable site. Using a recognizable domain tied to the organization's brand strengthens brand identity. It promotes awareness and makes it easier for users to associate the projects with the organization, reinforcing the brand's commitment to open source development. A dedicated top-level domain makes the website easier to find and remember. Users are more likely to visit a straightforward URL rather than a convoluted subdomain or hidden link, which can increase traffic and engagement.

During my time at Amazon, my team launched opensource.amazon. com. During my time at Apple, my team launched opensource.apple. com. Before my time at these companies, both companies have talked about their open source contributions in different open source events and through online blogs. Launching these websites provided a central focal point for sharing open source engagement at these companies. We had to craft a unified open source philosophy, navigate the company's internal processes to get the necessary approvals, and align the launch with strategic goals. Both of these were extremely joyful and fulfilling projects as it truly allows you to work across different parts of the company and establishes your team's thought leadership inside the company. opensource.amazon.com has continued to show progress over the years as their reliance on open source and contributions to the corresponding projects have only increased.

During my time at Intel, my team refreshed open.intel.com to showcase Intel's open source philosophy and highlight our extensive portfolio of projects. We launched a new podcast featuring discussions with leading Intel experts and open source community members, which was prominently linked on the website. Additionally, we published in-depth technical blogs, how-to guides, and tutorials from our developers, as well as contributions from external authors. We created dedicated landing pages for each major open source event where Intel was actively involved, and these pages featured our talks and demos from the events. A special section was also dedicated to profiling maintainers of open source projects from various developer communities.

When deciding on a home for a piece of content between an internal versus an external website, adopting an "external-first" approach is essential unless the content is specifically aimed at developers within the company. There are multiple benefits to this approach, such as a wider audience reach as the content is accessible to a larger audience, including potential users, contributors, and industry peers. This increased visibility can lead to greater interest in the organization's projects and initiatives. An external-first approach emphasizes transparency in the organization's operations and development processes. By sharing knowledge and practices openly, the organization builds trust and credibility with its audience. While the external-first approach is generally recommended, there are exceptions. If the content is exclusively targeted at developers inside the company, such as internal documentation, proprietary processes, or sensitive information, it is more appropriate to host it on an internal website. This ensures confidentiality, compliance, and focus on internal development needs without risking exposure to the public.

Interestingly, publishing content on the external repository often has a positive impact on fostering an open source culture within the company. When employees see their work showcased and utilized by the broader community, it reinforces the value of their contributions and encourages further participation. The external recognition and validation of their efforts foster a sense of pride and awareness among company employees, can boost morale, and motivate employees to engage more deeply with open source projects. Additionally, the feedback and collaboration from the external community can lead to new insights, improvements, and innovations that benefit both the organization and the open source community at large.

Integration with Employee Onboarding

The goal of new employee orientation, or onboarding, is to seamlessly integrate newcomers into the organization. This process serves various objectives, providing crucial information, fostering a positive atmosphere, and establishing the groundwork for a successful work experience. Incorporating the company's open source philosophy into onboarding ensures that employees understand the significance, relevance, and policies related to open source practices.

Here are some specific suggestions on what should be included in new employee orientation:

- Information on why and how the company uses open source and how it aligns with the overall mission and values.

- Existing policies regarding open source contributions, licensing, and usage.

- List of projects created by the organization and contributed to the community, and community projects that employees can contribute to.

- Process for employees to start contributing to a new project.

- Definition of success metrics for contributions. The criteria can differ widely across enterprises, but being explicit and transparent about it with your employees will help them to meet those objectives while serving the open source community.

- Policies regarding public speaking, leading working groups, and getting elected positions in the community.

- Guidance on how to engage with external communities, including communication norms and contribution etiquette.

- Different internal channels where open source is discussed inside the company and encourage employees to bring fresh perspective.

- Details around the mentorship program, if there is one.

- List of maintainers who work at the company, including prominent and visible open source influencers.

Consider publishing all of this to the central repository that was explained in the previous section. This cultivates institutional knowledge and makes it easy access to employees after the initial onboarding.

Cultivating Enthusiasm

As mentioned in the "Why companies may not contribute to open source?" section, there are multiple reasons for a resistance to cultural change to embrace open source principles. Addressing these sources of resistance involves effective communication, education, and demonstrating the tangible benefits of open source practices. Creating a supportive and inclusive environment that encourages learning and adaptation is key to overcoming resistance to open source culture.

Here are some effective strategies to cultivate enthusiasm:

- **Education and Training** – Provide comprehensive education and training on open source principles and practices. This helps dispel misconceptions, builds understanding, and equips individuals with the knowledge to actively participate.

- **Communicate Benefits Clearly** – Clearly articulate the benefits of open source, such as increased innovation, collaboration, cost-effectiveness, and community engagement. Show how open source aligns with organizational goals and values. This message should be repeated in company-wide meetings, newsletters by executives, and in direct 1-1s.

- **Address Security Concerns** – Address security concerns by highlighting the robust security measures, audits, and practices within reputable open source projects. Emphasize that the transparency of open source development often leads to faster identification and resolution of security issues.

- **Demonstrate Success Stories** – Share success stories and case studies of organizations that have successfully embraced open source culture. Highlight the positive outcomes, improvements in productivity, and innovative solutions achieved through open source collaboration.

- **Encourage Small Wins** – Start with small, manageable open source initiatives that allow individuals to experience success. These small wins build confidence and enthusiasm for larger, more ambitious open source contributions.

- **Provide Support and Resources** – Offer the necessary support, resources, and tools for individuals to engage with open source projects effectively. This includes training, documentation, and access to collaborative platforms.

- **Lead by Example** – Leadership support is crucial. Leaders should actively participate in and endorse open source initiatives. Their engagement sends a powerful message and sets a positive example for the rest of the organization.

- **Create a Collaborative Environment** – Foster a collaborative and inclusive work environment. Encourage teamwork, knowledge sharing, and open communication. Make it clear that open source values align with the organization's culture.

- **Recognize and Reward Contributions** – Establish a recognition and reward system for individuals who actively contribute to open source projects. Publicly acknowledge their efforts, celebrate achievements, and make it clear that open source contributions are valued.

- **Seek Feedback and Address Concerns** – Create channels for feedback and address concerns proactively. Encourage open communication and listen to the concerns of team members. Addressing issues promptly builds trust and demonstrates a commitment to the well-being of the team.

- **Offer Continuous Learning Opportunities** – Provide ongoing learning opportunities related to open source technologies and best practices. This helps individuals stay current, build expertise, and foster a culture of continuous improvement.

- **Promote a Culture of Experimentation** – Encourage a culture where experimentation is valued. Allow individuals to explore open source projects that align with their interests and expertise. This freedom to explore fosters a sense of autonomy and enthusiasm.

- **Create Community-Building Initiatives** – Facilitate community-building initiatives both internally and externally. Encourage employees to engage with open source communities, attend events, and contribute to discussions. This helps individuals feel connected to a larger community.

- **Measure and Showcase Impact** – Establish metrics to measure the impact of open source contributions on the organization. Showcase positive outcomes, whether they be improvements in software quality, faster development cycles, or cost savings.

Removing friction and streamlining processes for open source contributions, whether it's code, speaking, or leading a working group, will go a long way toward cultivating enthusiasm. By combining these strategies, organizations can gradually overcome resistance and create an environment where enthusiasm for open source culture becomes ingrained in the company's DNA. It's an ongoing process that requires commitment, communication, and a genuine effort to foster a culture of collaboration and innovation.

Incentive Mechanisms

To reinforce a culture of employee enablement, organizations should implement recognition and reward mechanisms for open source contributions. Acknowledging the efforts of employees who actively engage in open source projects fosters a sense of accomplishment and reinforces the organization's commitment to recognizing the value of such contributions. This recognition can take various forms, including internal awards, public acknowledgments, mentoring from senior leaders, exclusive lunch or coffee chat with senior executives, custom swag, and career development opportunities.

Create incentive mechanisms for employees to contribute to open source. Make this part of their annual focal targets and reward them for the behavior. Give them time to perform these activities in the open source. Sometimes, it may not directly correlate to your direct team goals, but it certainly helps with boosting employee morale. This helps with the overall employee retention too. Ensure the work-related assignments do not consume their entire time and create space for them to be able to contribute to open source effectively. Note that coding is only one part of contribution. Sustainable open source requires a wide range of contributions, such as leading working groups, writing up technical docs, reviewing conference talks, and running meetups.

Check in with employees to identify the friction points and work to streamline the process so that they are encouraged to participate. Establish regular feedback mechanisms, such as surveys, focus groups, and one-on-one meetings, to identify friction points like technical challenges, process barriers, cultural resistance, and time constraints. Streamlining processes can involve simplifying onboarding, improving tooling, optimizing workflows, providing clear guidelines, and allowing flexible time allocation for contributions. Ongoing support through mentorship, training, celebrating wins, and creating a safe environment encourages participation. Regular reviews, pilot programs, and leadership involvement are crucial for continuously refining and supporting open source initiatives.

Summary

This chapter explained how employees at different levels of the companies need to be enabled to foster open source culture. It provided specific training programs that can educate employees at the worker level as well as within the management. The relevance of a consistent language and creating an internal and external website are explained next. Finally, suggestions on incorporating the company's open source philosophy into employee onboarding, how to create a supportive and inclusive environment by cultivating enthusiasm, and creating incentive mechanisms to reinforce the culture are explained.

The next chapter provides concrete steps on how to get started on your open source journey. It provides concrete examples from my open source journey through multiple enterprises. The need to overcome a legacy mindset and build a collective strategy that gathers allies at all levels of the company is explained. A large part of the chapter is dedicated towards defining a framework to initiate a cultural change that favors open source philosophy within your enterprise.

CHAPTER 8

Getting Started on Your Culture Change Journey

You've read most of this book and found the techniques useful, pragmatic, and relevant. Some of them have been implemented in your enterprise and yet feel like not tapping the full power of open source. The stories from different enterprises inspire you to do more. Excited? Ready to be the fire starter to bring that cultural change into your organization?

By the end of this chapter, you'll have a comprehensive roadmap for navigating your open source journey, equipped with the knowledge and tools to make a meaningful impact in the open source ecosystem. Whether you're looking to contribute to existing projects, start your own, or integrate open source practices into your organization, this chapter will provide the insights and strategies you need to succeed.

This is going to be an exciting and a rewarding journey. It's going to be marked with challenges, but taking a mindful approach will allow you to solve one challenge at a time. The collaborative spirit of open source encourages creativity, resilience, and shared success, making the journey not just about achieving goals but also about contributing to a larger mission and experiencing the profound satisfaction of working together to create something meaningful.

My Open Source Journey

My last two decades have been about fostering open source culture and building developer communities. A large part of this journey has been during my full-time job where I was directly part of the team that was driving the change, started the entire team, or worked closely with the team driving the change. For example, my time at Sun Microsystems required me to build the developer community around Java EE and GlassFish. At Amazon, I was on loan to different service teams in helping craft their open source strategy. For example, I helped launch Amazon Elastic Kubernetes Service, Amazon Corretto, Firecracker, and OpenDistro (now called OpenSearch). At Apple, I started the Open Source Program Office. At Intel, I lead the team that is responsible for the overall open source strategy and execution across the company.

My first journey in open source was over two decades ago when GlassFish was converted from a closed source version application server to an open source one. We were very transparent and yet pragmatic in the team. It was made clear to the open source community that Sun was in charge of the project. The release cadence was documented on the website, and each subproject had some autonomy; in some the decisions were more collective, in some it was less. The weekly builds, the milestone builds, the release trains, and the support releases were all very clearly explained, including how features would show up in the free, public, and commercial releases. This helped clearly explain Sun's business case and get buy-in from the community. Open Source was a tool, and it was 100% synergistic with open communication. The blogging efforts, led by Tim Bray and Eduardo Pelegri-Llopart, were key to the success of GlassFish. I did my share of writing hundreds of blogs during that time as well. This could not have happened if the artifacts being discussed were not open source. Being open source also made it much easier to highlight the wins.

Publishing GlassFish's source code outside the firewall was an extensive effort as it required cleaning up the existing code, adding appropriate license headers, and removing any internal dependencies. However, that was only a part of the challenge. We had to bring a cultural change throughout the team that favors transparency and collaboration with the open source community outside the company. The date, time, and online location for the engineering meeting were shared on a public calendar so that others could attend. Any water cooler discussion that impacts the design of GlassFish was shared in a public email so that others can understand why that decision was made. The comments in the code were made more verbose so that others can understand the flow better. This created an inclusive culture for people from outside the company and enabled them to not only participate but take ownership of some of the modules.

Twenty percent of each employee's time was allocated to answering questions in the public forum and helping developers onboard. This was incentivized and rewarded in internal forums, emails, and annual focal reviews. The GlassFish team was given a Sun Presidential Award to grow the downloads from 0 to 5 million within three years. A large part of this was only possible because of the open source nature of GlassFish, and the culture that allowed collaboration across a wide range of communities. This award further excited the internal developer community about participating in this effort. In addition to GlassFish, during that time, several other open source efforts were happening at Sun. For example, OpenOffice, OpenSolaris, NetBeans, OpenJDK, and MySQL. There were common lessons learned and applied across these projects.

At Amazon, I was part of the open source marketing team. At that time, OSPO was mostly inward-facing to ensure compliance and building tools for streamlined consumption and contribution to open source by Amazon employees. There were several of us in the open source marketing team, and we were mostly outward-facing. We launched opensource.amazon.

com, describing Amazon's open source philosophy. This became a central point for everybody outside the company to learn about Amazon's participation. As the website became more popular, we started getting requests from the internal service teams to highlight their content on the website. We sponsored popular open source conferences and gave talks all around the world to explain how Amazon uses open source and contributes back to it.

The team launched a blog that published deeply technical articles on open source technologies used by Amazon customers. Amazon launched Elastic Kubernetes Service (EKS) the year I joined. Even before that, Amazon customers were running Kubernetes clusters on Amazon EC2 on a very large scale. It became apparent that Amazon should join the Cloud Native Computing Foundation to ensure sustainability of the cloud native projects. I wrote the six-pager for Amazon to join the foundation, ran it through the ranks to get approval, and have been on the Governing Board since then. We had to manage the optics of Amazon launching yet another managed service on an open source project. I still vividly remember reviewing the Amazon EKS six-pager and ensuring the tenets to keep us upstream compliant. The interesting part was, of course, how to bring that cultural change within the team. I clearly remember an incident where we talked about working through the social fabric of the open source community before filing a controversial change. These are all parts of bringing a cultural change in an enterprise.

Before my time at Apple, there were policies for Apple to consume and contribute to open source. This was mostly done by employees in their spare time, though. I was hired to create Apple's first Open Source Program Office and build the team to help execute the mission. We had extensive listening sessions from open source developers, middle management, and senior executives. This helps us understand why the current policies are defined the way they are, friction points in the system, and the impetus to change. We had regular meetings with different stakeholders and defined the gives and the gets. Delivering initial results for them allowed us to build a trustworthy relationship. This allowed us to set the basis for streamlining open source processes.

The team ran the first internal Kubernetes conference that gathered over 1,000 attendees across the company. The entire effort was very well recognized throughout the company and improved employee morale to talk about open source efforts happening inside their teams. The organizing team was recognized in internal emails and was invited for an exclusive lunch with the sponsoring executive. We started InnerSource practice inside the company that allowed us to improve the discovery of overlapping efforts and minimize them. We even ran an InnerSource Summit to educate employees and further break down silos across the company. A simpler process for Apple engineers to speak at open source conferences was defined as well. A public website at opensource.apple.com was launched to highlight Apple's open source philosophy and code releases.

Intel has been a prolific contributor to open source over the last two decades. I was hired to be the leadership voice for open source at Intel, both internally and externally. Hiring an executive to build a presence in the open source community was a clear message to internal employees and external developer community about the relevance of open source to Intel. It allowed me to connect with other executives in different business units, understand their goals, and define and refine existing processes for faster innovation and efficient delivery. A monthly forum was set up where executives from different business units shared their open source strategy, enabling a better understanding and the creation of a cohesive story across the company. A regular forum for open source developers allowed them to ask questions, raise concerns, and discuss the constantly evolving open source landscape.

The existing OSPO team was included as part of my team's charter. This ensured the governance, education, and advocacy of visibility of all inbound and outbound open source projects at the company to continue. An internal summit with over 2,500 attendees across the company provided a forum for employees to share their open source efforts and allowed further collaboration on similar efforts. We organized a hackathon around Intel's open source projects that allowed us to grow the internal open source skill sets. Mentors were assigned to developers new to the open source world. This allowed them to understand the tools and processes prevalent in the open source.

Intel employs hundreds of maintainers across 300+ open source projects as full-time employees. These maintainers are recognized by sharing their journey on open.intel.com. Acknowledging the personal journeys of maintainers humanizes the work, reminding the community that real people are behind these projects. These personal stories also inspire others to contribute to open source. When maintainers feel appreciated and seen, they are more likely to stay engaged and contribute over the long term.

The team sponsored multiple open source events and set up a streamlined process to get travel approvals of speakers and demo booth staff for the event. The team also managed and coordinated our presence in multiple open source foundations. We encouraged several folks from Intel to take leadership roles in these foundations. I personally talked to several managers to ensure continued support and encouragement of their team's role even when their work in the community is not adding to the corporate bottom line but required for sustainability of the foundation. You can also read about the Open Ecosystem Pledge in the Intel case study in Chapter 2.

Overcoming Legacy Mindsets

Bringing about cultural change in a company is always a complex and challenging endeavor, especially when the organization has a long history of success following a certain way of doing things. This challenge is amplified in the context of promoting an open source culture within an enterprise that has traditionally used open source software without contributing back significantly.

Cultural inertia is a formidable obstacle. In companies that have been successful for years, there is often a deeply ingrained belief that the current practices are the right or only way to do things. If a company has prospered without actively participating in the open source community, there can be a perception that this approach is sufficient, or even superior, to engaging more openly. This mindset creates resistance to change, as people may fear that adopting an open source culture could disrupt the established order or introduce unnecessary risks.

However, relying solely on past success can be shortsighted. The technology landscape is constantly evolving, and what worked well in the past may not be sufficient to sustain growth and innovation in the future. The global shift towards open collaboration, rapid innovation cycles, and community-driven development means that companies that remain insular risk falling behind. Encouraging a culture of contributing back to open source is not just about altruism; it's about staying competitive, attracting top talent, and ensuring long-term viability in a rapidly changing environment.

The transition to an open source culture requires a shift in mindset, from viewing open source as merely a tool to seeing it as a community where mutual benefit is the key to sustained success. This means moving from a consumption-oriented approach to a contribution-focused mindset. It involves recognizing that contributing to open source is not just a charitable act but a strategic investment in the company's future. When a company actively contributes, it gains influence in the direction of the projects it relies on, improves its internal development practices, and builds a reputation that can attract top-tier talent who value open collaboration.

Fostering an open source culture in such a company means helping it recognize that its long-term success depends not just on what it can take from the open source community but on what it can give back. This reciprocity is the foundation of sustainable innovation and is what will allow the company to continue thriving in an increasingly interconnected world.

Collective Success Strategy

As a runner, the African proverb " If you want to go fast, go alone. If you want to go far, go together" resonates deeply with your approach to fostering an open source culture within an enterprise. This proverb underscores the importance of collective effort and shared vision in achieving meaningful, long-term success – something particularly vital when trying to drive cultural change in a complex organizational environment.

Fostering open source culture is akin to running a marathon, not a sprint. The goal is not just to implement quick fixes but to build a sustainable, collaborative environment where innovation can thrive over time. To do this, you can't do it alone; you need to gather allies at all levels of the company who believe in your mission. These are the people who will help you spread the open source mindset, advocate for shared goals, and drive the collective effort needed to bring about real change.

Gathering folks at different levels of the company is crucial because culture change requires buy-in from a broad cross-section of the organization. Senior leaders can provide the necessary support and resources, middle managers can help align the open source initiatives with business goals, and individual contributors can bring the technical expertise and passion to make it happen. By bringing these diverse voices together, you create a coalition that's capable of navigating the challenges and resistance that often accompany cultural shifts.

This collective approach mirrors the dynamics of a successful long-distance running team. While each runner has their strengths and paces, the team's overall success depends on how well they work together, supporting each other through the ups and downs of the race. Similarly, in an enterprise setting, fostering an open source culture requires a united effort, where each person's contributions are valued, and the focus is on long-term progress rather than short-term wins.

In this way, your belief in the proverb informs your strategy as a change agent. It's not just about moving quickly on your own; it's about bringing others along on the journey, ensuring that the cultural shift towards open source is deep-rooted, widespread, and capable of enduring over the long haul. By going together, you ensure that the enterprise not only adopts open source principles but also integrates them into its very fabric, enabling the organization to go far in its innovation journey.

It's unequivocal that while individual efforts can lead to quick, isolated successes, the true power of open source lies in the collective effort. By working together, sharing knowledge, and building on each other's contributions, the enterprise can achieve greater, long-lasting success. This collaborative approach ensures that the solutions developed are not only innovative but also resilient and scalable, ultimately taking the enterprise farther in its goals.

Culture Change Framework

This section provides a framework to initiate a cultural change that favors open source philosophy within your enterprise. Some of these steps may have already been implemented at your work, but reviewing them holistically can help ensure a cohesive and comprehensive approach.

Find an Executive Sponsor

The role of an executive sponsor in fostering an open source culture within an enterprise is crucial. This person is a senior leader in the enterprise, preferably in the executive ranks, who ensures that the move towards an open source culture is strategically aligned, well-resourced, and effectively integrated into the organization. The sponsor articulates a clear and compelling vision for why adopting an open source culture is essential for the company's future. This vision helps align the open source initiatives with the company's broader strategic goals. They ensure that the open source strategy is not seen as a side project but as an integral part of the company's core mission. This alignment is critical for gaining buy-in across the organization.

An executive sponsor has the authority to allocate necessary resources – such as budget, personnel, and tools – to support open source initiatives. This might include funding for internal open source projects, participation in external communities, or training programs. They can facilitate the creation of cross-functional teams, providing the time and space for employees to contribute to and engage with open source communities without compromising their other responsibilities.

The executive sponsor champions the open source cause and acts as the primary advocate for open source culture at the highest levels of the organization. Their endorsement helps overcome resistance and skepticism, particularly in companies with established, traditional practices. By publicly supporting open source initiatives, the executive sponsor can inspire and motivate others within the organization to get involved, thereby building momentum for the cultural shift.

As a leader, the executive sponsor models the behaviors and values associated with open source culture, such as transparency, collaboration, and a willingness to share and learn from others. This sets the tone for the entire organization. They play a key role in addressing cultural and operational challenges that may arise during the transition, ensuring that the shift towards open source is smooth and sustainable.

The executive sponsor can help identify and mitigate risks associated with open source adoption, such as legal concerns, intellectual property issues, and potential security vulnerabilities. They work with legal and compliance teams to establish clear guidelines and policies. They ensure that while the organization embraces the innovative potential of open source, it also maintains necessary controls to protect its assets and intellectual property.

The executive sponsor helps ensure that the open source culture is not just a short-term initiative but a long-term, sustainable strategy that becomes embedded in the company's DNA. They may also play a role in building and maintaining relationships with key players in the open source community, ensuring that the company is seen as a valued and responsible participant in the broader ecosystem.

Identify Stakeholders

Identifying stakeholders is a critical first step in fostering an open source culture within an enterprise. By pinpointing the teams that are already using open source software, and understanding their experiences and challenges, you can gain valuable insights into the current state of open source engagement within the organization.

Begin by identifying the teams within the organization that are actively using open source software. These could include development teams, IT operations, data science groups, and others who rely on open source tools for their daily work. Understanding which teams are most engaged with open source helps you focus your efforts on those who are already invested in the ecosystem. Once these teams are identified, it's important to map out the roles and responsibilities of the key players within these teams. Who are the developers, maintainers, or project leads? What are their specific responsibilities in relation to the open source software they use? This mapping helps you understand the different perspectives and challenges each role might face.

Engage with the identified teams to understand how they are using open source software. What tools and platforms are they relying on? How integral are these tools to their workflow? This assessment helps in identifying how dependent the organization is on open source solutions and where improvements could be made. Investigate the friction points these teams encounter when consuming open source software. Are there difficulties in finding the right tools or ensuring compatibility with existing systems? Is there a lack of documentation or support for certain open source projects? Understanding these barriers helps in identifying areas where the organization could provide better support or resources.

Explore contribution challenges by finding whether these teams have the opportunity to contribute back to the open source projects they use. Are they developing patches, fixes, or new features that could benefit the broader community? If so, how often do they make these contributions, and what impact do they have? It's equally important to identify the challenges teams face when trying to contribute. Are there internal policies or processes that make it difficult to contribute? For example, do they need to go through multiple layers of approval before contributing, or are there concerns about intellectual property or legal issues? Understanding these barriers is crucial for making the contribution process smoother and more accessible.

Evaluate the contribution process by assessing how easy or cumbersome the overall process is for contributing to open source projects. Are the tools and workflows user-friendly, or do they require significant time and effort? Is there a clear understanding of the steps involved, from identifying an issue to submitting a patch? Evaluate whether teams have the necessary support and resources to contribute effectively. Do they have access to the right tools, training, and mentorship? Are there internal champions or experts who can guide them through the process? If not, what gaps need to be filled to make contributing easier and more rewarding?

Gather and analyze feedback by engaging with the teams through surveys, interviews, or listening sessions to gather detailed feedback on their experiences with both consuming and contributing to open source projects. This feedback should focus on what's working well, what's not, and what improvements they would like to see. Analyze the feedback to identify common trends or patterns across different teams. Are certain issues consistently mentioned? Are there particular open source projects or areas where friction is highest? This analysis helps prioritize areas for improvement and guides the development of targeted strategies to enhance the open source culture within the organization. More details on listening sessions are available in the next section.

Based on the insights gathered, develop actionable solutions to address the identified friction points. This could involve simplifying internal contribution processes, providing better training and resources, or improving communication and collaboration between teams. Finally, create a roadmap that outlines the steps needed to enhance both the consumption and contribution of open source software within the organization. This roadmap should include clear milestones, timelines, and responsibilities, ensuring that progress is tracked and momentum is maintained.

Collaborative Listening Sessions

Organize listening sessions with developers, middle management, and senior executives as it serves several important purposes when fostering an open source culture or driving any significant cultural or organizational change within an enterprise.

Listening sessions provide an opportunity to hear directly from different levels of the organization, ensuring that the unique needs, concerns, and ideas of developers, middle management, and senior executives are understood. This helps in identifying pain points, potential barriers, and areas of resistance that may not be apparent from a top-down perspective. Each group – developers, middle managers, and senior executives – has a different view of the company's operations and culture. Developers may highlight technical challenges and opportunities, middle managers may focus on process and resource allocation issues, and senior executives may provide strategic insights. Collecting these perspectives is crucial for developing a holistic approach to cultural change.

These sessions create a space for open and honest communication where employees feel heard and valued. This can build trust and demonstrate that leadership is genuinely interested in their input, leading to greater engagement and willingness to participate in the change process. When employees at all levels are given a voice in the process, they feel more ownership of the change. This empowerment can lead to higher levels of commitment and motivation to support and drive the cultural shift.

Listening sessions help in aligning the goals and expectations of different levels of the organization. For example, developers might be focused on the practical aspects of open source contributions, while senior executives might be more concerned with strategic outcomes. Bringing these perspectives together ensures that everyone is on the same page and that the initiative is tailored to meet the needs of all stakeholders. These sessions also provide an opportunity to address any misconceptions or misunderstandings about the open source initiative. This can help prevent misalignment and ensure that everyone understands the benefits and challenges associated with the cultural shift.

During listening sessions, you can identify individuals who are passionate about open source and who can act as champions or leaders for the initiative. These advocates can help spread the message, influence their peers, and drive the cultural change from within their respective groups. Middle managers and senior executives who show strong support for the initiative can be key allies in pushing the agenda forward. Recognizing and engaging these leaders early on can help in securing the necessary buy-in and resources.

The insights gained from listening sessions can inform the strategy and implementation of the open source initiative. For example, if developers express concerns about time constraints, the strategy might include dedicated time for open source contributions. If middle managers highlight resource issues, the initiative might include specific resource allocations. These sessions allow for a more responsive and adaptive planning process. By continuously gathering feedback, the organization can adjust its approach as needed to ensure the initiative remains relevant and effective.

Listening sessions embody the principles of collaboration and inclusivity that are central to an open source culture. By involving employees at all levels in the conversation, the organization reinforces the values of openness, transparency, and collective effort. These sessions can be part of an ongoing feedback loop where employees regularly share their experiences and ideas, ensuring that the open source culture evolves and improves over time.

Non-core Open Source Areas

When a company's primary product is not based on open source, it's still possible to identify and leverage areas within the organization where open source can thrive without conflicting with the core business. This approach allows the company to benefit from the advantages of open source, such as innovation, collaboration, and cost-efficiency, while maintaining focus on its main commercial objectives.

Identify non-core areas for the focus of open source. One of the best places to start is within the internal tools and infrastructure that support the company's operations but are not directly tied to the core product. This could include development environments, testing frameworks, deployment infrastructure, automation tools, and other internal systems where open source solutions might offer improvements in efficiency, flexibility, and innovation. Another area to explore is non-customer-facing applications, such as internal dashboards, data analytics platforms, or employee communication tools. These systems often benefit from the rapid development and community support that open source provides without affecting the company's main revenue streams. Open source can also play a significant role in the company's R&D efforts. By contributing to and leveraging open source projects, the company can experiment with new technologies and methodologies in a cost-effective manner, accelerating innovation while reducing risk.

Many industries have common challenges that are not tied to competitive advantage, such as compliance with regulations, cybersecurity, or environmental sustainability. In these areas, collaborating on open source solutions can help the company address shared challenges without compromising its competitive position. Open source is often used to create industry standards and improve interoperability between different systems. By participating in or contributing to open source projects in these areas, the company can help shape the standards that may benefit its core business while ensuring that its proprietary solutions remain distinct.

The company can explore open source opportunities in technologies that complement its primary product. For example, if the company's core product is a proprietary software application, it might contribute to or utilize open source libraries, APIs, or tools that enhance the functionality of that software. This approach allows the company to leverage the strengths of open source without diluting its proprietary offering. Engaging with open source communities in complementary domains can also be beneficial. By participating in these communities, the company can gain insights, influence the direction of key projects, and build relationships with developers and experts who may contribute to the company's innovation efforts.

It's important to clearly delineate between open source initiatives and the company's core intellectual property (IP). By defining what remains proprietary and what can be open sourced, the company can protect its primary business interests while still benefiting from open source contributions in other areas. The company can choose to contribute selectively to open source projects that align with its strategic goals.

For instance, contributing to a project that improves a complementary technology can enhance the value of the company's core product, while still maintaining control over the key IP that drives revenue.

By finding pockets within the organization where open source is the norm, the company can promote a culture of experimentation and innovation. Employees who are encouraged to explore and contribute to open source projects can bring new ideas and approaches back to the company, fostering continuous improvement. Involvement in open source projects can also be a valuable learning experience for employees, helping them develop new skills and stay current with industry trends. This, in turn, can benefit the company by ensuring that its workforce is knowledgeable and adaptable.

Open source initiatives can serve as a bridge to collaborate with external partners, such as other companies, academic institutions, or non-profits. By participating in open source projects together, the company can strengthen these relationships, gain access to new ideas, and explore potential synergies. Finally, even in areas where open source is not the basis of the company's primary product, contributing to the open source community can enhance the company's reputation as a leader in innovation and collaboration. This can be particularly valuable for attracting top talent and building trust with customers and partners.

Open Source Working Group

Setting up a cross-functional working group that meets on a regular cadence is a crucial step in driving the adoption and integration of open source culture within an enterprise. This working group should be composed of representatives from various departments and levels within the organization, including engineering, legal, IT, product management, marketing, and senior leadership.

The primary purpose of the cross-functional working group is to facilitate collaborative decision-making regarding open source initiatives. By bringing together diverse perspectives, the group can address the multifaceted challenges of open source adoption and ensure that decisions are well-rounded and aligned with the company's strategic goals. The working group should ensure that open source activities align with the broader business objectives of the company. This includes identifying opportunities where open source can enhance product offerings, improve internal processes, or contribute to industry standards without compromising the company's core business interests.

The group should include members from different departments and levels within the organization. Developers can provide insights into technical challenges and opportunities, legal teams can address compliance and intellectual property concerns, IT can assess infrastructure needs, and managers can align open source efforts with customer needs and market trends. Having senior leadership representation in the working group is crucial for ensuring that the initiatives have the necessary support and resources. Leaders can also help in removing roadblocks and championing the open source cause across the organization.

Establish a regular meeting schedule (e.g., biweekly or monthly) to maintain momentum and ensure accountability. Regular meetings allow the group to stay on top of ongoing projects, address emerging challenges, and make timely decisions. Each meeting should have a well-defined agenda that reflects the current priorities and challenges. The agenda might include progress updates, discussion of new proposals, risk assessments, and resource allocation. Flexibility in the agenda allows the group to adapt to changing circumstances and focus on the most pressing issues.

Clearly define the roles and responsibilities of each member within the group. For example, developers might be responsible for identifying technical hurdles, while legal advisors might focus on ensuring compliance with open source licenses. Assign specific tasks or projects to individuals or sub-groups within the working group. This fosters ownership and accountability, ensuring that action items are followed through and progress is made between meetings. Form smaller sub-groups within this working group to tackle specific issues or projects. For example, a sub-group might focus on developing open source contribution guidelines, while another might work on internal training programs.

The working group should serve as a central hub for communication regarding open source initiatives within the organization. This includes sharing updates, decisions, and progress with the broader company to keep everyone informed and engaged. Regularly report the group's findings, decisions, and progress to the executive team or other key stakeholders. This helps in securing ongoing support and resources, as well as aligning the group's efforts with the company's strategic direction.

Consider creating a sub-group and naming them Open Source Advocates. This group, made up of passionate advocates and a proven track record of involvement in open source projects or communities, will act as change agents by promoting the benefits of open source. They will drive the cultural shift towards open source by addressing varied concerns and challenges. Their enthusiasm will be crucial in driving the cultural shift. Regularly highlight their successes and milestones, share these achievements with the broader organization, and gather testimonials to showcase the benefits of open source. Encourage members to act as ambassadors, promote open source, and demonstrate commitment through active participation and advocacy.

Establish a mechanism for gathering feedback from the broader organization on the group's initiatives and decisions. This feedback loop allows the group to continuously improve its approach, ensuring that the open source strategy remains relevant and effective. As the company's open source culture matures, the working group should periodically reassess its goals and objectives. This ensures that the group remains focused on the most impactful initiatives and can pivot as needed to address new challenges or opportunities.

Develop Contribution Guidelines

Creating clear guidelines for contributing to open source projects is essential for ensuring that contributions are managed effectively and align with the company's objectives and values. By establishing comprehensive and clear guidelines for contributing to open source projects, companies can ensure that contributions are legally compliant, ethically sound, and strategically aligned with their objectives. This structured approach not only encourages active participation but also fosters a positive and productive open source culture within the organization. The definition of the policy and documentation at a well-known place are both equally important.

Ensure that the guidelines align with the company's strategic goals and values. Contributions should support the company's mission and enhance its reputation in the open source community. Determine which open source projects or areas are relevant for the company. Define the types of contributions that are encouraged, such as code, documentation, or bug reports.

Clearly outline the licensing requirements for contributing to open source projects. Ensure that all contributions comply with open source licenses and that legal teams review licenses for compatibility. Establish procedures for protecting the company's intellectual property. Specify how to handle proprietary code, confidential information, and IP rights when contributing to external projects. Implement contribution agreements or Contributor License Agreements (CLAs) to formalize the terms under which contributions are made. These agreements should cover ownership rights and the scope of use for contributed code.

Develop a code of conduct that outlines ethical standards for contributions. If the project where the code is submitted has a code of conduct, then make sure to follow that. This should include respect for community norms, professional behavior, and adherence to the project's guidelines. Ensure contributors are aware of potential conflicts of interest and provide guidance on avoiding situations where personal or professional interests may impact their contributions. Encourage transparency in the contribution process. Document and share the rationale for contributions to ensure accountability and maintain trust within the open source community.

Define a clear and streamlined process for making contributions. This should include steps for preparing, reviewing, and submitting contributions, as well as handling feedback and revisions. Optionally, consider implementing an internal review process where contributions are assessed for quality, relevance, and compliance before being submitted to external projects.

Make the contribution process as straightforward as possible to encourage participation. Reduce bureaucratic hurdles and provide clear instructions to facilitate easy and efficient contributions. Offer support to employees who want to contribute. Provide channels for asking questions, seeking advice, and receiving feedback on their contributions. Recognize and celebrate successful contributions both internally and externally. Highlight contributors' achievements in company communications and provide incentives for active participation. Build a culture that values open source contributions. Encourage teams to collaborate on open source projects and integrate contributions into performance evaluations or professional development opportunities.

Offer training sessions or resources to educate employees about the contribution process, legal considerations, and ethical guidelines. Ensure they understand the importance of compliance and best practices. Develop comprehensive documentation or a contribution handbook that outlines the guidelines, procedures, and resources available to contributors.

Define Public Speaking Policy

Maintainers and other leaders in open source projects are frequently sought after as speakers at developer conferences due to their expertise and deep involvement in the open source community. Their experience and insights make them valuable contributors to discussions on emerging technologies, best practices, and the future direction of open source. As influential voices in the field, they are often invited to share their knowledge, showcase innovations, and engage with other developers and industry professionals, further advancing the impact of open source in the tech community.

Having open source developers speak at conferences with their name associated with their company is crucial for enhancing the company's visibility and reputation in the open source community. It highlights the company's commitment to open source, attracts top talent, and builds credibility and trust with potential customers and partners. Such talks showcase the company's contributions and innovations, foster valuable networking and collaboration opportunities, and allow the company to promote its values and culture. Moreover, it enables developers to influence industry trends and guide the direction of open source projects, reinforcing the company's position as a key player in the field.

Defining a clear policy around public speaking involves creating a structured framework that governs how employees represent the company in external communications, such as conferences, webinars, media interviews, and other public speaking opportunities. This policy ensures that employees' external engagements align with the company's values, messaging, and strategic goals.

Specify who the policy applies to – whether it's all employees, specific departments, or designated spokespersons. Differentiate between internal speaking opportunities (e.g., company meetings, internal webinars) and external engagements (e.g., industry conferences, public panels). Include traditional media (e.g., interviews, press releases) and digital media (e.g., blogs, podcasts).

Establish a process for employees to request approval for speaking engagements. This might include submitting a proposal or request form detailing the event, audience, topic, and purpose. Designate a committee or individual (e.g., PR team, communications department) responsible for reviewing and approving speaking opportunities to ensure alignment with company policies.

Set up a content review process that requires employees to submit their speaking content (e.g., slides, speech drafts) for review before every event to ensure accuracy, consistency, and appropriateness. Provide feedback and request revisions as needed to maintain message consistency and address any potential concerns. The entire process should be lightweight and simple with a predictable turnaround time. Once the talk has been approved, the employee should be allowed to give the same talk at other conferences without explicit approval.

Promote Education and Awareness

Educate employees about the benefits of open source and how it can contribute to the company's success. This can be done through training programs, workshops, or internal communication campaigns. Highlight success stories and case studies where open source has had a positive impact. Work with the human resources team to integrate open source training as part of employee onboarding.

With the ever-changing landscape of open source, the workforce needs to be constantly educated and trained on new technologies, methodologies, and processes. Coordinate with your internal training team to develop and implement a robust training program that keeps employees up-to-date with the latest advancements in open source. This program should include regular workshops, webinars, and hands-on sessions tailored to different skill levels and roles within the company.

Establishing an internal website dedicated to sharing information is crucial for fostering a cohesive open source culture within the organization. This website should serve as a centralized hub where employees can access and review essential resources and policies related to open source. It should include sections for publishing open source policies, which outline guidelines for contributions, compliance, and intellectual property considerations. Additionally, it should feature the public speaking approval process, providing clear instructions for employees seeking to represent the company at conferences or other events. The site should also list the tools and platforms that developers are required to use, ensuring consistency and efficiency in their workflows.

Furthermore, the internal website should support collaborative communication by hosting internal forums where employees can discuss open source topics, share insights, and seek advice. It should provide coordinates for upcoming meetings, workshops, and training sessions, facilitating easy access to important events and ensuring that all team members are informed and engaged. By centralizing these resources and communication channels, the website helps streamline processes, enhance transparency, and promote a well-informed and connected workforce. This approach ensures that everyone in the organization has the tools and information needed to contribute effectively to the open source initiatives.

Measure and Celebrate Success

Establishing metrics to measure the success of your open source initiatives is crucial for assessing their impact and ensuring continued progress. Begin by defining key performance indicators (KPIs) that align with your open source goals. Track contributions by monitoring the number of code submissions, bug fixes, feature enhancements, and overall participation from your team in open source projects. Measure participation rates by analyzing engagement levels in both internal and external open source activities, such as forums, collaboration spaces, and community events. Evaluate the impact on innovation and efficiency by assessing improvements in development speed, product quality, and operational efficiencies that can be attributed to open source contributions and practices.

While code contributions are a critical and visible aspect of open source engagement, they alone do not provide a comprehensive measure of your involvement or impact within the open source community. Open source engagement encompasses a broader range of activities and contributions that collectively reflect a company's commitment and influence in the field. Appendix B highlights ten non-code ways to contribute to open source.

The CNCF gives out an annual "Chop Wood Carry Water" award to multiple folks from the cloud native community. The people dedicate countless hours to open source projects in non-code ways. They include people who host meetups and podcasts, are steering committee members, and are chairs of the Special Interest Groups and Technical Advisory Groups. By publicly honoring individuals who contribute to open source in non-code capacities, the CNCF highlights the diverse ways in which people can make a significant impact. This recognition helps to elevate the value of non-code contributions, such as community building, advocacy, and leadership, which are crucial for the health and growth of open source projects. Setting up an internal program to honor employees that are participating in these roles enables a diverse group of employees to participate in open source efforts.

To maintain momentum and demonstrate the positive effects of the cultural shift, it's important to celebrate both significant achievements and incremental successes. Recognize and reward individual and team contributions to open source projects, and highlight milestones reached in internal communications and company meetings. Additionally, publish an annual report that details your open source efforts, providing both internal and external stakeholders with a comprehensive overview of your initiatives. This report should include a summary of new projects created by the company, notable contributions to community-managed projects, leadership roles within open source foundations, and a recap of talks and presentations delivered at various open source events. By showcasing these achievements, you not only celebrate successes but also reinforce the company's commitment to open source, fostering continued engagement and support for the cultural shift.

Celebrate successes, both big and small, to keep the momentum going and to demonstrate the positive impact of the cultural shift. Publish an annual internal and external report highlighting open source efforts in the company. This can include new projects created by the company, top maintainers to community-managed projects, any leadership roles in open source foundations, a summary of talks across different open source events.

Continuous Feedback Loop

Implement a continuous feedback loop to ensure that the open source culture evolves and adapts over time. Regularly gather input from employees, stakeholders, and the broader open source community to refine and improve your approach. Use Listening Sessions to gather feedback, address them in Open Source Working Group sessions, and Open Source Advocates for spreading the solutions far and wide within the enterprise.

Set up office hours so that employees across the company can seek solutions and guidance on open source initiatives. These office hours provide a dedicated time for employees to address their questions, concerns, or challenges related to open source projects and contributions. By offering regular, accessible sessions with knowledgeable experts or open source champions, employees can receive personalized support and advice tailored to their specific needs. This approach fosters an open and supportive environment, encouraging more participation and engagement in open source activities. It also helps to demystify open source processes, streamline problem-solving, and build a more informed and confident workforce that is better equipped to contribute effectively to open source projects and align with the company's open source goals.

Consider setting up an advisory council with open source luminaries to provide strategic guidance and expertise on your open source initiatives. This council, composed of respected figures from the open source community, can offer valuable insights into best practices, emerging trends, and potential challenges. Their involvement can help shape the company's open source strategy, ensuring that it aligns with industry standards and leverages the latest advancements. By drawing on their experience and network, the council can also facilitate valuable connections and partnerships, enhance the company's credibility within the open source community, and support the development of innovative solutions. This advisory council acts as a bridge between your organization and the broader open source ecosystem, guiding your efforts and amplifying the impact of your contributions.

Summary

This chapter provided concrete steps on how to get started on your open source journey. It provided concrete examples from my personal open source journey through multiple enterprises. It explains why a legacy mindset may be holding you back from truly tapping the potentially of open source. It talks about how to build a collective strategy that gathers allies at all levels of the company is explained. The crux of the chapter is a framework to initiate a cultural change that favors open source philosophy within your enterprise.

Be the fire starter and lead the way to foster open source culture change in your enterprise!

APPENDIX A

What Is Open Source Software?

Contributed by: Jessica Marz, Director, Open Source Program Office, Intel Corporation (Note: This is from an internal Intel training document, shared for reference only.)

Introduction

The term "Open Source" emerged in the late 1990s, encompassing a broad spectrum of ideas – from software licenses to development practices. The origin of this term is explained on the Wikipedia page at `https://en.wikipedia.org/wiki/Open_source`. Since then, open source has transitioned from a fringe movement to a mainstream, even dominant, force in the technology industry. This discussion delves into what defines open source software.

Open Source Software, Defined

The Open Source Initiativeholds the definition of open source. It provides a framework for what constitutes "open source" from a practical and legal standpoint. The Freedom Software Foundation defines free software through a set of principles known as the Four Freedoms. While there are philosophical differences between the terms "open source software" and "free software," open source software commonly refers to any software made available in source code form under a license that grants users the following rights:

1. The freedom to study, use, and modify the source code

2. The freedom to distribute modified or unmodified copies of the code without the requirement to pay fees or royalties

3. No restrictions on the rights to copy, modify, or distribute the code

4. No discrimination against any potential users or uses

While this may seem straightforward, the term "open source" is often misused. Simply releasing software in source code form does not make it open source; it must be released under a license that grants the above-mentioned unrestricted rights.

Making software available to the public for free does not make it open source unless it is also available in source code form and under an open source license. Similarly, providing only binary-form software under an open source license does not qualify as open source because users must have access to the source code to exercise their rights under the license.

To reiterate, open source software is software released in source code form under a license that grants all users rights to copy, modify, and redistribute it without any fees or royalties. But there's more to open source than just these basic criteria. The health, success, and maturity of an open source project are often evaluated based on its community engagement, open development practices, and governance.

The Importance of Community in Open Source

A successful open source project thrives on community involvement, which ranges from sharing and improving code to using transparent, inclusive methodologies that involve collaborative decision-making and shared responsibilities. The more diverse and engaged the contributor base, the more open and innovative the project becomes. Community engagement is crucial for fostering collaborative innovation.

What Is a "Community"?

The term "community" in the context of open source often refers to core groups of professional contributors, whose time is subsidized by their employers. Alongside these core contributors, well-run projects empower contributions from users and developers addressing specific issues or making one-time improvements. A healthy community is self-sustaining, capable of not only developing software but also managing related activities like maintenance, security updates, documentation, and marketing.

Degrees of Openness in Open Source Projects

The evolution of an open source project can be described in stages:

> **Stage 0: Opening Up the Code** – Making the code available in source form under an open source license is the bare minimum. Projects at this stage are open in name only, lacking real community engagement.

Stage 1: Welcoming Input – True openness starts with accepting contributions. Projects should actively encourage and consider contributions from the community to gain new perspectives.

Stage 2: Developing in the Open – Encouraging community engagement involves developing in public repositories and holding open discussions about the project's direction. This transparency builds trust and enables higher-quality contributions.

Stage 3: Open Decision-Making and Neutral Governance – Extending decision-making beyond the original creators through governance structures like steering committees or advisory boards ensures impartiality and attracts diverse contributions. Some projects may transfer governance to specialized foundations for greater neutrality.

Time to Say Goodbye

When an open source project reaches the end of its useful life, maintainers should communicate its wind-down early, allowing users to adjust. Projects with a broad base of contributors may find new maintainers, but if not, the best practice is to archive the code, making it clear that the project is no longer maintained while keeping the code accessible for future use.

Conclusion

Not every open source project follows this exact path, but the most successful ones typically welcome input, develop in the open, and operate under neutral governance. The more open a project, the broader its reach and influence. For organizations transitioning from proprietary approaches, embracing open source principles is crucial for credibility and innovation. While proprietary models remain relevant, strategically leveraging open source can drive industry standards, foster partnerships, and enhance technological ecosystems.

Ten Non-code Ways to Contribute to Open Source

Do you need to know coding in order to contribute to open source? While coding is integral to open source, the "open" part means you can contribute in diverse ways. Here are ten non-code ways you can contribute to open source.

Documentation

Documentation plays a crucial role in the success and sustainability of open source projects. First and foremost, it acts as a guiding light for new developers joining a project by providing comprehensive insights into its architecture, coding standards, and setup procedures. This onboarding process ensures that contributors, regardless of their experience level, can swiftly comprehend the project's intricacies and contribute effectively to its growth.

Moreover, documentation serves as a user-friendly reference for individuals engaging with the open source project. By offering clear and accessible guidance on functionalities, features, and usage, documentation empowers users to navigate the project independently, fostering a self-sufficient and informed user base. This allows the project to scale and serves the global audience. Beyond user adoption, well-documented processes establish consistency and clarity within the project, breaking down tribal knowledge and ensuring that vital information is shared across the community.

Continuous improvement of documentation is vital for its ongoing effectiveness. Regular updates and enhancements reflect a commitment to accuracy, relevance, and accessibility, aligning the documentation with the evolving needs of the project and its community. Documentation serves as a dynamic and collaborative resource that fuels the success, inclusivity, and knowledge-sharing ethos of open source endeavors. You can help by writing, updating, and improving documentation, making it more accessible and understandable for users and contributors.

Translation

The global accessibility of open source projects is a key advantage that can be maximized through translation efforts. Making software and documentation available in multiple languages broadens the reach of a project, breaking down language barriers and fostering inclusivity. Translations enable individuals from diverse linguistic backgrounds to comprehend and contribute to the project, irrespective of their native language. This can significantly increase the project's user base.

Participating in translation initiatives goes beyond mere linguistic considerations; it plays a crucial role in cultivating a more expansive and varied user base. By translating documentation, user interfaces, and error messages, you contribute to a more user-friendly and accessible experience for a wider audience. This inclusiveness aligns with the collaborative spirit of open source, emphasizing that the benefits of technology should be available to everyone, regardless of their language proficiency. Your involvement in translation efforts helps create a global community around the open source project, enriching its ecosystem with diverse perspectives and insights.

Testing

Testing the project is a critical phase and ensures it is working as expected – meeting both functional and non-functional requirements. The unique testing needs and environments of individuals contribute to the diversity of the project, enhancing its overall quality. By actively engaging in testing processes, you play a vital role in identifying potential issues, ensuring that the software meets diverse user requirements.

The diverse perspectives brought by testing teams with varied backgrounds and experiences are instrumental in uncovering usability and accessibility challenges that may be specific to particular demographic groups. Your involvement in testing allows you to contribute to the project's overall inclusivity and user-friendliness. Whether it's testing functionalities, reporting bugs, verifying bug fixes, or participating in bug triage, your efforts directly impact the project's reliability and its ability to cater to a broad and varied user base. Testing thus becomes a collaborative effort that leverages diverse insights to enhance the project's performance and accessibility.

User Support

User support is a critical component of open source projects that contributes to user satisfaction, community growth, software quality, and the overall success and sustainability of the project. Contributing to user support involves actively engaging with users to troubleshoot issues, responding to questions across various platforms such as forums, mailing lists, or chat forums, and generously sharing your expertise with the community.

Your involvement in user support not only aids individuals in overcoming challenges but also fosters a collaborative environment where collective intellectual knowledge thrives. Open source projects thrive on the diversity of contributions, and by assisting users and sharing your insights, you contribute to the wealth of knowledge that defines the open source ethos. This collaborative approach to user support not only benefits individuals seeking assistance but also strengthens the community as a whole, making open source projects dynamic, responsive, and successful.

Design and UX/UI

Design and UI/UX are integral to open source projects because they directly impact user adoption, satisfaction, accessibility, and community engagement. Prioritizing design excellence in open source projects goes beyond mere aesthetics; it ensures that the software not only functions effectively but also offers an enjoyable and productive experience for users. This, in turn, significantly contributes to the project's long-term success and sustainability.

If you possess design skills, there are various avenues through which you can make impactful contributions. Creating or enhancing the project's user interface, designing icons, and improving other graphical elements are tangible ways to elevate the overall user experience. Additionally, your involvement in activities such as conducting accessibility audits, establishing design guidelines and style guides, organizing design sprints, and performing usability testing can further enhance the project's usability and accessibility. Your commitment to design excellence empowers the open source community to deliver software that not only meets functional requirements but also delights users, fostering a positive and enduring impact.

Community Building

Community building is not just about growing the number of project participants; it's about creating an inclusive, collaborative, and supportive environment. This environment becomes a breeding ground for innovation, sustainability, and overall project success. The process of building and nurturing a community is continuous, yielding substantial benefits in the form of enhanced software quality, increased adoption, and a more robust project ecosystem.

Your active participation in community building is instrumental to this process. Organizing events, meetups, or conferences provides platforms for community members to connect, share ideas, and collaborate. Organizing a successful open source conference is a substantial effort that involves meticulous planning, coordination, and execution. Conference organizers, despite their expertise, often rely on the support of dedicated volunteers to ensure the event's smooth operation. If you are passionate about open source and interested in contributing to the success of such conferences, reaching out to organizers and offering your assistance can be a valuable and rewarding endeavor. Volunteering for an open source conference can involve a diverse range of tasks, including helping with event logistics, assisting attendees during registration, supporting speakers, managing session schedules, or facilitating networking activities. Your active involvement can significantly contribute to the overall success of the conference, creating a positive and inclusive environment for participants.

As a moderator in forums and chat channels, you contribute to fostering a welcoming and inclusive atmosphere, ensuring that diverse voices are heard and valued. By engaging in these community-building activities, you play a vital role in creating an environment where collaboration thrives, knowledge is shared, and the open source project evolves into a resilient and flourishing ecosystem.

Project Management

Project management is essential for open source projects because it helps maintain order, maximize efficiency, ensure quality, and foster collaboration among diverse contributors. Effective project management is often the backbone that allows open source projects to thrive and continue providing valuable software to users and the broader community.

Contributing to project management tasks within open source projects involves a diverse set of responsibilities. This may include triaging issues, categorizing and prioritizing tasks, managing project boards to visualize progress, organizing collaborative sprints, coordinating communications among team members, and aiding in release planning and execution. Your involvement in these activities helps streamline project processes, enhance communication channels, and contribute to the overall efficiency and success of the open source endeavor.

Marketing and Promotion

Marketing and promotion are essential for open source projects to gain recognition, attract contributors and users, secure funding, and ensure long-term sustainability. An effective marketing strategy not only benefits the project but also contributes to the growth and success of the open source ecosystem as a whole.

You can promote the project through social media, blogs, or articles. Share updates, announcements, and success stories. Engage with community members and respond to inquiries or discussions related to the project. Whenever the project achieves a milestone or releases new features, share the news on your personal or professional networks. Positive word-of-mouth can significantly impact the project's visibility. Support the community by reaching out to relevant media outlets, influencers, or bloggers who may be interested in covering the project. Collaborate with the community to create press releases for major releases or events.

You can also help create marketing materials, such as posters, banners, or infographics, to raise awareness to attract more users and contributors and help attract sponsors and donors. Engage with other open source communities or related projects. Collaborate on joint initiatives, cross-promote each other, and expand the project's reach through network connections.

Engaging in open source research is a vital way to participate in the open source community. You can provide datasets, survey data, and qualitative insights to help the industry. Generating open source data is a shared activity and requires collaboration – – you can share surveys to your social network, provide financial support for creating insights, and so on.

Legal and Licensing

Legal and licensing considerations are essential for open source projects to ensure compliance with open source licenses, protect intellectual property, mitigate legal risks, and build trust within the community.

You can help to review the project's codebase, dependencies, and associated documentation to ensure compliance with open source licenses. Identify and address any licensing conflicts or violations. Assist in protecting the project's intellectual property by implementing measures such as Contributor License Agreements (CLA) or Developer Certificate of Origin (DCO). These documents clarify the terms under which contributions are made to the project. Collaborate with the community to establish clear processes for contributors to sign CLAs or agree to DCO terms. Help maintain records of contributors who have agreed to these terms to manage legal aspects effectively.

Periodically conduct license audits to review the project's compliance with licenses. Identify any outdated or problematic dependencies that may pose legal risks and work with the community to address them. Contribute to legal documentation within the project, ensuring that licensing information is clear and easily accessible. This helps both contributors and users understand the legal aspects of using or contributing to the project. Collaborate with project maintainers and the community to develop clear policies regarding licensing. Establish guidelines for contributions, use of third-party libraries, and overall project governance. In case of identified licensing issues, collaborate with the community to address and resolve them. This may involve reaching out to contributors, updating licenses, or seeking legal advice when necessary.

Financial Support

Contributing financial support to open source projects is crucial for their sustainability and overall success. Open source projects often operate on limited budgets, and financial contributions play a pivotal role in covering essential operational costs. These costs include hosting services, domain registration, and general infrastructure maintenance. By providing financial support, contributors help ensure the project's continuous availability to users, maintaining a stable and reliable platform.

In addition to operational expenses, financial contributions support the ongoing development efforts of open source projects. Developers dedicate their time and expertise to enhance features, fix bugs, and improve overall functionality. Financial support can fund development bounties, enabling contributors to focus on specific tasks that benefit the broader community, accelerating the project's growth and effectiveness.

Financial contributions also contribute to the broader health of the open source community. They enable projects to invest in community-building initiatives, events, and activities that foster collaboration, inclusivity, and engagement among contributors. Recognizing the importance of diversity and inclusion, financial support can be directed towards initiatives that encourage underrepresented groups to participate, ensuring a vibrant and diverse open source ecosystem.

Financial resources can help ensure that open source projects can continue to provide valuable software and services to users and contributors alike. Consider making a financial contribution to the project through platforms like Open Collective or GitHub Sponsorships to help cover hosting costs, pay for infrastructure, or fund development bounties.

Remember that open source projects thrive on collaboration, and every contribution, whether code or non-code, is valuable. Choose a contribution that aligns with your skills and interests, and reach out to the project maintainers to coordinate your efforts effectively.

Index

A

Aiven, 55–58

Amazon, 58–61, 247, 295, 307, 308

Amazon Elastic Compute Cloud
(Amazon EC2), 59, 308

Amazon Elastic Kubernetes Service
(EKS), 53, 306

Amazon Simple Storage Service
(Amazon S3), 59

Amazon Web Services
(AWS), 53, 58

Apache Software Foundation
(ASF), 59, 65, 256, 267, 277

Apache Solr, 267

Apache TomCat, 97, 99

Artificial Intelligence (AI), 3, 233, 246

Automotive Grade Linux (AGL),
145, 233

Ayushman Bharat Digital Mission
(ABDM), 274

B

Bitbucket, 157

BlackRock, 62–64, 113–116, 174–175

Bloomberg, 64, 66, 67, 263, 265–268

Bloomberg Women in Technology
(BWIT), 68

Business functions
code savings, 35, 36
community building, 40–42
compliance/security, 38, 39
customization/flexibility, 43
faster innovation, 30, 31
open source initiatives, 44–47
strategic initiatives, 37
sustainable codebase, 32, 33, 35

Business models
case studies
Aiven, 55–58
Amazon, 58, 60, 61
BlackRock, 62–64
Canonical, 69–71
Dell, 72–75
fidelity investments,
78–80, 84
Infosys, 85–89, 91–94
Red Hat, 95–97
SUSE, 99–103
sustainable open
source, 66–69
commercial license
model, 50, 51
consulting and custom
development model, 54
hardware sales, 53, 54

O

Printed in the United States
by Baker & Taylor Publisher Services